Advance Praise for *Believe in People*

"In many ways, *Believe in People* is one of the best arguments for the value of workplace diversity. Charles Koch and Brian Hooks make the case for the greater power of social change driven by a diversity of every kind of perspective. What makes it different from other, similar approaches is that this one is based, ultimately, on letting go. It is based on creating systems that allow for ingenuity to flourish and support the risk taking that leads to substantive change."

—ALBERTO IBARGÜEN, PRESIDENT AND CEO,
JOHN S. AND JAMES L. KNIGHT FOUNDATION

"Charles Koch's dismay about the crippling consequences of partisanship and the nostrums of politicians, businesspeople, and philanthropists is matched by his abiding faith in the way individuals can change our country for the better. *Believe in People* brims with the humility and humanity of a lifetime spent leading and learning."

—MICHAEL MORITZ, PARTNER, SEQUOIA CAPITAL

"*Believe in People* is more than a snappy title to an extraordinary book; it's a challenge to anyone who has ever tried to improve their own life, the lives of their loved ones, the lives of strangers, or the lives of all those with whom we share the planet.

This is not, however, a self-help book or a collection of bromides and platitudes—this is a deeply personal account of one man's remarkable determination to live the best life he can, by remaining true to the values his parents instilled into his very hard head, at a very young age.

Believe in People is a survival guide for the Social Entrepreneur in all of us—a manifesto for do-goodery—written by one of the greatest philanthropists to ever live, at a time in history like no other. I recommend you read it, and then, as time allows, live it."

—MIKE ROWE, EXECUTIVE PRODUCER,
HOST, AND CEO, THE MIKEROWEWORKS FOUNDATION

"I find Charles Koch's wisdom to be invaluable. His open-mindedness to changing society and giving people the opportunity to shine is so well written and explained.

Most of us know the word 'poverty' or 'underserved' but we don't understand how people got there. The insight of *Believe in People* is—to create change, we must help others. When serving people, we must seek out their needs. When something is broken, we must bond together.

Believe in People is a historical roadmap of inspiring people to inspire others. We all need a hero to follow and a game plan for success, awareness, and change. This is the DNA of who Charles Koch is! Lifting others when you rise."

—NANCY LIEBERMAN, BASKETBALL HALL OF FAMER AND
FOUNDER, NANCY LIEBERMAN CHARITIES

"Read about many men and women who changed themselves, the lives they touched, and hence became part of a wave of lives changed. The book is summed up in Charles Koch's own words: 'My North Star is a society in which every person can realize their potential.'"

—VERNON SMITH, NOBEL PRIZE-WINNING ECONOMIST AND GEORGE L. ARGYROS ENDOWED CHAIR IN FINANCE AND ECONOMICS, CHAPMAN UNIVERSITY

"Charles Koch is truly one of our great Americans, a man determined to make the world a better place. He is my friend. I know him as a searcher, a kind man, not content to sit back and enjoy the fruits of his personal journey. Instead, he felt it essential to encourage others to find their individual passions and what it is they love and do well. Encouragement like this can change the paradigm of people's lives, therefore empowering them to recognize the same in the next person. We all have something to offer, and the message such as in this book can be the spark that changes lives. We all want to know how Charles Koch did it. The answer lies within these pages."

—SUZANNE SOMERS, ACTOR, ENTREPRENEUR, ENTERTAINER, AND NEW YORK TIMES BESTSELLING AUTHOR

"*Believe in People* offers a unique look at how the fundamental features of entrepreneurship, and inspiring and investing in individuals who are passionate about solving problems creatively, are essential to overcoming long-standing economic and social challenges in the U.S. (and abroad). Charles Koch shares stories from his own life as well as those of other people and organizations that took risks, empowered from the bottom up, forged partnerships with unlikely partners, and used sound business practices to tackle entrenched problems. Charles offers a roadmap for how we each can harness the power of entrepreneurship and individual contribution to build more resilient communities and find real solutions to many of the problems we confront in America today. In the process, Charles shares lessons from which we all can learn and a means to achieve solutions-focused engagement with each other going forward."

—TONY WELTERS, EXECUTIVE CHAIRMAN, BLACKIVY GROUP AND CHAIRMAN EMERITUS, NEW YORK UNIVERSITY SCHOOL OF LAW

"*Believe in People* is a wise, thoughtful, and optimistic book. At its heart, it is a book about listening—to the quiet voice inside of each of us that whispers truths about finding our highest calling and discovering our best selves. A timely and important read."

—DAVID ISAY, FOUNDER, STORYCORPS

"Charles Koch's vision for a better America and his call to action for a new bottom-up movement make *Believe in People* a compelling and provocative read."

—MICHAEL LOMAX, PRESIDENT AND CEO, UNCF

"*Believe in People* is a celebration of the inherent dignity of every person—and a roadmap to move society closer to that ideal. It elevates the power of social entrepreneurs and hopefully will ignite more of them. In these difficult and unpredictable times, Charles and Brian not only see an expansive and inclusive future, but illuminate the path to get there."

—JONATHAN GREENBLATT, CEO, THE ANTI-DEFAMATION LEAGUE

"*Believe in People* is a book for anyone looking to make a difference by becoming the best version of themself. This is the book the country needs right now to help unite people and make progress together. Paying it Forward is the best self-gratification one can get while creating real change for humanity!"

—CORTEZ BRYANT, CO-CEO, BLUEPRINT GROUP AND
COO, YOUNG MONEY ENTERTAINMENT

"*Believe in People* is Charles Koch's most personal book, most substantive book, and best book—all wrapped up into one. Heartily recommended."

—TYLER COWEN, HOLBERT L. HARRIS CHAIR IN ECONOMICS AND
CHAIRMAN, MERCATUS CENTER AT GEORGE MASON UNIVERSITY

"If you don't believe in people, what do you believe in? This is a provocative book for the moment. Highly recommended."

—RYAN HOLIDAY, #1 *NEW YORK TIMES* BESTSELLING AUTHOR OF
THE OBSTACLE IS THE WAY AND *THE DAILY STOIC*

"Finally, an argument for a free and open society that meets the challenges of our time, head on! Charles and Brian make a clear case for why the future depends on truly living up to our country's founding principles. And how by uniting with anyone to do right, we can empower every person to realize their potential."

—TODD ROSE, FORMER DIRECTOR OF THE MIND, BRAIN, AND
EDUCATION PROGRAM, HARVARD UNIVERSITY AND
CO-FOUNDER AND PRESIDENT, POPULACE

"Forget everything you thought you knew about Charles Koch and read this book. Charles and Brian offer a clear path to success for anyone who wants to make a difference. An unrelenting picture of optimism that's a roadmap for solving our country's biggest problems."

—MARC ANDREESSEN, CO-FOUNDER AND GENERAL PARTNER,
ANDREESSEN HOROWITZ

BELIEVE
in PEOPLE

BELIEVE
in PEOPLE

BOTTOM-UP SOLUTIONS
for a TOP-DOWN WORLD

CHARLES KOCH

CHAIRMAN AND CEO, KOCH INDUSTRIES

with **BRIAN HOOKS**

CHAIRMAN AND CEO, STAND TOGETHER

 ST. MARTIN'S PRESS

NEW YORK

First published in the United States by St. Martin's Press,
an imprint of St. Martin's Publishing Group

www.stmartins.com

The Library of Congress Cataloging-in-Publication Data is available upon request.
ISBN 978-1-250-20096-9 (hardcover)
ISBN 978-1-250-20097-6 (ebook)

Our books may be purchased in bulk for promotional,
educational, or business use. Please contact your local bookseller
or the Macmillan Corporate and Premium Sales Department at 1-800-221-7945,
extension 5442, or by email at MacmillanSpecialMarkets@macmillan.com.

First Edition: 2020
10 9 8 7 6 5 4 3 2 1

Photographs on these pages are reproduced courtesy of the following:
Melony Armstrong: 201; Matt and Caitlin Bellina: 226–228; Café Momentum: 132–134; Madison
Jacques: 153 (bottom); Alice Johnson: 215; Charles Koch: 25–27, 49, 57–59, 70 (top); Antong Lucky: 110,
113; Kathaleena Monds: 97–99; The Phoenix: 139, 140; Dana Smith: 139; Rich Tafel: 239; the estate of
Sterling Varner: 69, 70 (bottom); Toiya Smith: 153 (top).

To the many people, whom I've known either
personally or through their works,
who have transformed my life.
And to the millions throughout history who have
had the courage to fight for justice
in making the world a better place for everyone.

CONTENTS

PREFACE

It was the middle of March. Our country was coming to the realization that the coronavirus was about to upend everything.

When the first restaurants and bars closed, almost overnight, millions of people were out of jobs—and it only got worse with each passing day. Families from coast to coast were suddenly facing a new struggle to put food on the table, provide for their kids, and pay the bills.

In Oakland, California, the team at the Family Independence Initiative (FII) watched with dismay. For nearly 20 years, they'd helped families in poverty connect with one another. Through mutual support and with a relatively small amount of financial assistance, the families would work together to rise above the challenges holding them down. Now, as the pandemic rapidly spread, Jesús Gerena and his team were beginning to realize that a lot more people would need help.

Jesús reached out to Stand Together, a philanthropic community that I founded. Stand Together had been working with FII for the past couple of years and was ready to support a national expansion, phased in over the next two or three years. Jesús knew that two to three years was now a lifetime away. It was time for fast action, and thanks to FII's technology platform, which made it possible to get cash donations directly into a family's bank account, they were in a position to help those hardest hit.

In a matter of days—and over several long nights—the two groups created a new project called #GiveTogetherNow. They designed it to get cash quickly to families who were struggling because of the coronavirus disruption. Verification takes about 10 minutes, and the money is transferred to their bank accounts within 48 hours.

Not only would this aid the families, it would offer people who wanted to help, but didn't know how, a chance to get engaged. Anyone could go to the website and give a few bucks. The initial goal was to try to rally enough supporters to aid 20,000 families. Nobody knew whether it would work, but it was worth a try.

I still find what happened next thrilling.

About six weeks later, as I write this, roughly 1,300 individuals, philanthropies, city governments, and businesses have donated more than $61 million and counting. They gave this money to an organization most of them had never heard of to help more than 122,000 families they don't know and will never meet.

This cash assistance enabled families most disrupted by the coronavirus to make rent, buy groceries, and generally just take a breath while figuring out what to do next. While FII's effectiveness ultimately comes from its community-based model—as I'll discuss in depth in chapter six—the quick support helped people who'd been knocked off a beneficial path by the pandemic. On its own, the project wasn't going to solve everything. But it was making a real difference at a vital time.

And this wasn't the only such effort underway.

Stand Together had spent the past four years working with nearly 200 groups like FII, community-based organizations that were helping those struggling with poverty to transform their lives. Once the coronavirus swept in, the work these groups were doing immediately became that much more important—and that much harder. In a world of social distancing and economic hardship, administering programs and raising sufficient funds could seem like impossible tasks.

So the team at Stand Together launched a GoFundMe campaign called "Help the Helpers," named after a saying from *Mister Rogers' Neighborhood*. It promised to match, dollar for dollar, the donations that the groups were able to attract from others, up to a total of $1 million. The assumption was that while most people wouldn't be able to focus on helping others when they were worried about their own situation, they might be more likely to chip in if they realized they could double their impact. It was a long shot, and it seemed like the million-dollar match would last a while.

It didn't. The groups maxed out the match in 24 hours. The sudden rush of donations enabled them to get much-needed resources to some of the most vulnerable people affected by the pandemic.

Seeing the swift response, the Help the Helpers campaign doubled down—surely another $1.5 million would keep this thing going. It did . . . for about a day and a half. Within 72 hours, people from all walks of life came together to get nearly $6 million to groups helping people in dire straits. As with FII, the quick action from people all across the country was incredible to see.

Meanwhile, in Tulsa, Oklahoma, someone else was looking at the widening crisis and wondering if there was some way he could pitch in. His name was Tim.

As an IT analyst in one of Koch Industries' businesses, Tim enjoyed working with the 3-D printers in his office. One day in March, he was reading a story about using 3-D printers to make face shields. He immediately downloaded a design file and tested it out. It worked.

This gave Tim an idea. He started tinkering with the design to fit several face shields onto a single printing plate. Since his office had five 3-D printers, Tim wanted to commit them all to making face shields. He did so with his manager's encouragement, and the company began donating the face shields to hospitals in Tulsa and elsewhere in the region. Tim's actions helped shore up the safety of health-care professionals, who were grateful for the sudden support.

Why am I telling these stories? Not to toot my own horn. They all happened spontaneously, with no input or involvement from me.

Instead, I tell these stories because of what they show. In each case, people turned on a dime and used their unique gifts to make a big difference in the lives of others. During the greatest crisis our country has faced in generations, they saw and seized opportunities to help. And they are not the only ones. Countless others across America have done the same, finding the best ways to apply their abilities to improve people's lives.

That's what this book is all about—the distinct and profound role that each of us can play in making our country a better place for everyone.

I started writing this book five years ago. I never expected to be finishing it in the middle of a pandemic. It has been surreal and deeply saddening to see the pain the coronavirus has caused.

But it has also been inspiring to see how so many people have reacted to help those most affected. Much of what I've witnessed since this crisis began has reinforced my confidence that the ideas discussed in this book work. It has further strengthened my deep belief in people and my commitment to the idea that all of us have a role to play in transforming society for the better, from the bottom up.

Of course, I wouldn't have felt the need to write this book if this belief in people's ability to solve problems from the bottom up was already widespread. As you'll see in the chapters that follow, a lot of how our society is organized today assumes that most folks aren't capable of much. People are often treated as problems to be solved, instead of being empowered to help address America's biggest challenges. In most cases, the general assumption is that major issues—like the coronavirus—can only be addressed from the top down.

Sadly, that approach is at least partly responsible for some of the biggest failures in the early days of the pandemic. It led to tests that didn't work, prevented the creation and supply of new and better tests, and stopped doctors and nurses from mobilizing quickly to see more patients.[1] Had universities, labs, businesses, and health-care providers been able to fully contribute from the outset, how much better might the response have been?

Empowerment could also have lessened the economic destruction that has ruined tens of millions of people's livelihoods.[2] It was clear from the start that to protect public health, businesses needed to change their operations—or, in some cases, to be suspended altogether (large sporting events are an obvious example). But the one-size-fits-all approach of naming some businesses "essential" and others "nonessential" was a huge missed opportunity. It failed to tap into the best knowledge in a way that would empower people to find ways to keep everyone safe and continue to employ millions who are now wondering how they will provide for their families.

As a result, many businesses stayed open even as they were unable to protect workers (some meat-packing facilities, for example), while others were told to shut down even though they could have operated safely (such as landscapers working outdoors with small crews).[3] If, instead, authorities had set clear health standards for businesses, imagine the innovative ways businesses could have found to meet those standards with fewer jobs lost and lives disrupted. This was the case, for example, with grocery stores that created special hours for the elderly and installed plexiglass partitions, as well as manufacturers that staggered shifts and took other innovative precautions.[4]

Unfortunately, this top-down approach falls short in many other areas, far beyond the coronavirus. As you will see in the pages ahead, this paradigm dominates in business, philanthropy, public policy, and much of our daily life, often with disastrous results.

What this book offers is a paradigm shift—actually, several paradigm shifts. It calls for all of us to move away from a top-down approach to solving the really big problems in society toward an approach that focuses on empowering people from the bottom up to act on their unique gifts and contribute to the lives of others.

The concept of paradigm shifts comes from the philosopher of science Thomas Kuhn.[5] He wrote that major transformations "are inaugurated by a growing sense . . . that an existing paradigm has ceased to function adequately."[6] A growing number of people in our country would agree that the current approach is not functioning adequately—to say the least.

But it's not enough to reject the status quo. Kuhn also wrote that "to reject one paradigm without simultaneously substituting another" is dangerous.[7] My experience tells me that we need to change our paradigms in at least three important ways.

First: Just because there's a big problem doesn't necessarily mean there's a big solution. In fact, most of the toughest issues can't be addressed by one-size-fits-all solutions, and the more we try, the more we find ourselves with a giant square peg in our hand, looking at a sea of small, round holes. Instead of looking for the one big answer, we must all look for many right-sized answers. The stories I started with are great examples of what this can look like.

Second: People aren't problems to be solved. They are often the source of the solution, and those closest to an issue are usually best suited to address it. The world needs experts, no doubt. But a little local knowledge and lived experience goes a long way. And a lot of humility is good to keep on hand when mandating a fix from a distance.

Third: Unite with anybody to do right. When times get tough, as they are right now, it's tempting to retreat to your corner, your team, your tribe, and to start to play the blame game—"us vs. them." Yet this limits how much we can do and all but guarantees that we won't overcome the challenges we face. We can achieve more together than we ever could apart—even and especially when we unite with those who think differently and bring different capabilities to the task at hand.

When you shift your paradigm in these ways, the entire world looks different. Where others see impossibilities, you see opportunities—or, to paraphrase Kuhn, the scales fall from your eyes.[8] I hope that after reading this book, you will be as persuaded as I am about the opportunities before us and what we can accomplish together.

More than that, I hope you will see that you have a unique and essential role to play—that you can help move our country toward a boundless future for all.

If that appeals to you, as it does to me, read on.

BELIEVE
in PEOPLE

THE PRINCIPLES OF PROGRESS

___

" The man who grasps principles can successfully select his own methods. The man who tries methods, ignoring principles, is sure to have trouble. "

HARRINGTON EMERSON[1]

___

I have had the good fortune to achieve more than I ever dreamed possible. When I consider what enabled my life's transformation, I inevitably turn to an epiphany I had when I was 28.

The year was 1963, and the place was Wichita, Kansas. My father, health failing, had recently convinced me to leave my first post-college job in Boston and come home to run the business he had helped start more than two decades earlier. I turned him down, but then changed my mind after he agreed to give me wide latitude to experiment and implement new ideas at the company.

Neither of us knew it at the time, but I had just begun what would become a lifelong journey to better understand the principles of scientific and social progress—principles proven throughout history to bring about progress, prosperity, and peace. I hoped to apply these principles to the business, to enable us to become much more successful.

But my vision didn't end at the company doors. As I learned the principles of social progress, I wanted to apply them to every facet of my life. Ultimately, this would turn into a commitment to help discover a better way for all of us to live well together as a society—a path of progress for all, a path to fulfill the promise at the core of our country.

So it was that I came to my epiphany: progress happens from the bottom up.

By bottom up, I simply mean that the combined efforts of millions of people, each using their unique knowledge and abilities, are what improve the world. Every person can make a difference, and everyone has something to contribute. All of us can discover, develop, and apply our talents to succeed by helping others. Our individual actions may seem small, but they're actually immensely meaningful. They can bring us a lifetime of fulfillment and, taken together, the best possible future—not only for ourselves, but for everyone.

Bottom up is not a statement of where people start, or a description of a specific socioeconomic status, but rather a vision of what every individual can do working with others. This includes those who start with many advantages—like me—as well as those who start with little or nothing. All of us have a role to play in improving our country.

Bottom up tends to work better for a simple reason. When people are empowered, they find solutions to the problems they are closest to, as they have the proximity and knowledge to do so. For this reason, the most important contributions often come from those who are overlooked or dismissed. As you'll read in the following chapters, the effective solutions to society's most pressing problems frequently spring from what might seem the most unlikely of places and then spread as others see their effectiveness.

Your success is essential to this process. And that's why I wrote this book. Because I want you to find how you can best contribute.

The more people do this, the better off we all will be. And if every person followed their own best path to contributing to the lives of others, then we could achieve a future beyond anyone's fondest hopes. It would be characterized by everyone cooperating to foster harmony and progress. Such a society would be more just and prosperous than any yet seen.

As I internalized this, my North Star became clear: do all I can to empower people so they can transform themselves—and the world around them.

This vision of openness, inclusion, and empowerment, based on a deep belief in people, has animated my life ever since. But realizing this vision is no simple task.

THE OPPOSITE OF EMPOWERMENT

Bottom-up empowerment is at odds with the prevailing ideas of our time, most of which are based on the paradigm of control. Look across society, and you'll see that millions are being impeded, directed, dominated, or worse. You'll see the widespread assumption that those at the "top" know best and the people they consider beneath them can't be trusted.

This vision of openness, inclusion, and empowerment, based on a deep belief in people, has animated my life ever since.

This leads to business projects, public policies, and philanthropic grand plans done *to* people rather than collaborative efforts that enable individuals to discover and apply themselves. This can be summed up as a top-down or one-size-fits-all approach. Far from a belief in people, it is predicated on distrusting and discounting them. At best, the approach says, "We believe in some people, but not others."

This is inherently unjust—and almost always counterproductive. People are being treated as problems to be solved instead of valued individuals worthy of help as they work to realize their potential. Unable to find and use their unique gifts, they're being denied the opportunity to contribute and succeed. They're stifled, trapped behind towering barriers. This obviously hurts them and, by holding them back, hurts us all.

History proves there's a better way. Rather than being controlled, our fellow citizens need as much support and encouragement as we all can muster—something all of us can do. Fostering that kind of society is my life's work. It has been so ever since that epiphany back in 1963.

The most obvious way I have strived to empower people is perhaps in my day job at Koch Industries. My goal has always been to enable our employees to develop and apply their talents to create value for others—to succeed by helping others succeed. Insofar as we have done this, the business has flourished.

I previously wrote the book *Good Profit* to help Principled Entrepreneurs™ do the same in their companies. It contained a detailed toolkit for anyone who wants to build a business that empowers its employees to contribute to society and the company's own success.

But transforming business was never my sole, or even primary, passion. My main motivation has long been the transformation of our country for the better. In fact, I see my work building Koch Industries into a business that creates value for others as helping to advance this larger goal. The same principles behind the company's success have helped me to achieve more in every facet of my life.

With this book, my goal is to further help those who want to empower people everywhere. Whereas in *Good Profit* I demonstrated how the principles of social progress can be applied to build a better organization, here I show how those same principles can help you build a better society where everyone has the opportunity to succeed.

My goal is to assist not just the entrepreneur in business but also the much larger world of Social Entrepreneurs. If you're reading this, I suspect you're a Social Entrepreneur—or perhaps aspire to be one.

AGENTS OF TRANSFORMATION

Words matter, and I chose "Social Entrepreneur" for a reason. An entrepreneur is someone who discovers (or wants to discover) new and improved ways of doing things. In the context of business, this means driving the innovation that improves people's lives through an enterprise. In a social context, it's a matter of finding new ways to break the barriers and overcome the injustices that prevent others from realizing their potential. These individuals disrupt the status quo to help others, especially the least fortunate, rise.

You can find these amazing people near and far.

Social Entrepreneurs are in our history books, ending some of history's worst injustices and inspiring us by their courage and integrity in the face of hardship, some of it beyond belief.

Today, Social Entrepreneurs are in the most challenged communities, helping families climb out of poverty and turning kids away from lives of addiction and crime.

They're at the pulpit, preaching about the values of tolerance and respect.

They're in the classroom, helping students unlock their unique passions and skills.

They're in the boardroom, telling executives that corporate welfare is not only bad business, it's self-destructive.

They're concerned citizens, mobilizing neighbors to support good policies and oppose bad ones.

They're elected officials—of any party—enacting laws that secure for everyone the opportunity to realize their potential and contribute to society's progress.

And there's a Social Entrepreneur in all of us—someone who longs to find the kind of fulfillment that comes from helping others improve their lives. Which brings us back to you.

Where do you have experience? Where have you learned what works? What's your passion? Is it tackling poverty, finding more effective ways for kids to learn, or fighting a harmful public policy that's affecting your family, friends, or neighbors? Maybe it's building a business that better satisfies its customers, empowers its employees, and contributes to its community.

No matter what your gifts are or what motivates you, I wrote this book to help you become more effective. In the pages that follow, you will find the principles of progress that transformed my life. They can transform yours too. And the more you understand and practice them, the more likely you'll help to transform society.

It's hard to fit the lessons of a lifetime between two covers, so I've organized my thoughts into three distinct sections. The first is my story. The second is our country's story. The third and final section is what I hope will be your story. Here's what you'll find, in brief.

MY STORY (CHAPTERS 1-3)

If I had to sum up my life in just a few words, they would be "trial and error," with an emphasis on "error."

I spent my formative years rebelling against my family and struggling to find what I was good at. High school and especially college helped me discover my unique gift, which is understanding and applying abstract principles in everyday life. I then set out on a learning journey, leading me to the epiphany that all people have unique gifts and the ability to contribute. (I use the word "contribute" frequently because it's part of a crucial concept—"contribution motivated"—as you'll see in chapter one.) I saw that the fewer barriers that stand in the way, the more likely people are to discover and act on those gifts. When they do, they make our society better.

I became a Social Entrepreneur the moment I realized this.

I reached this conclusion through years of studying ideas from all sorts of different disciplines and perspectives. History especially shows what's possible when people are empowered. Up until 1800, nearly everyone lived in dire poverty. There was basically no lasting progress of any kind. But then Social Entrepreneurs began to break down barriers, giving more people the chance to realize their potential.

The result has been more than two hundred years of unprecedented progress. Where we are now was unimaginable to our ancestors. If we keep empowering people, where we could be two hundred years from now is unimaginable to us.

My study of history and many other disciplines introduced me to the principles of social progress. As I discovered these principles, I applied them to every facet of my life, most notably Koch Industries. (This process continues today.) I believed it would help, but it proved more effective than I could have hoped. Empowering our employees to create value for others is the root of the company's success. Business succeeds when it's based on a deep belief in people too.

Koch Industries' value has grown 7,000-fold since 1961—43 times the growth of the stock market. An investment of $1,000 in the company when I came back to Wichita would be worth $10 million today. Where then we had revenues of $12 million, we now have annual revenues of around $120 billion—a one-million-percent increase. By the time you read this, our 130,000 employees will be contributing even more.

Koch's growth was generated by what we call "virtuous cycles of mutual benefit," or "cycles" for short. Because we focus on helping our employees find their greatest opportunity to contribute, they are continually looking for new ways to help the company and themselves succeed by contributing to society. As they build the capabilities to create value, they open the door to new opportunities, which allows us to build still more capabilities. Progress begets progress, in a never-ending cycle.

This phenomenon is the key not just to the company's success but to success at every level—for individuals, organizations, and societies. In fact, just as we have applied the principles of social progress to break down barriers and empower employees at Koch Industries, we need to do the same to end the injustices that prevent people from contributing to and benefiting from future progress.

OUR COUNTRY'S STORY (CHAPTERS 4–5)

One thing is certain: Americans from all walks of life are searching for a better way. This was the case before the coronavirus pandemic, and it's more true now. Despite the promise of new advances in medicine, communications, travel, and other fields, many people are terrified of what tomorrow holds—and understandably so. Even if they know a brighter future is coming overall, many don't see how they could possibly fit into it.

The signs are all around us. Entire communities are coming apart at the seams. Upward mobility is fading for huge numbers of people, especially those who need it most.[2] Suicide rates are rising, as are deaths from drug overdose.[3] This partially explains why life expectancy declined in the late 2010s, a phenomenon not seen in roughly a century.[4]

America is on a trajectory toward a two-tiered society—one in which fewer people get ahead and more fall behind.

These tragic realities are the result of a deterioration of the core institutions that people rely on, even in the toughest times. Those institutions—community, education, business, and government—are increasingly characterized by the same control mentality that held people back throughout history. As a result, they are falling down on the job, preventing millions from rising and finding fulfillment in their lives.

Transforming these institutions so they consistently empower people to succeed is the job of Social Entrepreneurs. Throughout American history, many inspiring people have applied their unique gifts to do that by ending injustices that kept people down. In this book, you'll meet well-known leaders like Frederick Douglass, who used his abilities to help end the most monstrous of barriers, slavery.

You'll also meet modern-day Social Entrepreneurs, many of whom are closest to the problems they're trying to solve. They are making headway on seemingly intractable issues, from failures in the criminal justice system to poverty to a lack of economic opportunity and many others, helping countless people realize their potential.

I am privileged to partner with many of the inspiring people you will encounter in these pages. They are demonstrating how to overcome some of society's toughest problems. Their lessons apply to me and you, and anyone else who wants to move America forward.

YOUR STORY (CHAPTERS 6–10)

As a Social Entrepreneur, you have the ability to transform society's core institutions so that more people are empowered and succeed. Whatever your gift may be, you can use it to help others improve their lives. But beware the temptation to double down on the failed approaches of the past. Many, if not most, Social Entrepreneurs risk becoming captive to the control paradigm. As a result, despite the best of intentions, their efforts can often hurt the people they want to help.

> Whatever your gift may be, you can use it to help others improve their lives.

In this section, we'll take a look at each institution and how the current approach holds people back. Then I'll describe a bottom-up method that actually helps people succeed. Many Social Entrepreneurs—some being those you would least expect—are using that approach, applying the principles of social progress to empower others. Whatever your own passion, these inspiring people hold lessons for us all as we work to bring about a society where every person can rise.

Take the institution of community. With nearly 40 million Americans living below the poverty line and many more teetering on the edge, essentially everyone agrees that large numbers of people are struggling to get by.[5] So why would we try to enact more one-size-fits-all programs and policies—whether from philanthropists or policy-makers—that treat the least fortunate as statistical problems instead of as individuals with unique abilities that can be unlocked with help?

There is a better way: believe in people, trust those closest to the problem, and empower them to transform their lives and those of others to escape poverty forever. Get ready to meet some truly inspiring people who are doing just that.

Within the institution of education, people recognize that more and more students are struggling to learn the skills and values necessary for success, especially in a fast-changing world. Unfortunately, the most common approaches in both public and private schools push students the wrong way. They tend to focus on a one-size-fits-all approach that limits both teachers and students.

A better approach is to think outside the typical classroom model (in both K–12 schools and universities) to foster individualized education. Meet each student where she is and help her get to where she wants and needs to be instead of forcing her to be something she's not. One of my favorite examples is a program called Youth Entrepreneurs. Its graduates tend to do markedly better than students who are stuck in a one-size-fits-all program.

Or look at the institution of business. Most Americans see businesses trying to enrich themselves at the public's expense, through corporate welfare. Corporate welfare, as we'll discuss in chapter eight, arises from collusion between businesses or other organizations (such as trade associations, unions, and nonprofits) and government. It allows the privileged to gain or keep power and wealth at the expense of everyone else. It is an insidious form of unequal treatment, which is to say, government-sponsored discrimination. The response to this very real problem is often more mandates, more handouts, and more opportunities for the wealthy and the well-connected to rig the economy in their favor. In other words, more of the same.

A better way is to unrig the system by ending corporate welfare, period. We must also cultivate and celebrate principled businesses that succeed by improving and enriching people's lives. This is "Good Profit," the title of my 2015 book. Companies that earn good profit are those that do well by doing good. More are needed.

Finally, there's government.

At this point, you may be thinking, "Oh no. Here comes the anti-government rant." Prepare to be disappointed. While it's true that government policies can hold people back, it's also true that government is a crucial institution with an important role to play. Sound public policy is essential to empowering everyone. A properly functioning government is a precondition for individual success and a thriving society—and a major focus of mine.

Unfortunately, decades of failed policies have made some of the worst ideas from history appealing to politicians from both parties. Nationalism, socialism, protectionism, intolerance, corporate welfare—ideologies and ideas predicated on controlling people and pitting them against each other are gaining ground.

They are the wrong answers to the right question—How do we help people who are being left behind?—and they are sowing division and discord that threaten to destroy the country. A better way is to unite people behind policies—not parties—that treat everyone equally and give every individual the opportunity and support they need to flourish.

Take it from me: it's easy for Social Entrepreneurs to use the wrong methods. As we'll discuss in more detail in chapter nine, the philanthropic community I founded temporarily took the typical, yet often counterproductive, partisan approach to politics.

In the lead-up to the 2010 elections, we started engaging directly in major party electoral politics. (I had steered clear of this for 45-plus years.) We did it to help cure the many ills caused by bad public policy, such as dangerous foreign interventions and wars, and debt-fueled government spending. We bet on the "team" whose policies we believed better enabled people to improve their lives. You only get two choices in our system, so we chose the red team.

By the mid-2010s, it was clear that this foray into politics wasn't going to be successful in helping to remove the biggest public policy barriers holding people back. The experience taught me what George Washington had warned two hundred years ago in his farewell address: partisanship is not the answer. It was a hard-earned lesson that has led to some big changes in how our philanthropic community engages in politics.

I'm still passionate about removing barriers in public policy, and that requires participating in politics, but not in the usual partisan way. A superior approach is partnership—cooperating with people to accomplish public policies that help improve people's lives regardless of which political party our partners belong to.

By building coalitions and looking for common ground with others—even those we disagree with on other issues—we have gotten much better policy results. I remain committed to engaging in politics as a way to help remove barriers and end injustices, but now we do it in a way that unites rather than divides and truly empowers people to be part of the change that's needed. The results have been remarkable, as you'll see in chapter nine.

No matter which institution you're focused on—communities, education, business, or government—progress is possible. But it won't happen on its own. Breaking the biggest barriers and transforming institutions requires movements of millions of people.

History shows that Social Entrepreneurs can inspire people from all walks of life to break down barriers and end injustices. It has

History shows that Social Entrepreneurs can inspire people from all walks of life to break down barriers and end injustices.

happened before, from the women's rights movement to the civil rights movement to the movement for marriage equality, all of which applied the principles of progress to achieve success. It can—and must—happen again if we hope to right today's wrongs, transform the institutions, and empower every person to chart their own path to success.

Can such movements happen today? Absolutely. As you will see, Americans are ready for a new approach. It's up to you to help demonstrate what it looks like, and how to make change happen.

STAND TOGETHER

I don't have the answers to our country's problems. No one does. Solutions will only come from empowering the millions of dedicated people across America who know we can do better.

I suspect you want to make this happen. If so, this book is for you. It contains the principles and lessons that I have learned over a lifetime of study and application—a toolkit that can help you transform yourself and empower others. It will enable you to better accomplish your goals and greatly increase your effectiveness, ultimately helping to transform society.

But my offer to partner with you extends far beyond this book. In 2003, I founded an organization now called Stand Together. Its mission is simple: find and empower the Social Entrepreneurs who are effectively tackling the biggest issues of our time.

To accomplish this goal, we unite people from all walks of life. At the time of this writing, we are partnering with:

- More than seven hundred of America's most successful business leaders and philanthropists.
- Over one thousand professors at three hundred universities and other organizations involved in postsecondary education.
- Tens of thousands of K–12 teachers and educators in the skilled trades.
- Nearly two hundred community-based groups helping over a million people struggling in poverty every year.
- Millions of grassroots public policy activists in all fifty states.

Working with so many different people, and learning from so many sources, has helped me understand much of what you'll encounter in this book. We have vastly different backgrounds, beliefs, and abilities. Yet whatever our differences, we share the desire to remove the barriers holding people back. We are using the power of the bottom-up approach to discover new and better solutions on issue after issue.

Through these partnerships, we have accomplished more in the past few years than I did in the previous 50. I have never been more optimistic about what can be achieved. A society of unlimited opportunity and prosperity—a society of mutual benefit, in which all of us succeed together—has never been closer, if we act on our deep belief in people.

I hope you will do your part to help reach that future. You have a role that no one else can play.

After my father died in 1967, I discovered a letter he wrote to his sons. In it, he expressed his hope that we would experience the "glorious feeling of accomplishment." No matter your passion, no matter your gift—no matter who you are, what you do, or where you live—you can help make this country better for everyone. When you do, you will find that glorious feeling that makes life worthwhile. My hope is that this book will speed you on that journey.

PART I

MY STORY

The Principles That Transformed My Life

1.

BUSY
BEING
BORN

" He not busy being
born is busy dying. "

BOB DYLAN[1]

For me, Bob Dylan deserved the 2016 Nobel Prize in Literature. He has a special way of expressing some of the most important facets of human life. The quote at left—from Dylan's song "It's Alright, Ma (I'm Only Bleeding)"—gets at the heart of one of my guiding beliefs: success in life mostly depends on discovering your particular talents, then developing and applying them. The moment you stop moving forward, for whatever reason, you start falling behind.

That's something I know from personal experience. Now, let me tell you what I don't know.

I have no clue what your unique talents are. Nor can I tell you which path to follow—that's unique too. In the pages ahead, I don't have all the answers, or even most of them. But I do believe that everyone has a special gift that can be used to bring them fulfillment by helping others.

This idea has animated the better part of my life, now more than eight and a half decades long. My hope is that my journey—and the lessons I've learned along the way—may awaken you to the joy that comes from understanding yourself and contributing to the world around you.

Every journey must start somewhere, and that somewhere is self-discovery. Mozart began composing music when he was only five years old, but for the rest of us, unearthing our gifts usually happens much later and takes far longer. It certainly did for me.

I was fortunate to grow up in a family that gave me every opportunity to succeed. I recognize that I won the birth lottery, for which I will always be grateful. My parents did their best to give my three brothers and me a head start.

My mother, Mary, was a talented silversmith, enamelist, and artist dedicated to helping struggling artists and performers get started. She felt a deep obligation to assist everyone who reached out to her. She was the best possible exemplar of the biblical idea that "for unto whomsoever much is given, of him shall be much required."[2] I'm sure that's one reason I came to demand so much of myself.

Every journey must start somewhere, and that somewhere is self-discovery.

My father, on the other hand, could be summarized by a different verse: "Spare the rod, spoil the child."[3]

Fred Koch was a successful businessman, and he had no intention of letting his kids become "country club bums." He was, for good reason, especially focused on me. When I was six, he started putting me to work doing all kinds of manual labor around our farm. It involved digging up dandelions and feeding animals, graduating to milking cows, shoveling manure, baling hay, digging postholes, and mending fences. I was often doing my farm chores within earshot of my friends, who were across the street yelling and splashing at the local swimming pool.

So went my afternoons after school, weekends, and summer vacations, year after year.

When I was 15, I spent the summer working at a line camp on a Montana ranch. My bunkmate was Bitterroot Bob, a volatile cowboy. Bitterroot bragged about his dishonorable discharge from the military during World War II for running from the line of fire. Some nights he would fire his revolver through the roof of our log cabin. When it rained, he'd get wet, but that didn't seem to deter him.

Most mornings, Bitterroot and I would ride out to fix fences and bring back bulls that had hoof rot. We started out at sunrise and usually put in at least a 14-hour day. It was one of the grittiest, most challenging work experiences I had as a teenager. It was also one of the most memorable.

When my father died, I discovered a letter in his safety deposit box, in which he told his sons that "adversity is a blessing in disguise and is certainly the greatest character builder." In retrospect, my father gave me many opportunities for character building. I now know that my father did me a hell of a favor. He wanted to keep me from having a feeling of entitlement and help me gain an understanding of what it means to be productive. As far as he was concerned, the earlier I learned this lesson, the better.

Research backs him up. Studies show that after age 30, your character and work habits are very hard to change.[4] Fred Koch would have argued that 30 is 24 years too late.

His manual labor regimen helped instill in me a strong work ethic—an essential element of my later success. My parents also made a point of teaching their sons the values of integrity, humility, courage, perseverance, and treating others with respect. Crucially, Fred and Mary Koch practiced these values in their own lives, showing us more by their example than their words.

Although that's not to say I actually learned the lessons at the time. Whether it was about a lecture over the dinner table or a day of digging postholes in a pasture, mostly I just grumbled—and rebelled. It didn't matter whether I was ignoring his instructions or—when I was older—sneaking out to bars with a fake ID. My father's answer was the same: get up early and work.

TRIAL AND ERROR—AND ERROR

Working at such manual labor also helped me understand where I *don't* excel, which is pretty much in anything that involves using my hands.

REMEMBERING MY FATHER

AFTER MY FATHER DIED, one of my responsibilities was to inventory his personal items, including those in his safety-deposit box. Not knowing what was in it, I drove to the bank and, with the area manager, opened the box, wondering what would be there.

What I found, along with a copy of his will and several valuables, was a letter. It was addressed to me and my older brother, my father having written it in 1936, shortly after I was born and well before our twin brothers came along. While the letter was more than 30 years old, in a way it contained my father's parting words.

Although I've frequently referenced the part about the "glorious feeling of accomplishment," that is far from the only line that has stuck with me.

Papa, as we called him, wrote that a "sound body" and a "good mind" are all the heritage a child needs. To that end, he left insurance policies, worth about $100,000 each, to help pay for our education.

He advised that we could use the money as a "valuable tool for accomplishment" or "squander it foolishly." As he put it, "If you choose to let this money destroy your independence and initiative, it will be a curse."

The letter ended by urging us to "be generous to one another and be good to your mother"—a piece of advice we could all hope to live up to.

Reading the letter touched me deeply. This was about as emotionally open as Fred Koch got. He came from a different generation that was very reserved. This was compounded by his stern upbringing without much outward affection in his first-generation Dutch immigrant family.

Of course, I never doubted for a moment that he loved us. He showed his love mainly by teaching values and through strict discipline. For him, raising us right was the most important thing.

To his credit, my father never prescribed a set path for his sons.

Jan. 22, 1936

My Dear Boys —

I am giving you these policies in your infancy to protect you and to ensure that you will receive a proper education. A sound body, a good mind developed by intelligent schooling is all the heritage a boy needs.

When you are twenty one you will receive what seems now to be a large sum of money. It will be yours to do with what you will. It may be either a blessing or a curse. You can use it as a valuable tool for accomplishment or you can squander it foolishly.

If you choose to let this money destroy your initiative and independence then it will be a curse to you and my action in giving it to you will have been a mistake. I should regret very much to have you miss the glorious feeling of accomplishment and I know you are not going to let me down.

Remember that often adversity is a blessing in disguise and is certainly the greatest character builder. Be kind and generous to one another and be good to your mother.

Your loving father,
Fred Koch

The messages in the letter I found after my father's death are with me always.

Instead, he sought to instill in us the character and principles that would enable us to succeed no matter what we chose to do.

He also practiced what he preached. For a young man trying to find my way in the world, few things impressed me more than his integrity, treatment of others, and commitment to learning. And, of course, his courage, which he expressed in one of his favorite sayings: "Don't take counsel of your fears."

While my wife, Liz, and I didn't agree with many aspects of his particular method of parenting, we did agree with his emphasis on values. We worked hard to instill them in our children, Elizabeth and Chase, and whatever our shortcomings, we were successful in that. We couldn't be more proud of our children, who they have become, and our relationships with them.

Raising my own children was well in the future when I first read my father's letter in 1967. Standing there, I realized I was holding in my hands something I would always treasure. My father's letter has been framed in my office ever since. Its message is with me always.

—CHARLES KOCH

My grandfather, Harry Koch, immigrated from the Netherlands in 1888. The three of us were at my father's Kansas ranch in 1942.

Top: Although my father could be stern, he had a great sense of humor. (Wichita office, 1958)

Bottom: My father didn't want his sons to become "country club bums," so he put me to work starting at age six.

Realizations like this are crucial for every person. As you try to develop skills, you're going to find a lot of areas where you just don't have the necessary aptitude. Trial and error is a principle on its own, and in my decades of experience, there's no such thing as too much error. Every dead end gives you a better sense of your best path.

My father embodied that principle better than most. We lived on an experimental farm—not a commercial one—on the outskirts of Wichita, where my father kept cows, horses, dogs, and chickens. He liked to refer to himself as a "half-baked chemist," and he loved to try his hand at finding new and improved ways to do things. "I figured out that we can live on $100 worth of food a year," he announced one day. "There are mixes of beans that provide all the nutrients we need, so that's all we're going to eat." Mercifully, that experiment didn't last long.

Another time, he created a concoction called "Tiger's Milk," made of buttermilk, orange juice, yeast, and worse, which he forced me to drink. It tasted even more disgusting than it sounds. Aside from enjoying a good laugh about my father's experiments now, the main thing I learned from them was that to find out what works, you first have to discover what doesn't.

Fred Koch was also living proof that learning is a lifelong pursuit. He regularly reminded me, "Learn all you can, son, because you never know when it will come in handy." I belatedly internalized that philosophy. I'm 85 and still trying to learn everything I can, every day and every hour.

Through all my early experiences, I was striving (sometimes unintentionally) to better understand my gift and how to apply it in a way that enabled me to contribute and succeed. It was a long struggle because I was mainly engaged in things I couldn't do well and disliked doing.

One of the earliest clues about my aptitudes came in third grade. The subject was something that many struggle with: math. One day, as my teacher wrote problems on the blackboard, I noticed that, while the answers were obvious to me, they weren't to any of my classmates. Although I didn't end up becoming a mathematician, it gave me some confidence and a sense of direction.

At that time, my intellectual curiosity still lay dormant. My nonconformist tendencies dominated, leading my parents to send me to eight different schools before college. My adolescent contrarianism peaked as a junior in high school at Culver Military Academy in Indiana. My parents sent me there for discipline, which I proved I needed after getting caught drinking with other cadets on the train back to school after spring break. We were all expelled the next day.

I vividly remember the fear I felt as I faced my father after an all-night train ride back to Wichita. His first words were, "Well, I see you made it, boy." His disappointment was obvious and penetrating. His next words terrified me: "I've been trying to decide what to do with you."

The punishment made it even clearer just how unhappy he was. He shipped me off to live with my uncle Anton, to complete my junior year in Quanah, Texas.

I'll say this much for Quanah: it was during my time there that I had a mind-set shift about school. The contrast between my aptitude for math and abstract concepts versus other subjects was becoming more apparent. In addition, as I was grounded for most of my stay and had few distractions beyond my job shoveling wheat in a grain elevator, I actually became diligent about doing homework. After finishing the school year in Texas, I was readmitted to Culver by agreeing to repeat the spring semester at summer school.

My experiences and unhappiness helped me begin to realize that I needed to change my life. I was learning that fulfillment doesn't come from instant gratification. I tried plenty of that, including, but not limited to, sneaking out with my friends to get drunk starting at age 14. Sure, it gave me a temporary mental reprieve from the things I didn't like—my father's tasks, bullies at school, boredom and confusion—but it didn't give me lasting pleasure. Aristotle wrote that "one swallow does not make a spring," and so it was with the passing fun I got from making dumb decisions.[5]

Finally, by the end of adolescence, I grasped that fulfillment comes from a much broader horizon. I could either do the hard work of applying myself and reach long-term success, or continue to pursue destructive instant gratification. This is the principle of "time preference." The higher your time preference, the more willing you are to sacrifice the future to get what you want now. The lower your time preference, the more you are willing to forgo gratification now in order to bring about a better future.

As this realization took root, I picked up an interest in reading—thanks to William Faulkner, Ernest Hemingway, and George Orwell—and began to have some academic success. It was just enough to get me admitted to a good university: the Massachusetts Institute of Technology. Both my parents and I were relieved: me, because I finally felt a sense of freedom; them, because I hadn't completely squandered the future they had worked so hard to give me.

A FULL-TIME NERD

I liked MIT because it spoke my language: math. It had been a full decade since my first inkling in third grade, but gaining a little maturity and success in school convinced me to keep at it. I still had little idea where I could succeed, so I followed my father's example and began to experiment, taking as many math and other abstract-concept-focused courses as possible.

At first I thought I wanted to major in chemical engineering. I quickly quit that track because it involved too much memorization. Next I settled on geology, which involved even more memory work—too many rocks. So I dropped that and signed up for courses I thought I would enjoy and do well in, such as the full range of physics, math, and thermodynamics. I was turning into a real nerd.

It became apparent to me that many scientific principles can be more broadly applied, including to individuals, organizations, and society. I was especially fascinated by the second law of thermodynamics, which holds that entropy virtually always increases in a closed system. Entropy is a measure of disorder or uselessness. In lay terms, this means that progress stalls or declines when something is walled off from the outside world.

Usually you hear this concept in discussion of technology, but it applies to every facet of life. People, as well as organizations, stagnate when they aren't open to new ideas or fail to experiment or learn new skills. Countries crumble when they shut the door to trade, immigration, and innovation. It was partially in the second law of thermodynamics that I came to see the principles of openness and exchange and their importance to progress.

People, as well as organizations, stagnate when they aren't open to new ideas or fail to experiment or learn new skills.

Such realizations, while interesting to me, did not constitute a path to graduation. My scattershot academic approach kept me from satisfying the requirements for a degree in a specific field, so I defaulted to general engineering. In the first two years, my performance was less than stellar, given the temptations of Boston and the freedom MIT offered. But that radically changed after my sophomore year, when my father threatened to stop paying my tuition unless I fully applied myself. That reality finally got through my thick skull, causing my grades to improve a full point.

During the summer, outside the classroom, I had some of my most valuable educational experiences. I worked on a geophysical crew for an oil exploration entrepreneur in Oklahoma, in the engineering department at Chrysler in Detroit, and for the Standard Oil Company of New Jersey (now Exxon) at their Bayway, New Jersey, refinery.

While working in Oklahoma, I was driving a water truck when its injection pump got low on oil. My response to the situation backfired: I accidentally added too much oil, creating an even bigger problem. It was one of the many signs that I'm better at understanding engineering concepts than operating things.

At long last, my abilities (and lack thereof) were becoming clear to me. It wasn't exactly engineering. And it definitely wasn't motor repair. I was best at—and found the most fulfillment in—understanding and applying abstract principles. It wasn't wrestling with abstract theories, like a philosopher or a professor. It was grasping them in a way that would enable me to productively apply them, with the goal being to solve concrete problems.

I wish there had been an "aha!" moment when all this became apparent to me. In fact, it took me a long time to articulate my skillset, and I'm still refining that understanding—it's a lifelong journey. Years later, I discovered the work of psychologist Howard Gardner, who developed the theory of "multiple intelligences."[6] I fall into the category of people he described as having "logical-mathematical intelligence."

The more important lesson I took from Gardner—as well as from his critics—is that people, by and large, are neither smart nor stupid. We are all both, at the same time: smart in some ways, stupid in others. We are smartest when we discover, develop, and apply our unique strengths—whatever they may be—and dumbest when we don't. There's an old joke that says you're unique . . . just like everyone else. And it's true: everyone has something special to contribute to the world around them.

This points to another important truth I slowly learned: partnership is essential to progress. One person's strengths compensate for another person's weaknesses, and vice versa. As you join with others who share your vision and values, you will accomplish much more, much faster. The possibilities are limitless in a community where people work together to realize their unique potential and help others do the same.

At the end of my undergraduate years, that discovery was still a long way off for me. I only knew that I wanted to use my aptitude for complex concepts to achieve something positive in the real world. So I took a master's degree in nuclear engineering because it seemed ripe with opportunity.

Nuclear engineering also appealed to my interest in abstract ideas: few engineering fields are more conceptual. In the 1950s, nuclear energy was in its early stages, so it seemed that it would offer plenty of entrepreneurial opportunities. It didn't take me long to see it offered little of the sort. Nuclear energy is so regulated that entrepreneurship and innovation are all but impossible. (Witness the decades-long construction of new plants, the massive cost overruns making them uneconomic, and the resulting dearth of new projects—which is tragic given the technology's potential, especially today, when zero-emissions energy is in high demand.)

Given that nuclear appeared to be a dead end, I thought chemical engineering might better meet my abilities and entrepreneurial interests. While pursuing that master's degree, I considered going even further and getting a doctorate in chemical engineering, since I was handling its abstract concepts well.

My first step was to get my department head's opinion on the subject. Fortunately, he had a clear-eyed view on the matter and asked me,

"What do *you* want to do?" I told him I wanted to be an entrepreneur. His response was blunt: "Then get the hell out of here. We'll just make your life miserable for nothing." I didn't need another nudge.

My next step was to find a job that would enable me to experiment. I wanted to find the kind of work that fit my aptitudes and would give me the best chance of finding success through entrepreneurship. I landed one at the consulting firm Arthur D. Little, which was in Boston and covered a wide range of disciplines.

I approached the job as one giant experiment, starting in product development, which wasn't a great match. I moved to a job in process development, where I could make a better contribution. This became a stepping-stone into management services, where I consulted on innovation and business strategy. This was by far the best fit, and it helped prepare me for a career as an entrepreneur.

The final confirmation that I was on the right path came via a graduate course in finance that the firm allowed me to take at MIT during the 1961 spring semester. The coursework came easily to me, and I found it enjoyable and fulfilling. Combined with the hands-on experience I was gaining at Arthur D. Little, the course helped me begin to understand that success in business depends on empowering employees to succeed by contributing.

I would later come to see that thriving communities and nations depend on the same principles—just replace "business" with "society" and "employees" with "everyone." That is, success in society depends on empowering everyone to contribute.

At this point I was consumed by the desire to become an entrepreneur. I hounded friends and professors at MIT about start-ups that I could get involved with. In fact, after moving back to Wichita to work in the family business, we did invest in several such opportunities. One was an innovative communications system developed by a former roommate. Another was with Ray Baddour, the chairman of the chemical engineering department, who had started what is now Koch Separation Solutions.

A SUDDEN SHIFT

What changed my direction and my life was two phone calls in 1961.

The first was in the summer. My father called and asked me to come back to Wichita to work with him. I turned him down. Given how tough he had been on me growing up, I didn't think I would have the opportunity to experiment and try new things. One of his favorite sayings, having strong Dutch ancestry, was, "You can tell the Dutch, but you can't tell them much." For Fred Koch, this was less of a joke than a statement of fact, especially in dealing with me.

A month later he called again, saying, "Son, my health is poor, and I don't have much longer to live. Either you come back to run the company, or I'll have to sell it." His blood pressure was nearly twice as high as it should have been, even with medication. He assured me that I could run Koch Engineering—a small, struggling equipment company— however I wanted. He also indicated that he wanted me to run our main business once I was ready. For a 25-year-old wanting an entrepreneurial opportunity, this was as good as it was going to get.

I accepted. I've been here ever since.

Whatever I've achieved in the intervening years is the result of what preceded it. For the previous 20 years, I had been on the long journey to discover, develop, and apply my talents, as well as develop the values required for long-term success. It happened in fits and starts, sometimes despite my best efforts to undermine it. But it happened nevertheless.

I was starting to see that personal success and fulfillment—in any field or endeavor—comes from helping others in a way that is mutually beneficial. Alexis de Tocqueville called this acting out of an "enlightened regard for [oneself]," which "constantly prompts [people] to assist one another."[7]

Tocqueville's wisdom points to one of the most important principles I ever learned: being "contribution motivated." This is a concept derived from the psychologist Abraham Maslow, one of the biggest influences on my life. He argued that individuals are motivated by the desire to meet our most basic needs: food, shelter, sleep, and so on.[8] Beyond that, we crave emotional security, friendship, community, and intimacy, as well as a sense of worth and self-esteem, among other things.

When we seriously lack any of these, we tend to be driven by the deficiency. (I call this being "negatively motivated.") In this state, people tend to act in unhelpful, even dangerous, ways—often understandably so. But when we satisfy these needs, we can begin to realize our potential and find fulfillment in our lives. Something remarkable then begins to occur.

Up to that point, selfishness and unselfishness struggle to coexist. After all, if you are hungry or homeless, it's highly unlikely you'll give up food or shelter for the sake of someone else. Once such needs are met, however, your natural desire to help yourself becomes entwined with helping others, making it easier to become contribution motivated. Your success is tied to their success, and the more you contribute to the world around you, the more you tend to be rewarded, both internally and externally.

Maslow called this fusing of selfishness and unselfishness "synergy." Once synergy happens, you become all that you are capable of becoming, using your gifts to help people in extraordinary ways. Maslow called it self-actualizing. While this looks different for everyone, it is the path by which anyone can find lasting, lifelong fulfillment.

I came to see this through my experiences as well as my studies, which took off once I was home. (More on this in the next chapter.) I also began to see that synergy is essential for the success of communities and countries. Maslow predicted it would be possible for a society to form in which people who pursue their own self-interest "automatically benefit everyone else, whether [they] mean to or not."[9] This means that creating a better society requires helping many more people to become contribution motivated.

The good news is that most everyone practices this concept in at least parts of their lives, even if the theory is foreign. An electrician who enjoys serving his customers is contribution motivated. So is a professor who likes teaching her students how to unlock their abilities, or an artist whose painting evokes a sense of wonder in those who see it. Someone who devotes time or treasure to a charitable cause also fits the bill—they gain fulfillment by helping others.

It's even possible for people who lack their basic needs to become contribution motivated. No one illustrates this more powerfully than Viktor Frankl, whom I discovered many years ago. He developed an entire school of psychiatric thought—"logotherapy"—dedicated to helping people discover what gives them joy and fulfillment.[10]

Frankl has influenced me in several ways.

In terms of theory, Frankl reinforced my belief that every individual, no matter the obstacles, can find meaning in their lives by contributing to the lives of others.

What's even more important to me than his powerful work are the lessons from his actual life—his actions during the series of tragic events that he endured while developing his theories.

You see, Frankl was Jewish and had the great misfortune of living in Austria during the 1930s and 1940s. After the Nazis annexed his country, Frankl found himself under the control of a regime that wanted to exterminate him because of who he was. The Nazis forced him into a ghetto and then shipped him and his family to Auschwitz. Yet even in a death camp, Frankl found a way to apply his unique abilities to help others.

The unspeakable suffering that surrounded him could not shake Frankl's desire to contribute. He strived to help others in ways big and small, sharing what little he had with those in greater need. He used his psychiatric training to counsel people who had lost everything and everyone they loved. While some were turning on fellow victims to survive, Frankl did whatever he could to help. In doing so, he not only enabled others to discover meaning in their lives, he discovered meaning in his own.

By all accounts, having a purpose gave him the will to survive the most dire conditions, and his example did the same for a number of his fellow prisoners.[11] In the darkness of Auschwitz, Viktor Frankl was a small yet blinding ray of light.

A VISION OF THE FUTURE

If everyone were contribution motivated, the result would be a society unrivaled by any in the history of the world. But the reverse is true as well: when people can't contribute, society is significantly worse off.

> If everyone were contribution motivated, the result would be a society unrivaled by any in the history of the world.

I was beginning to understand this by the time I came back to Wichita. My self-transformation was underway. The more I applied myself, the more success I found, and the more I wanted to contribute—a never-ending cycle that motivates me still. Ever since, a good day has been one in which I feel I have contributed. That drive is the main source of all the success and joy I've had, as it has resulted in my creating value for others, not just in business but more broadly as a Social Entrepreneur, helping others contribute.

Looking back, there's no question that I started with big advantages. But as I hope to show in the pages ahead, even people who have nothing and face seemingly insurmountable obstacles can rise farther and faster than they ever dreamed.

The path for each of us is unique, but the elements are the same—discover and develop our unique gifts and use them to contribute to the betterment of others and ourselves. That's the way I was heading when I came back to Wichita. I was trying to find a better path for my life and was about to discover one for business and society as well. And even now, at age 85, I'm still busy being born.

2.
UNLIMITED POTENTIAL

---

66 The possibility of men living together in peace and to their mutual advantage without having to agree on common concrete aims, and bound only by abstract rules of conduct, was perhaps the greatest discovery mankind ever made. 99

F.A. HAYEK[1]

66 I am sure there was no man born marked of God above another; for none comes into the world with a saddle on his back, neither any booted and spurred to ride him. 99

RICHARD RUMBOLD[2]

My self-transformation entered a new phase once I returned to Wichita. With fewer temptations on nights and weekends, I began to spend all my spare time reading every book I thought might help me.

In college, my studies of the hard sciences helped me develop my gift and taught me that we live in a universe governed by certain principles. Now I began to ask: Was all human life similarly ordered? My theory was that certain universal principles existed, and if I learned them, they would enable me to contribute and succeed.

My years of exposure to the scientific method motivated me to search out other theories and concepts that I could test in my life. Where once I dove headfirst into science textbooks, I was suddenly swimming in psychology, philosophy, history, economics, ethics, and many other fields. I journeyed through works from Abraham Maslow, Karl Marx, and Ludwig von Mises, Friedrich Hayek and John Maynard Keynes, Michael Polanyi and Karl Popper, Vladimir Lenin and John Locke, along with many others from a vast array of disciplines and philosophies.

No topic was off-limits; no author was out of bounds. Even those I radically disagreed with shaped my understanding of how things work. They pointed me to helpful principles and led me to the epiphany that progress happens from the bottom up, when everyone is able to contribute. This was the beginning of my transformation. I was 28 years old.

It would take volumes to share what I learned (and am learning still) from every author and source, and the lessons they taught me about individual empowerment. Instead, let's take a shortcut through recent human history—there you'll see the principles of progress in action. My hope is that they will inspire you and help guide your life, as they have mine.

THE GREAT ENRICHMENT

Around two hundred years ago, something mystifying happened: life started to get sharply better—and it hasn't stopped since.[3]

Nothing like that had ever happened. Before roughly 1800, the human experience was miserable. Nearly everyone was born in poverty, lived in poverty, and died in poverty.[4] A large percentage died during childhood, and the average life expectancy hovered somewhere between 30 and 40 years.[5] Even those who lived longer saw essentially no change in daily life between their youth and their death.

The most successful empires and civilizations failed to break free from this grim reality. The Egyptians, Greeks, and Romans built towering monuments and temples, while the ancient Chinese painted beautiful vases and created terra-cotta armies, but their accomplishments brought little change in the lives of the masses. At best, a couple of generations could expect modest improvements—perhaps a little more food or a little better shelter—only for this minor progress to disappear soon after.[6]

If you think of history as a chart of progress, then the overwhelming majority of the chart is a flat line, with only the tiniest bumps and dips along the way. But then that flat line turned into a hockey stick, suddenly curving and shooting upward.

After millennia of crushing poverty, more and more of humanity came into relative plenty. In 1800, the typical person earned today's equivalent of $3 a day. Now they earn $33 a day—and in the United States, it's $140 or more.[7] Our standard of living is more than 4,000 percent higher than it was two centuries ago.

Worldwide, in the past 30 years, more than a billion people have risen out of extreme poverty, while the number who are undernourished has fallen by half, even as the population has risen by 50 percent.[8] As the author Johan Norberg has shown, "Illiteracy, child labor and infant mortality rates are falling faster than at any other time in human history. Life expectancy at birth has increased more than twice as much in the last century as it did in the previous 200,000 years."[9]

Behind the numbers are amazing creations and advances of every kind. We've cured diseases, powered the world with electricity, discovered ways to instantaneously communicate over the farthest distances, and created many other things that once would have been considered magic. Where since time immemorial men, women, and children had trudged on foot from the hut to the field and back again, we suddenly had carriages, then trains, then cars, then passenger planes, and now people are talking seriously about commercial space travel.

All told, we are healthier, wealthier, and happier than ever before, and we're still advancing. The scholar Deirdre McCloskey calls it the "Great Enrichment"—I can think of no better term.

We now take it for granted, but we ought to ask: What happened?

The short answer is that, imperfectly, with many starts and stops, more people were empowered to realize their potential, enabling societal progress.

This is the essence of bottom up: people becoming what they could be.

Injustices were rolled back and barriers began to fall, allowing many more people to self-actualize and contribute. As people gained the opportunity to live as they saw fit (a process that was slow and uneven, and remains rife with injustice), they began to apply their unique abilities and knowledge to improve their lives and the lives of others. They solved problems that had bedeviled previous generations, devoted themselves to breaking barriers, and moved society forward through millions of everyday acts, some small, some large.

This is the essence of bottom up: people becoming what they could be.

The results were unlike anything ever seen.

Widespread individual self-actualization was essentially impossible before the late eighteenth century. Until that time, most everyone lived in societies that stifled people's innate abilities. Such societies were usually either authoritarian or totalitarian. They were premised on control—the antithesis of empowerment. (The control mentality was evident not just in government but in religious organizations, business—see: guilds—and essentially everywhere.)

In authoritarian states, an individual or a group of elites holds power, without any limits on what they can do to their subjects. Unsurprisingly, they typically use their power to oppress the people, strengthen their rule, and enrich themselves. Individual flourishing is out of the question: the well-being of the tiny upper tier is their only real concern.

Totalitarian states are even worse. Their rulers seek to control all aspects of life—not only what people do but what they believe, think, and say. For example, in theocracies, the rulers tend to treat those who question their dogma as heretics, using torture and threat of death to force everyone to submit. The fires of the Spanish Inquisition claimed two types of victims: the many who lost their lives and the many more who, through fear, lost their ability to pursue their aspirations and develop their aptitudes.

Both authoritarian and totalitarian societies are based on control. Those at the top decide how society should be ordered and how people should live their lives. This crushes learning and initiative, causing the immiseration of virtually everyone. Every society based on control undermines progress by preventing individuals from discovering, developing, and applying their talents.

Such societies still exist today, but there aren't nearly as many. That's due to a series of developments that began to weaken the hold of the powerful few over the oppressed many. Control started to give way to liberation and empowerment.

THE SHOULDERS OF GIANTS

This took the convergence of a variety of events, changes that occurred and compounded over a long period of time. As these changes took hold, people of all kinds began to adjust their mind-sets—recognizing that the world was understandable, that no one had a monopoly on truth, that life could be improved, and that many more people could contribute, each in their own way.

The roots of this transformation stretch all the way back to the ancient world, but there were some key incidents that helped set the stage.

One of the first was Johannes Gutenberg's invention of the printing press in 1440. The resulting availability of books allowed for the proliferation of literacy, giving a greater number of people the ability to learn and think for themselves. For the first time, people could discover firsthand that their rulers lacked justification. Not only that, they saw that their rulers were wrong about much else.

The printing press enabled Martin Luther to challenge religious doctrine and theocratic control in the first half of the sixteenth century. He preached what at the time was a radical egalitarianism, dignifying all productive work and offering a theory of individual empowerment. His ideas spread rapidly, partly because he had translated the Bible from Latin into German, which more people could read and understand.[10]

For this and other subversive acts, Luther was sentenced to death, beating the rap only by dying of natural causes.[11] William Tyndale wasn't so lucky. He was burned at the stake for translating the Bible into English.[12]

Another key driver was the development of science and the scientific method. The two scientists who contributed most to this transformation were probably Galileo Galilei and Isaac Newton.

Galileo directly challenged the professors and priests who believed that everything worth knowing had been written long before. He said they only studied "a world on paper," whereas he discovered the real world through his experiments.[13]

Among other things, he demonstrated that Aristotle's theory that heavy objects fall faster than light ones was wrong. Even more important was when he proved that the sun—not the earth, as church dogma dictated—is at the center of the solar system. Galileo's liberal, antiauthoritarian attitude helped destroy the myth that rulers were all-knowing.

Newton took science and the scientific method to the next level. His discoveries were key to moving the culture away from a closed mentality toward open inquiry, invention, and improvement. He also challenged aristocratic dominance, foreshadowing the recognition of individual rights. For his contributions, Newton has been called "one of the architects of our civil liberties."[14]

These advances built on one another, hence Newton's famous saying "If I have seen farther, it is by standing on the shoulders of giants."[15] His actions, like those of Galileo, Luther, Gutenberg, and many others, didn't (and couldn't) happen in a vacuum. Each one opened the door to other discoveries and developments—whether spiritual, scientific, social, economic, or otherwise. The application of those discoveries enabled further advances by contemporaries as well as later generations.

But the Great Enrichment wasn't driven solely by these rare, brilliant minds. If it was, then it would have started earlier—perhaps in the sixteenth or seventeenth century. Their work was necessary, but not sufficient. What was also needed was for people of all kinds—

supposedly regular and "common" people—to get in on the action. The cycle that started with a few scientists, philosophers, and theologians had to expand to encompass the rest of us.

Which brings us to Holland.

After the Dutch escaped from Spanish rule in the early seventeenth century, they entered a golden age during which they were the freest, most creative, and wealthiest people in the world. This happened for a specific reason, heralding a societal revolution.[16]

Unlike virtually every other nation on Earth, Holland let a relatively large number of its citizens live their lives as they saw fit. It practiced religious tolerance and respected intellectual differences while refraining from some of the worst discrimination against women, Jews, and other historically disenfranchised groups. This attracted dissidents from other countries, such as John Locke and René Descartes, who, together with native-born thinkers like Baruch Spinoza, advanced concepts like property rights, free speech, religious liberty, scientific inquiry, and trade.

These concepts were more than just ethereal ideas. The acceptance of property rights gave people of all kinds the confidence to work and save and make improvements. The acceptance of free speech and religious liberty allowed people to offer new ideas and interpretations, fostering intellectual development. Free trade enabled the Dutch to benefit from goods and ideas from all over the world and find new markets for their own. Scientific inquiry stimulated technological advances in a host of industries and fields.

All these changes led to meaningful improvements in people's lives. Merchants, artisans, scientists, philosophers, and workmen were allowed to pursue their interests without being punished. And so they kept trying, kept improving, kept positing, kept painting, kept innovating, and kept advancing wherever possible. This led to more livable cities, better health, and more educational and employment opportunities for those who had been excluded.

MEETING MY MATCH

NO ONE HAS CHANGED my life more than my wife, Liz. She is everything I'm not, and everything I need. Being so different has enabled each of us to learn from the other, and I believe we are both much better for it. I find her even more captivating now than when we were dating.

Our paths first crossed in the late 1960s. It was at a party—a very brief encounter sometime before we started dating. I remember thinking, "Too bad she's involved with someone else." She radiated a magnetic force that drew everyone to her, including me.

So when I learned she was free from that relationship, I immediately called her for a date. It was apparent from the beginning that she was unlike anyone I'd ever met. The more I got to know her, the more taken I was.

Liz grew up in a family with an old-world Italian culture in which girls were to focus on being attractive, developing social graces, then getting married and raising children. As someone who was steeped in

principles, including Maslow's mandate that "what one can be, one must be," I thought she could be so much more.

Some of her gifts were already apparent: her world-class people skills and her style. She was rising fast in her career in fashion, working as a buyer for women's separates at a local department store—a prestigious position for a 22-year-old. And she was an amazingly quick study on most everything.

She had never tried sports, whereas I was into skiing, tennis, and running. At first she hated them all, especially skiing. She was delighted when my knees gave out and we stopped going.

Tennis grew on her when our son, Chase, started playing. She now loves it, playing every day, and is still winning tournaments.

Not too long ago, I ran into a tennis friend of Liz's at the gym who complimented us on how well we had danced together at a party the previous Saturday night. I corrected her—Liz dances well, I don't. I only

Liz and I met in the late 1960s. I knew she was special from the moment I met her.

We've been together for more than 50 years.

look good when Liz leads. Her retort was, "Yes, Liz leads us all." When I told Liz, she laughed and said, "That was not a compliment."

But it's not just dancing and tennis. And it's not just me. Liz has developed her extraordinary people skills such that she leads everybody, and I mean everybody, without fear. I can't tell you the number of times I've seen successful, famous people sit still for some needed Liz logic.

And why? Because they knew she was right, and later told me so. Everyone who knows her regularly seeks her counsel, including our children, as did my mother when she was alive.

I give part of the credit to the principles I was encouraging her to learn that were transforming my life. At first, she considered that too heavy a burden. Then, as she witnessed the principles helping me, she began applying them herself and saw that they aided her as well.

I'm so grateful she did, as she uses the principles daily to support me. For example, years ago she cured me of using cocktail parties to hone my ability to apply and debate them, which wasn't making

me any friends. And over the years, she has improved my ability to communicate their benefits by encouraging me to use more stories.

More than 50 years later, I can say unreservedly: Liz has transformed my life. She has always compensated for my flaws and has been a tremendous source of joy.

No wonder I love her still. But why does she love me? I asked her. Her answer was classic Liz. She told me that in the beginning, "it wasn't exactly fireworks." Instead, it was because she had never met anyone like me, "someone who was so dedicated to his cause, to his North Star. Someone who invariably did what he said he would, who so faithfully lived up to his commitments."

We love each other even more today than when we fell in love. And that's because we have dedicated ourselves to helping each other become what we are capable of being.

—CHARLES KOCH

This is not to say that the Holland of 1690 was without tragic flaws. Dutch society was still riven with injustices and mistreatment of individuals and ethnic groups. Despicably, it followed suit with nearly every other nation at the time and allowed slavery. The lost human potential from that injustice is incalculable. While Holland showed what even a small increase in liberty and justice can do, especially compared to the other countries of that era, we cannot look to it as an ideal model.

Despite its injustices, though, the Dutch experience gave a glimpse of what's possible. If Holland could thrive by only partially implementing principles such as equal rights, openness, individual liberty, global trade, and scientific inquiry, then countries that more fully practiced such principles could do even better and go farther and faster.

Which is exactly what happened. The ideas that transformed Holland made their way to England in about 1700, then to Scotland, and on to parts of France, Belgium, and Germany. Those ideas also found their way to the New World—to 13 colonies on the North Atlantic coast.

Those colonies then did what no other nation had done to date: founded a new country, the United States of America, dedicated to the proposition that all people "are created equal" and possess "certain inalienable rights," among which are "life, liberty, and the pursuit of happiness."

A NEW COUNTRY, A NEW VISION

In these simple, elegant words, human history was turned upside down. America articulated a vision unlike anything that had come before.

It's hard to overstate how seismic this shift really was. Where once all societies had been divided between the few rulers and the many ruled, now there was a nation that said, in principle, no such distinction exists. Of course, America inexcusably and widely violated this principle from the start through slavery, the treatment of Native Americans, restrictions on women, and many other egregious injustices. (I will expand on this shortly.)

Unlike any other nation, however, America had established a standard that made these injustices obvious and abhorrent. That standard, enshrined in the Declaration of Independence, ultimately empowered those who would break so many barriers over the next two-hundred-plus years. It opened opportunities for the Social Entrepreneurs who went on to help millions more contribute.

The economist-historian-philosopher Friedrich Hayek perhaps best captured this transformation in his quote at the beginning of this chapter. The "greatest discovery mankind ever made" refers to a system of equal rights. Prior to this discovery, societies were ordered on the assumption that control was essential to communal stability—that society had to make a choice between the harmony of the community and the autonomy of the individual.

But this was (and is) a false choice. In a system of equal rights, empowered people realize that helping others is the way to help themselves. As equal rights spread, so did empowerment.

The result was the Great Enrichment.

As more people began to discover, develop, and apply their abilities, they improved the world around them and found fulfillment in their own lives. They combined their ideas with the best ideas of others, creating something greater still. This has always been the story of material advances, from the wheel to the automobile to the airplane. That it took us so long to get from the wheel to the automobile, but not from the automobile to the airplane, is a testament to the progress that's possible. When more people are engaged, the result is much more progress, much more quickly.

The dizzying speed of progress over the past two centuries was directed by no one and predicted by no one. The opposite is true: it often came from the most unlikely places. People who would have previously been considered ordinary could act on their ideas, and it turned out they could do extraordinary things. A pair of bicycle mechanics with little formal education invented the airplane. A college dropout founded the company that led the digital revolution. Other examples are everywhere.

This points to a profound lesson, one that seems obvious in retrospect: *all* of us are smarter than *each* of us.

We are all better off when we add our voices to the larger conversation. We all benefit when each person has the chance to make their mark on society. When we transform ourselves, we simultaneously help transform the world around us.

PROMISES BROKEN

The progress of the past two centuries is nothing short of breathtaking, yet the story is not one of all progress and no pain.

The extent to which we have followed the principles of the Declaration of Independence has made the United States the most successful country in the world. Sadly, America has also violated its principles in appalling ways. For many people, the promise of equal rights has been denied in whole or in part, thereby limiting—or eliminating—their ability to apply themselves and contribute. The consequences of these violations continue to haunt us today.

Slavery is the most horrific example. For nearly a century after the Declaration was signed, millions of African Americans toiled in degrading, dehumanizing conditions. Fathers, mothers, and children were considered property, and as such, were bought and sold, separated, beaten, and worse.

After slavery's abolition, segregation, violence, and racism prevented many African Americans from fully participating in American life. Racism still shackles people—and limits our country.

Native Americans faced many injustices as well. Like African Americans, their rights and humanity were also denied. Most were stripped of their land and driven from their homes. Many were victims of organized violence and even genocide, as expansionist settlers, military officers, and politicians sought to eradicate Native American culture and Native Americans themselves. A continuing system of control and dependency has led to a legacy of struggling individuals and communities in many areas today.

Injustice also marred the treatment of women. At the Founding, women were excluded from full participation in society. For decades, women were prohibited from attending college or defending their rights and, when married, from controlling their own property. For more than a century, they couldn't vote. Unjust expectations rooted in this history and culture continue to hold women back.

Throughout American history, there have been many other grave injustices, targeting religious and sexual minorities, immigrants, and others. They are all destructive, and wrong for at least two reasons.

The first and most important is the profound harm to the individual. When people are denied their rights, they have less opportunity to discover and apply their abilities. Every person deserves the chance to find fulfillment, meaning, and personal success—to self-actualize. One of the great tragedies in life is being denied the opportunity to become all you can be.

The second reason is the harm to society. When people are prevented from realizing their potential, we are all poorer for it, and not just materially.

The Great Enrichment happened because more and more people were allowed to contribute. Each such person added to the advances of the last two hundred years. Every time someone was excluded—for whatever reason—it subtracted from our possible achievements. Just as our progress was unimaginable to previous generations, where we could have been right now is unimaginable to *us*.

This puts in perspective the injustices of our time. Many have been around since before America's Founding.

In subsequent chapters, I will more fully explore many other modern-day injustices. They include corporate welfare, protectionism, and a broken criminal justice system, among many other wrongs. The first two rig the economy in favor of the well-connected and especially harm the least fortunate, preventing them from contributing. The last—the criminal justice system—disproportionately holds back those with little or nothing. While they are in no way equivalent to the much more egregious and obvious harms of slavery or abuse of Native Americans, they nonetheless stifle people's ability to find fulfillment and to contribute, undercutting social progress. Just as previous generations have removed the most pernicious violations, it is up to us to remove those that persist today.

The Great Enrichment will remain unfinished so long as even one person continues to be sidelined.

There is another important similarity between the injustices of the past and those of today: their defenders say the system can't be changed, so we shouldn't try.

At our nation's Founding, no less than Thomas Jefferson declared that slavery simply couldn't be eliminated. The author of the Declaration of Independence himself wrote, "We have the wolf by the ear, and we can neither hold him, nor safely let him go."[17] It wasn't that Jefferson didn't understand the evil of slavery. He did, as shown by his statement, "I tremble for my country when I reflect that God is just."[18] Instead, as was prevalent at the time, he was blind to the potential of those who suffered the horrors of slavery.

RAISING OUR KIDS

LIZ AND I HAVE BEEN blessed to have two amazing children, Elizabeth and Chase. Starting when they were very young, I wanted to help them transform their lives using the principles that were transforming my own. I was so passionate about it that I would frequently wake up in the middle of the night filled with emotion about wanting to pour everything I had into empowering them.

Which is exactly what I tried to do. In their early years, I especially focused on helping them discover their unique gifts through trial and error. My approach was much stronger on the error side, making it extra difficult for our children.

The first real talent Elizabeth revealed was at summer camp in Missouri as a preteenager. One of the activities at graduation was a race. Liz and I were amazed— Elizabeth didn't just win it, she blew the others away. Afterward, I got her to join a local junior track team, the Shocker Striders, which provided training and coaching, and got the kids to meets throughout the state.

Wanting to ensure that this experiment succeeded and helped Elizabeth increase her confidence, I provided additional training and coaching on the side. (My usual tendency is to overdo, e.g., 5 a.m. runs on family vacation, wind sprints in a blizzard on Christmas Eve.) I also went with her to every weekend meet. She developed rapidly, winning second in the state championship in both the one- and two-mile races after just a couple of years.

But when Elizabeth became a teenager, her performance began to slip. To see what was wrong, I watched one of her training sessions, and the problem was obvious. She wasn't giving her all.

When I confronted her, she said she no longer wanted to do track. I said that's fine, but you need to do something to which you will give 100 percent. She had totally accepted the idea that to be happy, you have to discover your gifts, fully develop them, and apply them constructively.

She said, "Look, Pop, I'm a bohemian. I do not enjoy athletic competition.

We worked hard to help our children discover their own unique paths. After a lot of trial and error, Chase now leads Koch's investments in transformational technology. (Africa, 1985)

Left: Elizabeth is devoting her life to helping others find their way, as she did. In 1984, we were having fun at our home in Wichita.

Right: Our family on a fishing trip in Alaska in 1986.

When our kids were young, I'd wake up in the middle of the night filled with emotion about wanting to pour everything I had into empowering them. (Father's Day, Wichita, 1984)

I'm passionate about writing and painting." I said, "So you're going to push yourself as hard at writing and painting as I pushed you in track?" She said, "Absolutely." She was true to her word. She became as committed as possible to applying all of herself to everything she did. She won national painting and writing awards. She was also one of the top students in her class. But it didn't make her happy.

In fact, the harder she worked, the less happy she was becoming. She tells me the reason for this was that her extreme industry wasn't driven by curiosity or the desire to grow but by an unconscious desire to "earn" all the privilege she was born with. She kept thinking that each paper or work project would be the magic ticket to self-confidence and respect, but none were. It took many years before she realized that she had missed part of the puzzle—all that industry would not be fulfilling until it was attached to a North Star.

Thankfully, she discovered hers. Central to that was founding an organization called Unlikely Collaborators in which she uses her story of being lost, combined with a wide range of therapeutic tools and introspective practices, to help others transcend limiting beliefs and find their own unique way, as she did.

Chase's path was quite different but also involved trial and error and being lost for a lengthy period. Chase demonstrated good coordination at an early age, and since I was into tennis then, we got him into a tennis program.

He developed quickly, doing well in Kansas District and qualifying for Missouri Valley regional competition in his age group. In the 12-year-old category, he made the national championship tournament in San Diego, performing well enough to be ranked in the top 100. He and his superstar teammate Matt Wright did so well over four years of high school that they were written up in *Sports Illustrated.*

After several more years of a life consumed by tennis, Chase's performance began to slip. Liz tried to encourage him, but at a Missouri Valley tournament in Kansas City, it was obvious it was all over. He threw both of his matches in a double-elimination tournament to get out of there as quickly as possible.

Liz's seventieth. Our family is fortunate to still be close after all these years.

When they got home, Liz had me talk to him. I told him he could quit tennis but that he would need to do something else to which he would give his all. He immediately said, "I'd rather have a job."

I think he believed he could get an easy job in Wichita, allowing him to party with his friends. So he was surprised when the manager of our feedlot in Syracuse, Kansas, pulled up in a pickup the next day to take him to his new job.

Chase spent the next six weeks sleeping on a couch in his manager's trailer, working 13 hours a day, 7 days a week, shoveling manure, treating sick animals, and repairing facilities. He made friends with all of his coworkers, who didn't exactly share his background.

Chase came back feeling better about himself than he ever had. He was transformed, as he could see he was capable of much more than he had ever imagined. He spent the rest of his summers doing tough jobs at company facilities throughout the country. Upon graduation, he worked at another company in Austin, Texas, for a couple of years before joining Koch Industries.

After 11 years with us, in many roles, Chase was named president of Koch Fertilizer. That only lasted a year before he fired himself, taking a lesser position. He believed he wasn't the right person for the role, that others could do a better job.

Three years later, in 2017, pursuing his North Star, he founded Koch Disruptive Technologies to acquire cutting-edge innovations that would enable Koch Industries to better serve customers, employees, and society. I'm happy to say that both Chase and KDT are off and running.

Liz and I are so grateful for our two children. They have taught us much about how we're all unique and how we all need to find our own best path. Discovering that path is never easy, but it's worth the struggle.

—CHARLES KOCH

Jefferson and those like him, who had such a strong belief in *some* people, simply could not bring themselves to believe in *all* people. This view, that certain groups lack innate worth or ability, is at the root of so many other injustices throughout history, many of which I'll describe.

Gratefully, other Social Entrepreneurs have had the courage of their convictions, from Gutenberg to Luther, Galileo to Newton, Frederick Douglass to Martin Luther King Jr., and all the pioneers who opened the door to the progress of the past two centuries. It's also true for the *billions* of others who contributed by applying their own gifts to do what was right. As I was learning, no barrier is too big to break, so long as principled people have the courage to take it on.

APPLYING THE LESSONS OF HISTORY

My studies exposed me to the wonders of individual empowerment. It and the other principles I was learning consumed me to such an extent that I wasn't satisfied with simply understanding them intellectually. I felt compelled to apply them in every facet of my life. Doing so, I believed, would enable me to achieve much more and have greater fulfillment than I ever would have otherwise.

I didn't think of myself as a Social Entrepreneur at the time—certainly not in those words—but I definitely wanted to share what I was learning so others could benefit as I did. From my experience, history, and other studies, I could see a future of boundless possibility.

I see it still. The Great Enrichment will remain unfinished so long as even one person continues to be sidelined. If we can empower everyone to contribute and realize their potential, there will be no limit to what our country can become. The progress of the past is nothing compared to the promise of the future.

As you will see, this was about to be demonstrated in the transformation of the family business, Koch Industries.

3.

TRANSFORM-ING KOCH INDUSTRIES

" The philosophers have only interpreted the world . . . the point is to change it. "

KARL MARX[1]

---

was 31 when I succeeded my father as chairman and CEO of the family business.

The year was 1967, and my elevation was no cause for celebration. Fred Koch had just died. A heart attack early in the year had put him in the hospital. A second heart attack had followed, and the third, in November, proved fatal. To honor my father's memory, we renamed Rock Island Oil & Refining, our parent company, after him. The business has been Koch Industries ever since.

I wanted to honor my father in another way: by transforming his company and bringing it to new heights. Because of my studies in so many disciplines, I was swimming in a sea of concepts and principles—ideas that I wanted to apply to the company to make it better and grow.

My idea was to apply the theories I was learning to enable Koch Industries to succeed by empowering our employees to succeed. I envisioned our employees using their aptitudes to better serve our customers and society—benefiting themselves and building the company from the bottom up.

Simultaneously, I was applying these principles outside the business. In the 1960s, I began speaking on college campuses and elsewhere about how best to foster human flourishing. (This included arguments against America's involvement in the Vietnam War, among other issues.) I also took my first steps in philanthropy, focusing on helping students apply these ideas to realize their potential.

Business took most of my time, especially in those early years, but my goal was to get those newly acquired concepts into practice in every part of my life.

In the 1960s, our businesses consisted of a company that made a specialized chemical separation product (Koch Engineering), a crude oil–gathering company (Rock Island Oil), and cattle ranches. I first worked at Koch Engineering, which my father turned over to me carte blanche. At my father's request, I also quickly got involved in the oil-gathering business, which generated the bulk of the company's income.

I dedicated all my spare time to learning the principles of progress, and a good part of my company time to figuring out, through trial and error, how to apply them to get results. It gave me great insight into the company's strengths—and its weaknesses.

A STRUGGLING COMPANY

What I discovered both saddened and motivated me. My father's failing health had prevented him from effectively managing the business. The company had neither the vision nor the willingness to work to improve and better serve our customers. It was on a fast track to nowhere, which would eventually end in us going out of business.

Worse, I found miniature versions of the paradigms and approaches that had held back humanity for millennia.

For one, control and protectionism ruled the day. Managers thought they always knew best, believing that their ideas were naturally superior to those of the rank-and-file. There was a near-total unwillingness to ask for or listen to feedback.

For example, the president of Koch Engineering would send questionnaires weekly to his subordinates, making them explain each expense item, no matter how small. As a result, they had much less time for productive work. So not only was there no innovation, the office equipment was obsolete and the bookkeeping was six months behind. His attempts to control and micromanage people held the entire company back.

As for protectionism, the company resisted changes to the status quo and had an aversion to trial and error and risk-taking of any kind.

Case in point: it refused to let customers verify that its custom-designed product would deliver the promised benefits. They feared customers would copy its design methodology. In another attempt to avoid competition, the company had also contracted with multiple shops in Europe, with each making different pieces of the product, and still another shop assembling them. The whole system was extremely costly and wasteful, leading to sizable losses. Such are the consequences of protectionism.

If our employees had the opportunity to transform themselves, they would transform the company, and in turn help transform society.

The oil-gathering company, Rock Island, was hardly better. Its management opposed extending the business beyond southern Oklahoma, so our little piece of business, while profitable, was essentially frozen. The managers were afraid to compete with the major oil companies, so they settled for what they had. This is just another form of protectionism—the unwillingness to try new things out of fear they may fail.

The more involved I got, the more problems I found, giving me more opportunities to improve results by applying the principles of progress. Mercifully, I wasn't the only one to see them. Many employees knew we could do things better and had constructive suggestions—ideas that, when combined, could begin to transform the company from the bottom up. They were just being stifled, ignored, and controlled.

This counterproductive approach created a destructive downward cycle: when employees know that no one will listen to them, they keep their ideas to themselves. Worse, they stop looking for ways to improve things and opportunities to apply themselves. This resulted in a stagnant company, just as control and protectionism had caused countless societies to stagnate.

The lessons of history should have been obvious: everyone is capable of contributing. When they are empowered to do so, the results are far superior.

UNLEASHING OUR EMPLOYEES' POTENTIAL

In the mid-1960s, we had about 300 employees, and every single one had abilities they could apply to benefit the company and themselves. They simply needed a better environment, one in which they could discover their aptitudes, develop them into valued skills, apply them to maximize their contributions, and then do it all over again. Individuals who follow this path—it is unique for each person—continually learn, grow, and contribute at a higher level, greatly increasing their ability to succeed, whatever their calling.

My task was clear: change the company's culture to one of empowerment, not control.

I knew this was the key to Koch's future. If our employees had the opportunity to transform themselves, they would transform the company, and in turn help transform society. I believed employee empowerment would allow Koch Industries to experience a Great Enrichment of its own.

My task was clear: change the company's culture to one of empowerment, not control.

In my early conversations with management and employees, I was explicit about my intentions. My goal wasn't to give all the answers, which I didn't have. Rather, it was to provide the vision, philosophy, and tools for our employees to find answers themselves, to solve problems using their own unique abilities and knowledge. We needed to ask, not tell; to experiment, not stifle.

The most important person who had the same vision was Sterling Varner. He is proof that everyone can contribute, and that so-called "ordinary" people are capable of extraordinary things. He became the greatest success story in the company's history.

Sterling was born in an oil-field tent and delivered by his grandmother, since no doctor was available. Throughout his life, he stuttered and was beset with serious health problems, including a botched appendectomy and lung damage. His college education consisted of two years at the Murray State School of Agriculture in Tishomingo, Oklahoma. He came to the company as a clerk in a 1946 acquisition.

Sterling was the sort of fellow most folks wrote off until they got to know him. He had great people skills and a first-rate entrepreneurial mind. I immediately recognized it when I started working with Rock Island. Unlike many others, including nearly all the management, he thought we should aggressively expand our oil gathering, and he had great insights on how to do it. So, together, we pushed to make it happen.

We aggressively bought trucks, trucking companies, and pipelines, in addition to building our own pipelines in every new oil field anywhere in the United States and Canada. Far from just trying to maintain the existing business, Sterling and I dreamed of becoming the largest oil-gathering company in North America. By the 1990s, we accomplished our goal, moving about a million barrels of oil a day.

A PROFILE IN PARTNERSHIP

IT'S HARD TO EXPRESS just how much Sterling Varner meant to me.

That's true, even though we had quite different aptitudes. In fact, it's that difference, combined with our shared vision and values, that made us so close. We made each other better.

Our differences were many.

Born in a tent, he faced steep barriers from day one. I didn't.

He was a people person. My strength is concepts.

He could turn a phrase in any situation. I prefer paragraphs—long ones. In fact, his one-liners are so legendary in the company that we call them "Sterlingisms."

One of many that I remember is, "Don't confuse motion with progress."

It was precisely because of our differences that we were able to accomplish so much together. Sterling's quiet but powerful influence can be seen behind so much of the company's early success.

We did share some similarities. Both of us were raised in families that prized integrity. That was probably what drew me to Sterling in the first place.

Sterling's character was evident to all. At a meeting in the early 1970s, after striking a particularly good business deal, a few of our salespeople started joking and laughing about how they had outsmarted the customer. Sterling blew his stack.

He came down hard on them: "Stop it! You boys are way out of line! Our customers are our friends. They are the ones who keep us in business, and we don't take advantage of or laugh at our friends. It's not right. And if we do, we won't have any friends and we won't have any business. . . . We have to earn their trust, and that starts by treating them with respect."

Sterling, as usual, had said exactly what needed to be said when it

Sterling was born in a tent at an oil field. He overcame early hardships to become president of Koch Industries.

Sterling was an ideal partner and friend. In 1968, we were working on opportunities in Alaska.

After retiring, Sterling loved being at his Shadow Valley ranch in eastern Kansas.

needed to be said. And he certainly said it better than I would have. I have lost track of how often that was the case.

Sterling taught me many lessons over the 60-plus years I knew him, and I'd like to think I did the same for him. None was more vital than the importance of partnership.

He was living verification of my theory that you accomplish the most when you surround yourself with people who are good at the things you're not. People who bring a different perspective. Sure enough, that's who Sterling was to me.

But, as I said in my eulogy at his funeral in 2009, he was much more than that: "He was a mentor, and my closest advisor and confidant. He was one of the best friends I ever had . . . like an older brother that I loved and respected."

—CHARLES KOCH

In Sterling's story, we see how anyone can become contribution motivated. He overcame tremendous personal barriers and unearthed his gift, enabling him to better his life and the lives of others. By the time he retired, that son of an oil-field mule contractor was president and COO of Koch Industries, and he was a contributing board member until his death in 2009.

Sterling didn't build our oil-gathering business by himself. Just as he was empowered to use his gifts, we were all empowered to do the same. Our salespeople, our pipelayers, our truck drivers—all employees were given the chance to act on their ideas, see and seize opportunities, and better serve customers, and were rewarded in turn. Their success spurred them to find more ways to contribute, in a cycle of continual transformation and value creation. All of us focused where we could accomplish the most in the spirit of bottom up.

One of the greatest lessons I have learned is that people who are overlooked may have the most to contribute.

Like Sterling, nearly all our employees have come from humble roots. This often surprises people, especially those who assume that success comes from grand plans and so-called great leaders rather than regular folks. We found that a great leader is someone who empowers those they work with, which describes Sterling Varner perfectly. One of his favorite sayings was, "I get things done through people."

An Ivy League–educated journalist from a famous New York business publication once asked me, "Doesn't your location in Wichita make it hard to attract top talent?" She probably meant no offense, but her subtext was clear: "How do you convince Harvard and Yale grads to come work for you?"

The answer is, we don't (or, I should say, we rarely do). Other companies might prefer to hire Ivy League graduates, but we've had much more success hiring from Wichita State, Kansas State, and Oklahoma State. Sure enough, the four employees who succeeded me as president of the company hailed from Murray State School of Agriculture (but didn't graduate), Texas A&M, the University of Tulsa, and Emporia State University.

One of the greatest lessons I have learned is that people who are overlooked may have the most to contribute. This is true not only of those who went to colleges you have never heard of but also of college dropouts and those with high school diplomas or less. You'd be astounded how often they have the virtue and talents we need, more so than the most credentialed Ivy League grads.

MORE IDEAS, MORE PROGRESS

My efforts to empower employees regardless of education, background, or belief have always been grounded in a simple reality: different people have different abilities and knowledge. The history of innovation encompasses different ideas combining to create something better (think back to chapter two). The success of the company depends on the same thing.

That is why we encourage our employees to proactively share their ideas. We got this concept from the scientist-philosopher Michael Polanyi, who coined the term "Republic of Science." He theorized that progress comes from individuals in different disciplines and with different perspectives freely sharing knowledge and challenging one another, which spurs innovations (a great illustration of bottom up).

To benefit from everyone's unique knowledge, we liberate and urge our employees to proactively offer suggestions. Supervisors at every level are held accountable for soliciting their employees' ideas and applying those with merit.

This is central to what we call the "Challenge Process." It can be summed up simply: anyone can challenge anything—ideas, recommendations, ways of thinking, etc. We encourage rigorous questioning and brainstorming, in a spirit of intellectual humility and constructive improvement.

This is essential to overcoming the natural tendency to defer to authority. Empowerment also demands it: one of the biggest problems throughout history has been a hostility to challenge by those at the top. Generally, the rulers and powerful refused to listen to others, especially those they thought beneath them. Worse, they took challenge as a threat to their dominance, often punishing or executing the challenger. While they may have had a monopoly on power, they never had a monopoly on truth or knowledge.

No wonder humanity muddled on for millennia without any meaningful improvement.

The lessons of history apply to business. CEOs don't have a monopoly on good ideas, either. You never know where—or whom—a brilliant idea will come from. But if you stifle even a small portion of people, chances are the idea will never arise. The principle of openness is non-negotiable for progress.

For the record, this practice of challenge applies to me the same as anyone else. Informally, it's a daily part of my work life. Formally, the leaders of Koch's various companies and capabilities typically meet every two months in what we call a "Discovery Board." Any of the 30 or so participants can bring up a problem or opportunity, and the rest of us respectfully challenge it. Most of the time my ideas get pushback from quite a few people. I never leave the room unscathed, or without a better solution.

Some time ago, another reporter asked me why I tolerate this. She asked, "You don't fire them?" I laughed out loud! "There's no place for fragile egos here," I said. "What damages your self-esteem more: being shown the flaws of your proposal early, or failing to seek objections only to endure a massive failure?" Challenge is critical for everyone in any organization, the leaders especially. As I told the reporter, "I love it."[2] I also depend on it.

A CULTURE OF CONTRIBUTION

As Koch has expanded, our top priority has been to implement the principles of progress within our company. This is a difficult process, especially when we acquire companies dominated by the control mentality.

One of my earliest challenges as CEO took place in 1969 when we acquired full ownership of an oil refinery in Minnesota. Its culture was so hostile to new ideas that a number of employees went to extremes to prevent any change. People nearly died from the violence of the ensuing strike.

It was a brutal nine-month struggle, but in the end, we were able to begin to gradually change the culture from control and protectionism to empowerment. Today, the Pine Bend refinery is much larger, much safer, and more environmentally friendly, and it uses fewer resources, primarily because our employees have become contribution motivated rather than negatively motivated. It has been transformed, with employees leading the way, in innovation and superior performance.

We encountered another setback in implementing our bottom-up philosophy at our metal fabrication plant in Bergamo, Italy, in the 1990s. Its union leaders rejected the approach, saying: "This might work in the United States, but it's not going to work in Italy. Here, managers think. Workers work. You're asking us to do the manager's job."

They were right about that last part—we wanted them to think creatively and constructively instead of doing everything as they had in the past. If they did, they would find success and fulfillment by making innovations that created more value for others. And they ultimately did.

Similarly, after acquiring Georgia-Pacific in 2005, we began implementing the principles of empowerment at its many locations, including a substantial manufacturing plant in Green Bay, Wisconsin. As was the case with those at our Italian facility, most of the Green Bay employees were being controlled rather than encouraged to contribute.

One example stands out. The employees running the machinery on the shop floor had the best knowledge of those machines, but only senior managers could push the "stop" button in an emergency. If non-management employees saw something wrong, they had to find a manager instead of addressing the safety matter immediately themselves.

This illustrates one of the dangerous consequences of control. That rule was the first to go when we began empowering employees. It was an early sign that we trust employees to do what's right, and we wanted them to see themselves as partners in the company's success.

We have found that control is ingrained in essentially every company we acquire. When Koch purchased Georgia-Pacific, its senior management worked on the top floor of a 51-story building, which had a special elevator just for that floor. No employee was permitted on the floor without a jacket and tie, even though the rest of the company had a "business casual" dress code.

We knew this wouldn't do. It sent the signal that managers were set apart, somehow better than everyone else. So we moved these leaders downstairs with their teams and converted the fifty-first floor into meeting rooms available to all employees.

Similarly, at Koch's headquarters in Wichita, we don't have an executive dining room or anything like that. When I get lunch, I go to the cafeteria, pick out my food, and pay like everyone else. Employees regularly approach me with their ideas. That's exactly what should happen in a culture of empowerment.

Some of our greatest successes have come from our acquired companies, as employees who were once held back became empowered to discover how they can best contribute.

Take Mike Cooper, a master technician at Georgia-Pacific. With a career spanning 40-plus years, he used to worry about whether his job would be automated. That's a legitimate fear, and many companies stoke it by failing to help their employees find new ways to apply themselves. By contrast, as we implemented our principles at GP, Mike came to see that automation could create more opportunities for him, not fewer. The company supported Mike by providing him training, recognizing that we all need assistance to succeed.

Soon, Mike's facility was filled with laser-guided vehicles that did his old job, loading pallets of paper into shipping trucks. One day, he noticed that costly mistakes were being made on the back end, so he used his own skills to design a solution on the front end. He created a device to adjust the vehicles' sensors, making them more precise when loading.

Mike was rewarded and now holds a patent for his invention, which is used across the company and saves a lot of money that we invest more effectively elsewhere.[3] He is one of a great many Koch employees over the years who saw a problem and used their talents to solve it. (The company did its part by removing barriers in his way.) Every employee who succeeds moves the company and society forward.

One reason for our progress is that it is widely known at Koch Industries that the reward for success will be greater than the penalty for failure. Throughout history, inventors and entrepreneurs have experimented for the same reason. To encourage our employees to do the same, we have cultivated a culture of prudent risk-taking—asking employees to experiment—and we ensure that they share in the profits if they find a better way to serve customers. The same is true when they find a way to use fewer resources, which we can then devote to other needs.

In practice, this means that even the most junior employee can dramatically increase their income. Recently, two technicians at our Wichita analytic lab together doubled their normal income by developing a test method that enabled us to significantly increase throughput at one of our plants. At Koch, anyone can earn more than his boss by creating more value. We put no limits on incentive pay, which is entirely dependent on an employee's contribution.

Once again, this is essential to empowerment: if you know you'll succeed by helping others, then you'll focus on doing so. That, after all, is the story of progress.

A COMPANY TRANSFORMED

What has been the result of the application of these principles? Nothing short of the transformation of Koch Industries.

When I returned to Wichita, the company was relatively small. We had one low-volume manufactured product, a small oil-gathering system in Oklahoma, and a ranching business. We weren't doing very much, and we weren't doing it very well.

Empowerment changed everything, slowly at first and then faster than I anticipated—just like the Great Enrichment. Our employees began to see new opportunities, applied themselves to make the most of them, and then found still more opportunities. Not only did they improve the existing parts of the business, they also found new businesses to enter.

Just as employees applied their abilities to find new success, the company applied its capabilities to do the same. Up and down Koch Industries, we have continually worked to succeed by increasing our contribution to customers, employees, and other key constituencies.

Where we are now looks nothing like where we started.

Recall my first assignment at Koch Engineering, which was failing in the 1960s. Now it's a leader in separation and combustion technology, pollution control, engineering and construction, and many other fields. One of our oldest and stodgiest businesses is bursting with new ideas. Its revenue has increased more than a thousandfold—and its net income even more—for the simple reason that it's filled with employees who want to contribute, and do.

Remember that small oil-gathering system? As you already know, we turned it into the nation's largest. That successful transformation required building a trading capability that turned into a large commodity-trading business. We then took the lessons learned and applied them to gas liquids and natural gas. Next we used our gathering capabilities to create distribution businesses in energy, asphalt, and fertilizer, among others. Fertilizer distribution also gave us the opening to build a much broader fertilizer business. Once again, our expanding success flowed directly from our employees' expanding contribution, a process that continues today.

These are the never-ending cycles I mentioned in the introduction—what we call virtuous cycles of mutual benefit.

Without going into too much detail, a virtuous cycle starts when a person discovers, develops, and applies her unique ability to create value in the lives of others. The more she develops and applies it, the more she expands her horizons and discovers new opportunities to succeed. As she uses her abilities to a greater degree, she reaches new levels of achievement in a process that repeats over and over. While individuals create these cycles with the development of their aptitudes, a company does so by applying and expanding its capabilities.

Beyond the two mentioned above, we have created these cycles in three other areas.

The Pine Bend refinery is the foundation of our largest cycle. What started with oil refining has grown into chemicals, nylon, paper and building products, glass, and renewable energy, putting us in the business of everything from airbags to paper plates to energy-efficient construction materials. We've also created a cycle with investments that help other companies improve their businesses.

Our most recent is perhaps our most exciting: electronics and data technology. Through technology, much of what used to be dull or dangerous work at an office, chemical process plant, or manufacturing facility can now be handled by a technological solution, freeing employees to do higher-value, more challenging, rewarding work. This gives employees in all kinds of roles a much better chance to self-actualize.

Our employees' success has always been the source of our success. And what a success it has been. As I mentioned in the introduction, Koch Industries has grown 7,000-fold since 1961—43 times the growth of the stock market, an increase of up to four orders of magnitude. An investment of $1,000 in the company when I came back to Wichita would be worth $10 million today. Where then we had revenues of $12 million, we now have annual revenues of around $120 billion—a 1,000,000 percent increase.

These numbers surpass everything I thought possible. In fact, shortly after I joined, I plotted out my vision for the company's growth. By 2019, we had exceeded my lifetime goal eightyfold.

While it's tempting to look at this transformation and think that it all happened because of top management, I give the lion's share of credit to our employees, as would any other executive, past or present. We certainly played our part—everyone does in bottom-up progress—but so did our employees. Whenever you read this, they will still be innovating, creating, and challenging on every front. That's what empowered people do, and the results are amazing.

It may also be tempting to look at Koch Industries and see nothing but good outcomes. This is false. The path of progress is never straight and is always full of pitfalls. The biggest ones have been homemade—when we failed to follow, or pretended to follow, the principles of progress, such as openness, empowerment, and mutual benefit.

From the beginning, I personally had more failures than successes. As for the company, we've made many bad bets, from animal feed to pizza dough to tankers to drilling rigs. In that respect, the company's experience was no different from that of an individual. What's more important than the setback is the lesson you learn from it. Far from stopping you, setbacks should cause you to rethink the path forward.

I often recall Thomas Edison's response to being consoled over the lack of results in his nearly 10,000 attempts to develop a new battery: "I have gotten a lot of results. I know several thousand things that won't work!"[4]

To this day, we continue to search for new ways to succeed, not only through innovation with our products but also with how we empower our employees. Over the years, we developed a framework called Market-Based Management® to help every employee understand the principles of progress and contribute to a greater degree.

Since describing this framework in my book *Good Profit*, we have made significant revisions in the spirit of continual transformation, all of which are reflected in my recent short book, *Continually Transforming Koch Industries Through Virtuous Cycles of Mutual Benefit*. The last of our Guiding Principles has been changed from fulfillment to an even more powerful concept—self-actualization. (All our Guiding Principles can be found in an appendix in this book.) It has helped our supervisors at every level better enable our employees to realize their potential.

What was true in the 1960s is still true today: we thrive when our employees flourish, and their contributions move society forward.

THINKING BIGGER

America certainly needs a better business culture. As I describe in chapter eight, many companies still control their employees, rig the system instead of creating value, or both. I will continue to advocate for more businesses to break down the barriers that hold them, their employees, and our country back. I will always call on all companies, and all business leaders, to practice Principled Entrepreneurship™—doing well by doing good.

Yet to me, transforming business is just one part of a larger opportunity: transforming society for the better. At the same time we were breaking down barriers holding back our employees, I was working to break down barriers holding back people from all walks of life. The control mentality was alive and well across so much of America. (It still is, as we'll discuss.) So, just as I applied the principles of progress to foster the company's success, I sought to help implement them to spur a new era of progress in our country. My goal was, and is, the same in philanthropy as in business: to empower people. Enable them to build a better future for themselves and everyone else.

This looks a lot different for our country than it does for Koch Industries. The principles are the same, but their practical application has to be much more widespread. The control mentality takes many more forms—and holds back many more people—in society than it does in a single company. Overcoming it requires an even greater effort, from even more leaders—Social Entrepreneurs like you.

That brings us to the big problems in our country, and how you can help solve them.

PART 2

OUR COUNTRY'S STORY

The Long and Winding Road

4.

THE CORE INSTITUTIONS OF SOCIETY

" Change is the law of
life. And those who
look only to the past
or present are certain
to miss the future. "
JOHN F. KENNEDY[1]

W
hich do you think sums up America today:

Prosperity or poverty?

Thriving communities or struggling individuals?

Upward mobility or economic decline?

In each case, the answer is both.

On the one hand, there's never been a better time to be alive. Think back to the Great Enrichment. The past two hundred years have delivered us to an age of incredible opportunity, and the future holds the promise of even greater progress.

On the other hand, millions of people aren't sharing in that progress. They're being left behind. This discredits everything our country stands for, weakening America more every day. Moreover, it threatens to tear us apart.

Our country was founded on a deep belief in people—the idea that everyone has something to contribute. As you read in chapter two, ours was the first country in history to extend the promise of the pursuit of happiness to everyone, not just the privileged few. The story of America's progress is one of continually struggling to live up to the principles enshrined in the Declaration of Independence. We have spent more than two hundred years moving toward, and sometimes away from, our ideals. The journey has been a bit like someone who periodically gets lost because they lose the North Star behind the clouds.

Thankfully, many of the worst injustices in our history are gone. But their legacies remain, in the form of racism, sexism, and other deeply destructive attitudes. At the same time, new barriers have been built, preventing millions more from realizing their potential.

Of course, the challenges we face today differ greatly from the injustices of the past. They are not as brutal as slavery or as all-encompassing as the many limitations put on women in U.S. history. They nonetheless ruin individual lives and limit society's progress by preventing people from contributing.

These injustices are the source of America's current predicament. Whereas for most of our history more and more people became empowered, now, increasingly, many are being held back—and falling behind. America is sprinting toward a two-tiered society.

The difference between the two tiers could hardly be starker.

America is sprinting toward a two-tiered society.

In the first tier, many people are thriving, doing better than they ever thought possible. They're usually affluent and educated, with strong families, good schools, and well-paying jobs. In places where this holds true, there is low unemployment, rising income, and other indicators that things are generally going well. Fortunately, this is still the case for the majority of our country. A recent study found that just over half of Americans—52 percent—live in strong communities. Another 24 percent live in areas that are doing relatively well.[2]

But it's a completely different story in America's other tier.

There, people are struggling, often in dire circumstances. In about one in five ZIP codes, you'll find a quarter of the population living in poverty, on average.[3] The unemployment rate may be low, but labor force participation is also low, meaning people are stuck without jobs—either because they have stopped looking for one or don't have the skills to fill those that are available. In these communities, millions of

Americans don't know how they'll get by for the next week, let alone the next year. And in many areas, this experience is characterizing life for more and more families.

The country is divided about what the future holds. In some places, parents have optimism—even confidence—that their children's lives will be better than their own.[4] Chances are they're right. In other communities, people have little reason to think the next generation will be any better off. They're right too.

Children born in the 1940s had a 9-in-10 chance to earn more than their parents. By comparison, it's more like 50-50 for the children of the 1980s, and it's probably worse for younger generations.[5]

Poll after poll shows that Americans are losing hope—and for many, their lives.[6] Suicide rates have been rising for more than two decades. There haven't been this many suicides since World War II.[7] Drug overdoses are also skyrocketing. In 2017, a record 70,000 Americans died from drugs, a number that has nearly quadrupled in the past 20-plus years.[8] Alcohol-induced deaths have also greatly increased—by 50 percent since 1999.[9]

The economist Anne Case and Nobel Prize–winner Angus Deaton call these "deaths of despair."[10] Such deaths claim the lives of people who are struggling to find fulfillment and personal success. Without a path up, they look for a way out.

These developments help explain why U.S. life expectancy declined for consecutive years in the late 2010s.[11] The last time our country saw this kind of sustained multiyear drop was during the Spanish flu outbreak of 1918.[12] (While this worrisome trend halted in 2018, the toll the coronavirus pandemic may have taken in 2020 is not yet clear.[13]) This is despite a century of cures, vaccines, and incredible medicinal advances. Considering these breakthroughs, and with the promise of even more radical developments in the near future, life expectancy should be rising without interruption. The fact that it's not should worry us all.

THE PACE OF CHANGE

These stories and statistics should cause us all to ask: Why are more and more Americans falling behind and feeling left out?

The most common answer is rapid social and economic change.

It's definitely true that the pace of change is faster than ever. Developments in software, artificial intelligence, data analytics, communications, robotics, biotechnology, and other fields are improving lives in extraordinary ways, but they're also profoundly disrupting people's day-to-day experiences.

"Creative destruction"—a term coined by the economist Joseph Schumpeter in reference to innovation—is all around us, destroying much of what we had come to rely upon in the process of creating the new. Those who bear the brunt of this disruption understandably see more downside than upside.

For example, automation is upending manufacturing. Robots and machine learning are paving the way for self-driving vehicles, which may soon completely change how we drive and transport things. What a frightening thought for truck drivers especially, since in many states that's one of the most common occupations.[14]

Even without automation, the nature of work is profoundly shifting. A couple of generations ago, there was a widespread expectation that you'd be able to hold a job for life. Now the median duration for a job is less than five years, and it's still lower for younger workers.[15]

No wonder so many people, facing constant disruption and dislocation, are falling behind. Even if they believe a brighter future is coming overall, they don't see how they fit into it. They see a society that doesn't need or care about them. Sadly, they have a point.

But disruption isn't the real problem. After all, progress is impossible without this kind of major change. The underlying issue is that society is failing to help people adapt to these rapid and radical social and economic advances.

While it's tempting to blame seismic change, it's dangerous to buy into the argument that progress is bad. This fearful mind-set looks at creative destruction and only sees the destruction. When this fear turns into action, progress suffers, harming the least fortunate most of all.

The most telling example is the Luddites of the nineteenth century. They smashed textile machinery in a desperate attempt to keep weaving clothes by hand. Yet the textile industry made clothes affordable for virtually everyone, providing many more jobs, reducing poverty, and improving quality of life.

This is the story of the Great Enrichment, past and present. Every material, technological, and social advance in history upended whatever preceded it. We see it in the car replacing the carriage and the cell phone ending the era of landlines, and on and on it goes.

But major change only becomes progress if we as individuals are able to keep up with it—and if the benefits are widely shared. True progress requires all of us being able to contribute more, not less, as the world shifts. We can't allow a future that leaves some behind.

We also shouldn't discourage progress. Few things would be more disastrous for Americans' future well-being. Rather than trying to limit economic or social advances, we need to empower those who are struggling in the second tier to succeed like those in the first. The latter aren't inherently better; many just have the right support. Every person deserves the opportunity to realize their potential.

Which brings us to the core institutions of society.

WHAT ALL OF US RELY ON

When I say "institutions," I mean the aspects of society that are most essential to our ability to live well together. My view of them has been formed through decades of personal involvement and study. There are different ways to categorize these institutions. For ease of analysis, I do so as: community, education, business, and government.

These institutions play an essential role in helping each of us find our purpose, develop our skills, and apply them in a way that enables us to contribute and succeed.

How the institutions function also profoundly affects how we respond to change. When change affects us positively, they help us reap the benefits and build on them. When change affects us negatively, the institutions help us get back on track. When they're working, they instill in us the principles and practices that are essential to success and provide the support we need to keep pace with progress.

While each one plays a different and distinct role, the goal for each institution is the same: empowering us to discover and continuously develop and apply our unique abilities in a productive way. That's how we become contribution motivated and find fulfillment, making a better life for ourselves by benefiting others.

At least that's what they're supposed to do. When the institutions perform well, they engage and empower people, strengthening our country. When they fall short, they create barriers that prevent us from contributing to and sharing in society's progress, hurting us all.

America is on the trajectory toward a two-tiered society because the institutions are breaking down. They're no longer helping an increasing number of people find their gifts and best path.

The institutions' failures don't affect everyone equally. Some are injured more than others. For example, failing schools mean that students who can't afford an expensive alternative suffer more than those who can. Similarly, corrupt business practices based on corporate welfare can make it difficult for companies to compete, especially small ones and start-ups.

If the failures of our core institutions are the primary reason people are falling behind, then it stands to reason that we need to address those failings to help them succeed. That is, we need these institutions to break, rather than build, the barriers holding people back.

This is a tall task. We're not talking about tweaks at the edges. Transforming these institutions is the key to changing our country's current trajectory, which should be a major project for Social Entrepreneurs. First, however, we must understand what each institution is, and why it matters. Then we can turn to how you can make a difference.

Part 3 of this book addresses these institutions in much more detail, but here is a snapshot of each:

Community: Community includes all aspects of civil society, from neighborhoods to families to religious organizations to voluntary associations and more. Most simply, it is where each of us lives. It is supposed to be where people come together to solve common problems, support each other during difficult times, and discover and develop their gifts and aptitudes in a friendly and loving environment.

Education: Education is the primary way people identify their gifts, their passions, and their path to fulfillment. Rightly understood, education is three-dimensional. It helps students learn to *be*—who they are and what they do and don't do well. It helps them to *know*—finding out how the world works and the principles that undergird it. And education helps them to *do*—experimenting to discover what they will be rewarded for and find fulfilling.

Business: The role of business is to create products and services in a manner that helps people improve their lives. This requires creating an environment where employees thrive and find fulfillment by developing and applying their knowledge and skills to satisfy customers' needs. A business's profit ought to reflect its contributions to its various constituencies—customers, employees, suppliers, investors, communities, and society—and nothing else.

Government: Government is a powerful institution with an important purpose: keeping people safe and securing equal rights. In America, the vision of a government is best articulated in the Declaration of Independence: "We hold these truths to be self-evident, that all [people] are created equal, that they are endowed by their creator with certain unalienable rights, that among these are life, liberty and the pursuit of happiness," and that "to secure these rights, governments are instituted."

THE PATH TO EMPOWERMENT

Each institution is badly broken, as you will also read in part III. Rather than consistently empowering people to contribute and succeed, they too often erect barriers that hold people back. The institutions are also interconnected: a failure in one usually creates problems in the others.

For example, when government policy distorts the criminal justice system, it causes many businesses to steer clear of hiring individuals with criminal records; it locks up young people at a time when they most need good mentors and a good education; and it shatters communities by tearing apart families and perpetuating poverty and crime. At every point, individuals are prevented from rising, cut off from contributing and pursuing happiness. The longer those barriers stand, the wider the chasm in our country grows.

Fortunately, none of the institutions are irreparably damaged. Each can still be transformed to change America's trajectory and empower every person to succeed by contributing. As we have seen time and time again in our country, this kind of progress can only happen from the bottom up. The task falls to you and me, and to millions of other Social Entrepreneurs.

If transforming these institutions sounds like a tough task, that's because it is. I have spent the better part of my life working to understand the role that institutions need to play and how to transform them for the better. Through trial and error, study, and challenge from people I've partnered with, I have learned a lot about what it takes. It has helped me see that the path to transformation is grounded in the principles of progress, and it starts with us—you and me.

What injustice do you want to end? Which barriers do you want to break down? This is your motivation, your starting point. Perhaps you want to end poverty or fix the failing school your own kids attend. Perhaps you're sick and tired of special-interest handouts to businesses or upset about a terrible policy that pushes people down instead of enabling them to rise.

As a general rule, the people best suited to end an injustice are those closest to it.

Once your sights are trained on a specific injustice, you need to accurately diagnose the problem. The most common response to injustice is to double down on the approach that created and compounded it—usually one based in controlling, not empowering, people. This is no solution, no matter how well intentioned, and it usually causes more problems and ruins more lives. You will soon see how this same sad trend is playing out in each institution today.

The alternative—the real solution—is to empower people. This looks different with each injustice and within each institution. In broad terms, the right approach is the one that enables people to discover, develop, and apply their gifts so they can succeed by contributing.

KATHALEENA MONDS
FINDING MY PATH AND HELPING
OTHERS DO THE SAME

KATHALEENA MONDS IS A PROFESSOR AT ALBANY STATE UNIVERSITY. SHE RECEIVED A UNCF SCHOLARSHIP IN 1984 THAT ENABLED HER TO ATTEND COLLEGE.

It's tough going back home to Detroit. Most of my childhood friends are still there, and they are not doing so well. It's hard to see their struggles.

It's kind of a miracle that I got out. After all, we were all in the same boat back in the day. We hung out in the same places. We went to the same schools. For all intents and purposes, we were on the same track, and it wasn't a great one.

Maybe I had a better shot because of my family. My mother emphasized the importance of hard work and community, and she did her best to raise us seven kids with those values. One of my earliest jobs was helping my brothers fold the *Detroit News* and *Detroit Free Press* in preparation for their paper routes early, early, early in the morning. I learned a lot of good lessons at a young age.

Even so, by the time high school ended, I didn't know what to do next. I went back to a counselor and asked if she thought I could go to college. She told me there was a school in Atlanta, Georgia—Spelman College—where I might be a good fit.

I applied. A few weeks later, I got accepted.

I should have been excited, but instead I freaked out. No one in my family had ever gone to college, and we didn't have the money for tuition. We didn't even have a car, so I didn't know how I'd get down to Atlanta.

Two weeks after I graduated from high school, my family was evicted.

Kathaleena is dedicating her life to helping others discover, develop, and apply their gifts, as she did.

My mom asked her employers— the family she worked for as a domestic—to provide some support in renting a car to get me from Detroit to Atlanta. My mom and eldest brother dropped me off, turned the car around, and went home.

There I was, at a school I couldn't afford, and with nowhere else to go. So I went to the financial aid office and told my story.

That's when I learned about UNCF. They gave me a scholarship. I couldn't believe it. I could stay at Spelman. I could get the education I wanted.

Spelman helped me discover what I was best at, putting me on a completely new path. It awoke my passion for inspiring young adults.

I now teach and lead the Center for Educational Opportunity at Albany State University, where we focus on research to help fragile communities build stronger schools so children can thrive. My goal is to help as many young adults as possible find their own upward path through the education that's right for them. Just like I did.

—KATHALEENA MONDS

Kathaleena grew up in Detroit, where she faced many challenges.

Spelman College

350 Spelman Lane SW • Atlanta, Georgia 30314 • 404/681-3643

Dr. Donald M. Stewart
President

March 30, 1983

Miss Kathaleena Edward
9026 Burnett
Detroit, Michigan 48204

Dear Miss Edward:

The Admissions Office has informed me of your acceptance to Spelman College. Congratulations. You will become part of an institutional tradition of excellence, one which focuses on the roles of black women, and one which encourages its graduates to attain great heights in professions of every kind.

May I personally welcome you to Spelman and wish you every success in the future.

Sincerely yours,

Donald M. Stewart
President

DMS:ejw

Kathaleena graduated from Spelman College with the help of a UNCF scholarship.

As a general rule, the people best suited to end an injustice are those closest to it—a crucial component of bottom up. Consider your own aptitudes, skills, and experience when figuring out where and how to apply yourself. I'll soon report on this concept in action—and the people who are getting results from it.

After you find what works—what enables people to contribute and succeed—support it in whatever way you can. Not everyone can start an organization from scratch, and worthwhile projects need volunteers, funders, promoters, and others to help them grow. The project with the most potential in the world is not transformative if it only empowers a handful of people.

As you help these efforts succeed, others will start to take note. The positive results will put to rest the bankrupt ideas that have long held people back. (You'll encounter these ideas in chapters six through nine.) You, in turn, will find new avenues to apply yourself, new opportunities, and new partnerships that will enable you to better help others. You can create the sort of never-ending cycle that expands your effectiveness by orders of magnitude.

This road map is grounded in sound theory, but results also require sound practice. In the chapters that follow, you'll meet many Social Entrepreneurs who are beginning to transform each institution. Their experiences are enabling me to improve my own efforts to empower many more people. It is my hope that their experiences will provide the same benefit for you.

THE COURAGE TO ACT

At the beginning of this chapter, I asked you which description fits America today—prosperity or poverty, thriving communities or struggling individuals, upward mobility or economic decline. The answer is both, but it doesn't have to be.

The path we take depends on the choices we as Social Entrepreneurs make— on how we lead, empower, and inspire others to tackle society's most pressing problems.

We are not locked into our country's destructive path, where fewer people will be able to realize their potential. Nor are we promised a future of opportunity and fulfillment for all. The path we take depends on the choices we as Social Entrepreneurs make—on how we lead, empower, and inspire others to tackle society's most pressing problems. As we do, we help transform the institutions from the bottom up.

The past and the present are filled with examples of these pathfinders—Social Entrepreneurs who can inspire and inform our work today. There are many more than you think. It's time we meet a few.

5.

SOCIAL ENTRE-PRENEURS

" There is hope of change. [We should not] feel hopeless and powerless when we realize that we can make only a small change in the society as a single person . . . that single person is the best there is. "

ABRAHAM MASLOW[1]

Where can you find Social Entrepreneurs? All around you. It's remarkable how many people are striving to break the barriers holding others back. It's even more remarkable how many people want to but don't know where to start or, despite their best efforts, aren't making much of a difference.

If you recall from the introduction, a Social Entrepreneur is someone who looks for new ways to help others realize their potential. Like the rest of us, they have unique gifts. Like the rest of us, they can attain fulfillment through the principled application of those gifts. And like the rest of us, they succeed when they discover where they can make the greatest contribution. The more of us who do, the more likely we will be able to transform the core institutions of society so that they enable every person to rise.

I began to see the importance of Social Entrepreneurs through my studies of social progress and history, although at first I didn't use those words to describe them. Gutenberg, Luther, Galileo—these and so many others used their talents to topple the obstacles that held virtually everyone back.

The more I studied, the more examples I found. History is filled with people whose contributions enabled many others to succeed. While we remember the most famous ones, there are countless others whose names and deeds are not recorded. Many Social Entrepreneurs labor in obscurity, although my goal is to change that, as the pages ahead show. We owe history's progress as much to them as we do to those who are honored with statues and memorials.

STAND BY THOSE PRINCIPLES

Of all the inspiring change-makers I have encountered—either on the page or in person—none represents the ideal more fully than Frederick Douglass.[2]

Douglass is held up as an American hero for good reason. Born into slavery, he escaped to freedom and dedicated his life to realizing our national ideal of equal rights and life, liberty, and the pursuit of happiness, saying, "Stand by those principles, be true to them on all occasions, in all places, against all foes, and at whatever cost."[3] Douglass lived by his words, helping to bring about the abolition of slavery and committing himself to the elimination of many other injustices. Few Americans have accomplished more, especially considering where he started.

Douglass's life is worth exploring in brief because of the lessons it teaches. To be clear: while I have learned much from him, it is not my intention to claim that Frederick Douglass thought about the world in the same way that I do (a claim that various others have made about themselves). Rather, I view his accomplishments as a model for Social Entrepreneurs. His actions show how self-transformation can lead to societal transformation—something all of us can strive for.

If you look closely at Frederick Douglass's life, you can see everything that defines a Social Entrepreneur.

Douglass's desire to help others was an elemental part of his character. Like Viktor Frankl, whom we discussed in chapter one, he strived to contribute even while he was being deprived of his most basic needs. Like most enslaved people, Douglass was estranged from his family, usually hungry, perpetually in physical danger, and continually denied any sense of belonging or self-worth.

His first opportunity to develop his gift came at age eight, after he was moved from the plantation where he was born to work in a house in Baltimore. Upon hearing the slave owner's wife reading the Bible, Douglass persuaded her to teach him to read. When the slave owner discovered this tutoring, he exploded with rage, screaming words that made a profound impact on the young Douglass: knowledge would "forever unfit him to be a slave."[4] In that moment, Douglass realized that he wasn't a slave because he was inferior. But he was purposely being kept ignorant.

This realization caused a profound mental shift in Douglass. He became filled with an unquenchable desire to learn, which led, in time, to the discovery and development of his unique talent for writing and oratory.

One book in particular—Caleb Bingham's *The Columbian Orator*—inspired his passion for freedom and opened his eyes to underlying principles about the moral dignity of every human.[5] The book also showed him how to employ his natural abilities in a way that would help himself and others, teaching him that orators must practice and constantly improve.

After being sent back to the plantation at age 17, Douglass began teaching other slaves to read and write at a Sunday school he helped organize, one of his first opportunities to empower others. He wrote later about the experience: "Here, thought I, is something worth living for; here is an excellent chance for usefulness."[6] Even as a slave, he was contribution motivated.

When Douglass's efforts were discovered, he was sent to a notorious slave-breaker. The man's brutal attempt to break his spirit failed when Douglass fought back and won. With the slave-breaker's reputation and business hanging in the balance, Douglass escaped the usual fate of death. This incident further transformed him. He wrote, "I was *nothing* before; I *was a man* now." This gave him "a renewed determination to be a *free man*," which he accomplished at age 20.[7]

Douglass settled with his new wife in Massachusetts, where, despite rampant racism, he felt liberated. He now had the opportunity to contribute and be rewarded for doing so, rather than punished. His elation at earning a dollar for putting away a pile of coal was almost indescribable: "I was not only a freeman, but a free-workingman."[8]

Douglass then began to apply his extraordinary gift for communication to the area where he could make the greatest contribution: eliminating slavery and other injustices. At the Massachusetts Anti-Slavery Society convention in 1841, he was asked on the spot to give a speech. Although he was petrified, Douglass's remarks inspired the crowd. It marked the beginning of his career as one of the most famous and effective abolitionists in America.

Over the course of the next 50 years, through triumphant highs and excruciating lows, Douglass's fame and influence grew. He honed his skills as a speaker and writer, the better to persuade others of the justice of his cause. He became the most photographed American of the nineteenth century. He published his own newspaper for 16 years. He was also appointed to prestigious government positions, and after befriending Abraham Lincoln during the Civil War, he met with each subsequent president through Grover Cleveland.

Ultimately, Frederick Douglass played a leading role in catalyzing the movement that led to the abolition of slavery. He then lent his skills to the struggle for equal rights, not only for black people but also for women, immigrants, and religious minorities. He said in a speech in 1869, "In whatever else other nations may have been great and grand, our greatness and grandeur will be found in the faithful application of the principle of perfect civil equality to the people of all races and creeds."[9] Through this spirit, he contributed mightily to the foundation on which future reformers built.

If you look closely at Frederick Douglass's life, you can see everything that defines a Social Entrepreneur.

Unlike others who have suffered injustice, Douglass didn't succumb to negative motivation, and he refused to seek vengeance. From the beginning, he was contribution motivated, a characteristic that strengthened as he succeeded. He discovered, developed, and applied his unique gifts in service of others. The fulfillment he then found caused him to keep looking for new ways to make a difference. This led him to diverse partnerships that helped make progress possible.

> # Frederick Douglass helped transform society because he continually transformed himself. He demonstrated that just one person who inspires others can set the country on a better path.

Douglass's efforts contributed to the transformation of society's core institutions—community, education, business, and government. Each had been constrained by discrimination and control, keeping all but a minority from exercising their gifts. Those barriers began to fall as Douglass and others confronted them. Of course, many injustices remained following his death in 1895, and many are still with us today. But his actions as a Social Entrepreneur enabled others to make progress toward a more just country.

In the end, Frederick Douglass helped transform society because he continually transformed himself. He demonstrated that just one person who inspires others can set the country on a better path.

YOUR NORTH STAR

I never cease to draw inspiration from Douglass's life. He still helps me gain a deeper understanding of fundamental principles. One that his story has reinforced in me is the importance of a "North Star." (*North Star* was also the name of his newspaper.) It is the vision that guides a Social Entrepreneur's efforts, the yardstick by which one measures her actions, determining whether she is going in the right direction, whether she is making progress.

Every effective Social Entrepreneur I have ever known has a North Star. It goes with the territory: you envision a world without the barrier (or barriers) you seek to break. Your inspiration and persistence come from moving closer to making that vision a reality. For Douglass, it was a society that fulfilled the promise of equal rights.

Now, none of us is Frederick Douglass. I don't know anyone who faces challenges of the same magnitude as slavery. But that fact alone should fill us with hope. If it was possible to eradicate slavery in America, then how much easier should it be to overcome even our worst problems today? In Frederick Douglass, every Social Entrepreneur has a role model.

There are many inspiring people today who are blazing their own unique trails in the fight against injustice. Their paths are different, but the steps they're taking are the same.

They're discovering, developing, and applying their gifts to help others. They're learning through trial and error how to discover a North Star that will give meaning to their lives. And these Social Entrepreneurs are inspiring others to get involved. They can create—and in some cases are already creating—the kind of excitement and energy that can transform the institutions to empower more and more people.

Take a man I met a few years back. His name is Antong Lucky.

Antong grew up in the projects in a rough part of Dallas. Before Antong's first birthday, his father went to prison on a 50-year sentence. Although he had some good influences in his life—his grandparents chief among them—he was often pulled in the wrong direction. He saw it as a matter of survival.

Antong was knee-deep in drug dealing by the time he was a teenager. He saw plenty of other kids take a similar road—starting out washing dealers' cars, then becoming a lookout scanning for police, and finally graduating to selling drugs on their own. For someone who grew up in poverty, the money he found helping people get high seemed too good to pass up.

It wasn't long before he got involved in gangs. The Crips dominated most of Dallas at the time, but Antong wasn't interested in following an established gang. Instead, he started and led the Dallas chapter of their hated rival, the Bloods. He wasn't even 15 years old, yet Antong Lucky sat atop a pyramid of drugs, violence, crime, and suffering.

All the while, the life he had chosen was claiming the lives of those around him. Antong was fortunate he didn't get killed himself. Instead of a body bag, he wound up in prison.

Behind bars, Antong Lucky had two options. The first—and easiest—was to keep heading in the same direction. He ruled the streets on the outside and became one of the most powerful men on the inside. His fellow inmates either looked up to him or feared him—the legend who started the Dallas Bloods.

But something gave Antong pause. He noticed that many young men were committing crimes to get into prison thinking it would impress him. Instead, it destroyed him inside. He could see their lives were taking a tragic turn, in large part because of him. As a gang leader, he had tried to protect the people under him, but now he was seeing that he couldn't do that from within a gang. While others wanted to be like him, Antong wanted to be someone else entirely—someone who could help others, not hurt them and the community.

Antong Lucky founded the Dallas Bloods when he was just 14.

ANTONG LUCKY

DISCOVERING MY NORTH STAR

A FORMER GANG LEADER, ANTONG LUCKY TURNED HIS LIFE AROUND IN PRISON AND IS NOW TRANSFORMING INNER-CITY CULTURE AS THE MASTER EDUCATOR OF URBAN SPECIALISTS.

The things I did before I turned 21. . . The gangs. The violence. The drugs. I was running the streets of South Dallas. And after I got busted, I was on my way to running the prison.

Even behind bars, everybody wanted to be around me. They flocked to me, followed me everywhere I went. Kids were committing crimes just to get to prison to meet me. They wanted to be like me and impress me. If I said something, they listened. If I did something, they did it too. And if I gave an order . . . man, they jumped.

I didn't really understand it at the time. I barely noticed what was going on. I was too young and dumb to see the power I had. Then one day, an older guy pulled me aside. Willie Flemming was his name. He'd been there like 10 years.

I remember what he said like it was yesterday.

He said, "Little brother, let me holla at you."

He goes, "Man, you elite." Then he kept going: "All these guys in here do everything you tell them to do. They always trying to impress you and meet you and blah blah blah." Then he got quiet and looked right at me. He said what my 20-year-old self needed to hear:

"If you can lead these dudes to do wrong, you can lead them to do right. You are a leader."

I had never heard that before. It set off an explosion in my head. I realized he was right. I'd been leading young men like me to do terrible things. Now, for the first time, I saw that I could lead them in the opposite direction.

If he hadn't said that, there's no way I'd be doing what I'm doing now. What he said opened my eyes, and once that happened, I started seeing things. Things I never saw before.

That's why I paid attention a few weeks later when this news story came on the TV in the dayroom. There was a man on the screen named Omar Jahwar. He was talking about gang intervention.

Then two of my cousins showed up on the screen, because they were working with this guy. I was like, "This is crazy." So I wrote my cousin a letter that said, "Man, whoever this guy is, hook me up with him."

I met Omar just a few days after getting out. We've been working together ever since. He gave me a beat-up car, not like the ones I used to drive. He gave me a salary that was a lot smaller than what I made on the streets. But he also gave me something way more valuable: a purpose in life.

Now, I know that kids will emulate those around them. When I was running the Dallas Bloods, they wanted to be like me. Now I'm showing up in their neighborhoods, in their schools, showing them it doesn't have to be that way. They still want to be like me.

I've got a lot of lost time to make up for. I messed up a lot of kids and a lot of lives. I can't undo the damage I did. But I can go to the streets I used to run and show kids how to take a different road in their own lives. That's what I do. That's where I am, every single day.

—ANTONG LUCKY

Watch a video about Antong's work with Urban Specialists at BelieveInPeopleBook.com/stories

Now Antong is using his firsthand experience to end gang violence and help kids find a better path.

Something the judge said at Antong's trial stuck to his soul—that Antong was a "menace to society." When he heard this, he didn't want to be that man. It wasn't long before a mentor in prison convinced Antong that if he could lead others to do wrong, he could also lead them to do right. He was beginning to discover his North Star. His internal barriers began to fall.

The challenge was discovering what to do next. In his search for a different path, Antong began reading as many books as he could get his hands on, one of which was Plato's *Republic*. Plato's story of the cave—where people thought the shadows on the wall were reality because they had never seen the light outside—made Antong realize that he was in that exact place. More important, it made him realize that he could *leave* the cave. As he tells it, one of the great lies of being in a gang is that it's permanent—"blood in, blood out," as Antong says.

Suddenly he saw through this. He wanted to step into the sun and help others find their way out of the darkness. He didn't know it, but he was on his way to becoming a Social Entrepreneur.

One day, on the prison TV, Antong saw something that resonated: a profile of a local pastor, Omar Jahwar. (You'll meet him in chapter six.) Pastor Omar (now Bishop Omar) was working to break the cycle of gang violence in local communities. This immediately struck Antong, who was just a few weeks shy of parole. After his release, he went straight to Pastor Omar. He was determined to help solve the problems he once created.

He's been on that journey ever since. Antong Lucky is now the master educator and lead trainer at Urban Specialists, a group that Bishop Omar founded about two decades ago specifically to "transform urban culture," with a focus on ending violence. He works in the same communities—on the same streets—where he was once a gang leader. The difference is that he's now applying his skills to help people instead of hurt them. Using his leadership gifts, he's guiding them down a productive path, not a destructive one.

Antong's unique skills and background allow him to make inroads where once he saw dead ends. He forges truces between warring gangs by building personal relationships with their members. He shows kids, many of whom are a reflection of his old self, that they have other options and a future of opportunity, if they're willing to reach for it. He works to restore trust between inner-city communities and the police. In everything he does, Antong Lucky empowers people to break the cycle of drugs, crime, and violence. (I'll share more about what Antong is achieving in the next chapter.)

Antong Lucky is a shining example of a Social Entrepreneur. He's using his personal knowledge to address a major problem: violence in communities. As he makes progress, he constantly develops and applies his unique abilities in new ways, enabling him to make a bigger difference. He is truly contribution motivated: the more he helps people, the more people he wants to help.

DO WHAT YOU KNOW

Antong Lucky embodies many of the characteristics of successful Social Entrepreneurs.

First, he is close to the problems he's trying to solve. He has first-hand knowledge of the crisis in so many of our country's urban communities. Who better to mentor troubled kids in those environments, providing them with the guidance and support they need to take a better path? He could have devoted himself to tackling other barriers, but he likely would have found less success.

This holds true for every Social Entrepreneur: embrace who you are and what you know, because that's how you can make the greatest contribution and find fulfillment. Don't, and you will struggle to help others or find the success you crave. Your natural abilities—and the firsthand knowledge you have gained from your experiences (and, yes, from your mistakes!)—are central to what you can be and what you want to be.

Second, Antong unites with others to make progress, even those who seem to be unlikely allies.

Embrace who you are and what you know, because that's where you can make the greatest contribution and find fulfillment.

Look no further than his partnership with me. It seems odd at first glance: the fortysomething former gang leader from South Dallas working with the wealthy eightysomething businessman from Wichita, Kansas. Yet whatever our differences, both Antong and I know that we can achieve more together than we ever could on our own. Sure enough, Antong is working with me and many others to expand his effectiveness in Dallas and beyond.

Finally, Antong Lucky has a North Star. He envisions urban neighborhoods free from violence, gangs, drugs, and crime. He also sees the kids he serves as leaders who can achieve far more than they might imagine. Antong uses his North Star to guide his decisions, enabling Urban Specialists to continually expand its effectiveness and reach.

I have a North Star too. It's what I described in the introduction: a society in which everyone can realize their potential and find fulfillment. My pursuit of this vision is why I partner with Antong Lucky and so many others. My greatest ability—understanding and applying abstract concepts—means I could never do what Antong does. Instead, I use my capabilities to help him and other Social Entrepreneurs increase their effectiveness and scale. When Social Entrepreneurs' North Stars align, it enables them to accomplish much more, much faster.

Consider another Social Entrepreneur I've come to know: Scott Strode.

Scott's North Star is simple but profound: a world without drug and alcohol addictions. This is deeply personal for him, because he's in recovery from substance use disorder himself. He lost track of the number of times he woke up in an unfamiliar place, reeling from his actions the night before. Fortunately—for himself and others—his years of drug and alcohol misuse did not cost him his life. Realizing he would die if he didn't get clean and sober, he vowed to break free of the drugs that had such a hold on him.

Scott soon found that he could rise through exercise. The day after he gave up cocaine and alcohol, he stepped into a boxing ring at a local gym in Boston and never looked back. He climbed mountains, competed in races of every kind, and pushed himself harder and farther every day. More than two decades later, Scott Strode is still sober.

But Scott didn't just want to help himself. He wanted to empower people in similar straits. He came to see a connection between exercise and community in helping people recover. He saw it in the gym, on the mountain, while cycling, and on the track. His experience led him to start a nonprofit called The Phoenix. It was Scott's hope that others struggling with addiction would be able to follow the same path of recovery through an active, sober community of peers.

The Phoenix is named after Scott's own journey. Like the mythical creature, he burned bright, and then burned out. But from the ashes, Scott was reborn. He had discovered his unique gift: helping others who share his struggle.

Founded in 2006, The Phoenix employs instructors who are in recovery from substance use disorder themselves. This gives new members a sense of acceptance, safety, and trust. The only membership requirement for The Phoenix's free programs is that participants have at least 48 hours of sobriety. The first workout helps people start to realize they have a new support system—one that believes in them.

Alive with encouragement, their first day turns into two days, then two weeks, two months, two years, and more if needed.

Scott started small, in Colorado, with only one location. But he kept developing his model and his own abilities, enabling him to expand his operation to help more people. Though over 21 million individuals need treatment for a substance use disorder, only 17 percent are able to access care.[10] About half relapse within the first few months, if not the first few weeks.

By contrast, less than 20 percent of participants in The Phoenix relapse in their first three months of recovery. A stunning 80 percent stay sober. Think what this means: The Phoenix is well over *twice* as effective as traditional recovery efforts.[11] (I'll share more detail about The Phoenix in chapter six.)

I could name many other Social Entrepreneurs who are valiantly—and successfully—pursuing their North Star. Whatever it may be, it's important to realize that it's a guide, not a destination. Just as navigators of old used Polaris—the North Star in astronomy—to mark their passage across the seas, you can use your North Star as the critical reference point on your journey to discover your innate abilities and apply them to help others.

NOT JUST ANY PATH WILL DO

What is your North Star? Be wary that however praiseworthy it may be, *how* you pursue it matters just as much as what it is. Not every Social Entrepreneur uses his or her skills for good.

For example, several years ago, I attended an event where a well-known philanthropist spoke about education. His North Star was excellent: dramatically improving the public education system to help more students discover their gifts. I share this goal.

Then he got to his suggested path forward: shutting down every private and charter school in America and forcing all kids into traditional

You can use your North Star as the critical reference point on your journey to discover your innate abilities and apply them to help others.

public schools. His reasoning was that once the children of influential parents had to endure failing schools, they would finally force the system to reform. This is the antithesis of a bottom-up approach!

The philanthropist admitted that a generation or two of students would suffer from the loss of some good schools, but he suggested that the benefits would outweigh the pain—that is, it's okay to hurt some people now on the chance that it will help other people later. Unfortunately, that perspective isn't all that unusual in philanthropy and public policy. But I wholeheartedly reject the "you have to break a few eggs to make an omelet" approach to social change.

I pressed the philanthropist on his views during the Q&A session, and he publicly admitted that there were probably less destructive ways to help improve public schools (more on this in chapter seven). But the entire exchange rattled me. It showed how easy it is for Social Entrepreneurs to use top-down control instead of bottom-up empowerment. As you will see throughout this book, that approach has never worked—it *cannot* work—and it causes much suffering.

Fortunately, there are many Social Entrepreneurs who show there's a better way, people like Antong Lucky and Scott Strode. As with Frederick Douglass, they both discovered a North Star that enabled them to use their gift to help others. They broke down the internal and external barriers that held them back, becoming contribution motivated. In Antong's case, he left behind gang life. In Scott's case, he left behind addiction. Now they're empowering others to do the same.

While many who rely on an approach based on control are well intentioned—like my philanthropist friend—they will never find the kind of success they seek. Or the fulfillment that comes from empowering people.

EVERYTHING IS POSSIBLE

Social Entrepreneurs like Antong Lucky and Scott Strode are helping to transform the institution of community. They are already transforming themselves, accomplishing more than they imagined. Their belief in people's potential enables them to better help others rise.

But they can't do it by themselves. Communities suffer from a host of problems, going beyond violence and addiction to homelessness, alienation, and poverty, to name a few. Breaking these barriers requires a greater number of creative problem-solvers applying the principles of progress. Without more Social Entrepreneurs growing in effectiveness and showing a better way, we can't overcome the many crises that afflict America's cities, towns, and neighborhoods.

That's what we need: more people working together to transform community and every other institution—education, business, and government. My journey to discover how to accomplish this began when I first became a Social Entrepreneur in the 1960s. As I was applying principles to transform Koch Industries, I was also focusing my efforts to foster a society where everyone can thrive. I was looking for ways to empower everyone in our country, just as we were empowering our employees at the company.

As with my experience in business, I don't have all the answers, or even most of them. Instead, my work has brought me into hundreds of partnerships that have helped me see what's possible.

Stand Together, the organization that I founded in 2003, partners with nearly 200 community-based programs that unite millions of people helping others rise. Antong Lucky and Scott Strode are among them. The people we work with are making progress on every front. They are transforming themselves and the core institutions, with the goal of transforming society for the better.

In the pages that follow, you will meet more of these amazing people. You will see them practicing the principles of progress and applying the road map I laid out at the end of chapter four.

Most important, you will see how you can help them and others like them, join them, and be like them, using your own unique gifts. As I share their experiences across each of the institutions, I hope that you will see opportunities to apply those lessons in your life. I hope that you will make social change your story.

Only 25 years after he became free, Frederick Douglass helped break one of the tallest barriers in American history. Now imagine what the Social Entrepreneurs of today could accomplish in 25 years.

Antong Lucky could put an end to senseless violence in so many of our cities.

Scott Strode could enable millions of people to beat addiction.

And you could be on the cusp of ending the injustice you're most concerned about. There is no limit to what you can accomplish if you approach it by empowering people from the bottom up.

YOUR STORY

A Brighter Future for All

6.

PEOPLE AREN'T PROBLEMS

> 66 In the end, a good society is not so much the result of grand designs and bold decisions, but of millions upon millions of small caring acts, repeated day after day, until direct mutual action becomes second nature and to see a problem is to begin to wonder how best to act on it. 99

RICHARD CORNUELLE[1]

What would you do if you had to struggle to put food on the table? How about if you were addicted to drugs and not sure how to break free? What if you were shut out of basically every job you ever applied for? And what if you didn't know where you would end up every night because you had no place to call home?

Thankfully, these questions are hypotheticals for most of us. Sadly, they're a daily reality for tens of millions of Americans. Many communities are filled with people struggling to get on their feet, let alone stay standing. Such was the case with Abillyon, a young man I met a few years ago.

Abillyon grew up in Dallas, Texas. He never knew his dad, and his mom was in and out of his life, so his grandparents raised him. They both worked to make ends meet. When his grandfather passed away and two incomes became one, life got a lot harder. Abillyon tried to help his grandmother however he could.

As Abillyon puts it, he did "things I wasn't supposed to do to get money." He believed he had no other choice. It wasn't long before he ran afoul of the law.

Abillyon wound up in the Dallas juvenile detention system when he was only 14 years old, and he was stuck there for two months. That short stay threatened to derail his life to an even greater degree. Abillyon was well on his way to becoming a statistic.

The juvenile justice system is notorious for ruining kids' lives. Nearly 60,000 young Americans are incarcerated at any given time, and about two million are in and out of prison or jail every year.[2] Most of these kids never committed a violent crime.[3] Once they leave, they tend to become repeat offenders. Exact figures are elusive, but reasonable estimates indicate that more than 50 percent of those leaving the juvenile justice system are arrested again within 12 months.[4] It's a vicious cycle of joblessness, crime, and unrealized potential.

The people who work in juvenile detention facilities have a name for their charges: "throwaway kids." It speaks volumes about the expectations our society has for rehabilitation and personal transformation once a kid makes a mistake. The assumption is that they're a lost cause, worth little in the eyes of others.

But there's no such thing as a throwaway kid. Abillyon and his peers have unique abilities and the capacity to contribute. We're talking about teenagers who should be learning what their gifts are and how to constructively apply them rather than wasting their talents in detention facilities. Instead of making them feel worthless, the juvenile justice system should be helping them recognize their innate self-worth and constructively apply their abilities. For many, guidance and mentoring should be tried first, not sentencing.

That's where the institution of community comes in.

DEFINING COMMUNITY

If you recall from chapter four, community is what's all around us, all the time. It includes every aspect of civil society, such as family, neighborhoods, religious groups, nonprofits, volunteer groups, clubs, sports, entertainment, and much more. (Schools will be covered in the next chapter.) This definition is expansive, but so is our need for community.

Individual success depends on the health of our communities. A good community provides us with a sense of belonging and a safe environment. It's the relationships—love and friendships—that define a huge part of who we are. It's the bonds with those around us that cause us to support each other in both cases. It's recognizing our common interests and concerns, which enables us to join together to solve common problems. It's learning at an early age what mutual benefit looks like in practice. Community provides the first safety net we turn to—those nearby who can assist us when we fall on hard times.

Individual success depends on the health of our communities.

From the day we're born until the day we die, community is all around us, influencing our ability to grow, contribute, and thrive.

To those of us who have benefited from strong community bonds, this sounds commonplace. But for many people (maybe some of you reading this now), this description of community sounds fanciful.

Community is flourishing in certain places and floundering in others. The places where it's thriving share similar characteristics—strong families, strong friendships, strong involvement in social organizations like service groups and churches. People come together, supporting each other in times of need.

Where community is struggling, those qualities are either deteriorating or nonexistent. Families are broken; friendships have given way to distrust; violence and crime are spreading; social organizations are withering; gang membership is more appealing than school or church. Where this is the case, people are hurting, not helping, one another.

In his book *Alienated America,* Tim Carney documents the consequences.[5] In strong communities, people's needs for friendship and self-esteem are met, giving them the foundation to discover their skills and find fulfillment. The result is more opportunity, more optimism, and healthier habits. Problems like addiction still exist, but the community provides support for those afflicted. A strong community quietly but powerfully points people toward a mind-set of contribution, shaping their lives for the better.

The opposite is true in struggling communities. About 60 percent of Americans now report feeling lonely and isolated, and for Millennials, the feeling tends to be more acute.[6] (This was prior to "social distancing" and self-isolation during the 2020 coronavirus outbreak.) Absent the strong bonds we all crave, and often in the face of harmful external conditions, people develop self-destructive habits and attitudes. The consequences ripple outward, hurting job prospects, earnings potential, and mental health while pushing people toward crime, addiction, and dependency.[7]

Carney also shows that no one is immune to a community's collapse. We're so heavily influenced by our surroundings that even people who are doing well in a struggling community eventually start to exhibit the psychology of their neighbors—alienation, addiction, anger.[8] Some might escape these places, but that's not a long-term solution. It's tragic when the only option to save yourself is to leave your community.

Both types of community are self-reinforcing—one headed up, the other spiraling down. Yet the latter isn't foreordained to collapse. If some communities are healthy due to strong relationships and social cooperation, then rebuilding those bonds can save struggling ones.

This can't be mandated from the outside; it must evolve from within. Strengthening communities depends on building on their

A strong community quietly but powerfully supports people and points them toward a mind-set of contribution, shaping their lives for the better.

essential nature, which means empowering their members to assist one another. It depends on, in the words of the innovative thinker Richard Cornuelle, "millions upon millions of small caring acts, repeated day after day."

THE TYRANNY OF EXPERTS

Sadly, empowerment isn't the approach of the vast majority of anti-poverty efforts.

Take the War on Poverty, which President Lyndon B. Johnson launched in 1965. He declared the aim was "not only to relieve the symptom of poverty, but to cure it and, above all, to prevent it."[9] The government created dozens of agencies and programs designed to lift Americans from poverty to prosperity. Philanthropists largely adopted the same approach, assuming that people outside, not inside, struggling communities know the best way to fix them.

More than a half century later, the poverty rate has barely budged, and intergenerational poverty is still a massive crisis.[10] For example, Tom Fletcher—the impoverished man whom President Johnson met in 1964, moments before launching the War on Poverty—died essentially destitute in 2004, despite decades of government support.[11] And his family has continued to struggle.

All told, our country has spent $15 trillion and counting in this titanic struggle, and what do we have to show for it?[12] Poverty has become easier to endure but harder to escape.

Public policy failures are not the only failures—far from it. Foundations and individuals have spent enormous sums trying to lift up the least fortunate, with little to show for it. In 2018 alone, philanthropists gave more than $50 billion to poverty-related causes, and tens of billions more to issues that indirectly address poverty, such as education and healthcare.[13]

I know many of them personally and can attest that their intentions are good. I can also attest, after brainstorming with quite a few, that they are disheartened by their lack of effectiveness.

Why do such efforts fail, whether governmental or philanthropic? Why are so many Social Entrepreneurs trying and failing to make a difference? Because they generally view the people being helped as problems that need to be solved, rather than as the source of the solutions. Their efforts are based on top-down control, not bottom-up empowerment.

The "logic" behind top-down control is that the smartest people can design a program that will make everything right. Adherents to this idea truly believe they have the best knowledge, enabling them to create a one-size-fits-all formula capable of fixing anything. They may not come right out and say it, but it is clear from their actions.

This mentality is nothing new. People have always fallen for simple solutions to complex problems. For some, it reinforces their self-esteem. For others, it feeds the desire for power and prestige. Either way, both policymakers and philanthropists have bought in to top-down control. The people they intend to help are paying for it.

William Easterly calls this approach the "tyranny of experts."[14] The tyranny stems from the so-called experts' control mentality, leading them to force their "solutions" on others. Convinced of their own superior abilities, philanthropists and policymakers impose their vision, their values, and their plans on the downtrodden, without understanding the facts on the ground. They fail to account for the infinite complexity that stems from each individual's unique needs and talents. The least fortunate, who are typically seen as needing a caretaker, pay the price.

Additionally, the people and programs devoted to helping the least fortunate are typically measured on inputs (dollars spent) instead of outcomes (individuals empowered). Similarly, those who are charged with supporting the poor are generally focused on managing them instead of enabling them to rise. I've read that some members of the Black Panthers had a name for this in the 1960s—"poverty pimping."[15] They predicted the slew of programs would help the anti-poverty workers more than the actual poor. They were right: dependency has become the standard for these programs, not self-sufficiency.

Fifty-plus years of such efforts demonstrate that this approach doesn't work. America has a poverty-industrial complex that uplifts shockingly few people at a shockingly high price. More than 75 percent of Americans agree this approach has failed.[16] There's got to be a better way.

EVERYONE HAS POTENTIAL

The poverty-industrial complex is almost entirely focused on people's deficiencies. Sadly, this convinces them that they really are deficient. (Remember young Abillyon and the idea of "throwaway kids.") Over time, such a negative approach destroys their self-belief and motivation and reduces their aspirations.

Yet by focusing on what the least fortunate *lack*, policymakers and philanthropists miss what they *have*—the potential to overcome the obstacles holding them back. Even the most downtrodden are capable of unique and valuable contributions.

Just ask Mauricio Miller, who grew up in poverty. Having spent his professional life in the field, and having firsthand experience with the anti-poverty programs created by politicians, bureaucrats, and philanthropists, he argues that the entire system basically "hides [the poor's] talent and potential."[17]

The introduction to Mauricio's book, *The Alternative,* is aptly titled "Disrupting the Deficit View." *The Alternative* is a powerful argument against the status quo and a call to action for anyone who really wants to help the least fortunate succeed. For his novel way of thinking,

Mauricio won the MacArthur Foundation's Genius Grant in 2012. The organization he founded, the Family Independence Initiative (FII), is a great example of his ideas in action. More on FII shortly.

Mauricio's wisdom bears on every Social Entrepreneur who cares about issues like poverty, addiction, or any other ailment afflicting communities.

If you're focused on deficiencies rather than contributions, your efforts will reflect it. You'll double down on the wrong approach—more good money after bad, more control, more programs that prevent people from becoming the best version of themselves. You'll hurt those who are struggling, even as you try to help them.

Conversely, if your focus is on potential, you'll approach people in a spirit of support and encouragement, helping them find how to contribute and succeed. You'll empower, not stifle—and therein lies a better way.

More than half of the kids coming out of juvenile detention go back within a year. Less than 15 percent of those who go through Café Momentum have ended up behind bars again. (Los Angeles, 2019)

COMMUNITY REIMAGINED

Which brings us back to Abillyon.

Abillyon doesn't see himself as a throwaway kid. When he introduced himself to me, he said, "I'm Abillyon—that's easy to remember because I'm going to be a billionaire." Whether he makes a lot of money or not, what he's thinking and doing will give him a more fulfilling life. He's discovering his abilities and contributing, leaving a life of debilitating financial hardship and crime behind.

Why? Because he was fortunate to find a transformative project that empowers people: Café Momentum.

Café Momentum is the brainchild of Chad Houser. Once ranked among Dallas's best up-and-coming chefs, he bought in to a restaurant in 2007. Then in May 2008, through a volunteer program, he taught a few young men in juvenile detention how to make ice cream. One of them told Chad how much he enjoyed it, saying, "I just love to make

Chad Houser founded Café Momentum, a transformative restaurant that helps kids coming out of juvenile detention believe in themselves. (Colorado Springs, 2019)

food and give it to people and put a smile on their face." Chad left a changed man, a Social Entrepreneur, and it wasn't long before he founded his own restaurant—one with a very specific mission.

Café Momentum gives young adults with criminal records a job, enabling them to get back on their feet and build a foundation for future success. Instead of telling the kids that they'll never amount to anything, which they hear constantly and come to believe, Café Momentum shows them they have talent. Then it demonstrates, day in and day out, that there are people willing to help them develop and apply it in a positive way.

Abillyon started in a 12-month internship at Café Momentum. He did basically everything there is to do in a restaurant, from prepping food to waiting tables to the back office. By working in a variety of positions, he learned where he excelled and where he didn't. He also wrote a résumé and went through mock interviews.

All Café Momentum interns go through the same experience. Many, if not most, won't end up in the food industry. But the lessons they learn

Abillyon's story shows how Café Momentum enables people to overcome barriers. (Super Bowl LIV, Miami, 2020)

at the restaurant prepare them for a life of contribution, no matter what they choose to do.

Abillyon knows that Café Momentum transformed his life. He says that if it weren't for the restaurant, he "would probably be in jail or on the streets or dead right now." Instead, he says, "I feel like I have a purpose, like I'm doing something that's actually helping people."

Nor is Abillyon alone. In Dallas, while more than half the kids coming out of juvie end up back in the justice system within a year, less than 15 percent of those who go through Café Momentum end up behind bars again—ever. Empowerment instead of punishment puts them on an upward path.

But Café Momentum is doing more than just helping these kids. It's challenging the "throwaway kid" mind-set—and changing people's perspective on how to uplift the least fortunate.

Most of us write off kids who go through the juvenile justice system, if we ever think of them at all. That changes the moment Abillyon steps up to a table to greet diners and take their orders. When he looks his customer in the eye, smiles, and asks what they'd like, they no longer see a throwaway kid. They soften and realize these kids can contribute, just like anyone else.

What makes this story even better is that Café Momentum is consistently ranked among the best restaurants in Dallas.[18] These kids don't just contribute—they do so at the highest levels!

Furthermore, many benefits arise from the tens of thousands who eat at Café Momentum every year. Employers may look at a job application from a kid like Abillyon a little differently next time. Teachers may react differently when a kid acts out in class. Others may tell friends about the extraordinary meal and mind-set change they had and encourage them to check it out themselves. I can attest that once you experience Café Momentum, there's no chance you'll keep it to yourself. It creates a ripple effect of changed lives and minds.

This is already happening. Chad and Café Momentum caught the attention of the NFL, leading to a national profile on *NFL 360* and multiple pop-up restaurants in cities with NFL teams.[19] One pop-up was organized in conjunction with the NFL draft in Nashville, causing the city to consider changes to its juvenile justice system. Another pop-up restaurant was established through a partnership with the Los Angeles Rams. It, too, spurred some serious rethinking.

These efforts led to Café Momentum doing a Super Bowl event and forming a partnership with the Players Coalition, a player-led initiative to fight injustice. These are only a few of the ways that Café Momentum is changing the conversation about helping kids in the juvenile justice system.

SOLUTIONS, PLURAL

In Café Momentum, we see the seeds of institutional transformation. Transforming communities involves finding projects that empower, celebrating success, and challenging others to get engaged.

Whatever problem you're focused on, know that there is no single solution. That's a paradigm that must be dispelled—that one approach, one program, or a one-size-fits-all initiative can make everything right. When you look at these issues from the bottom up, you don't go to communities and tell them what works. You go there to *find* what works and learn how you can help it improve and spread.

Café Momentum is far from the only transformative project out there. In the past five years, Stand Together has discovered groups with a similar philosophy in more than 200 cities in 47 states. We support nearly 200 community-based initiatives, and we're just scratching the surface. Each one focuses on how people in poverty are the source of the solution, rather than problems to be solved.

Take the Family Independence Initiative, founded by Mauricio

Miller, whom I just mentioned. His years of work in top-down, control-based anti-poverty projects completely disheartened him. He knew that approach didn't work, and he saw what did in the families that refused to participate in the programs he ran.

This led him to found FII, which has a simple guiding principle: believe in people. Instead of telling people how to live, it supports them in pursuing their own path while helping them build community.

The results: On average, families that stick with FII for two years see their monthly incomes rise 27 percent, their savings jump over 200 percent, and their dependence on government assistance drop 36 percent. Nearly 90 percent of students in these families do better in school. Such results are unprecedented in the anti-poverty space. Recently, FII introduced a technology platform that has enabled them to begin scaling nationwide.

Or take Safe Families, which is focused on foster care. An estimated 437,000 kids are presently in the U.S. foster care system, a number that grows larger every year.[20] Kids in foster care are more likely to struggle with education, employment, and emotional stability.[21]

Safe Families helps prevent that from happening. When parents fall on truly tough times, it partners them with families who temporarily take care of their kids. They don't have to give up parental rights, as they would in the traditional foster system. Remarkably, 93 percent of families are reunited, compared to less than half of those in foster care.[22]

REAL RESULTS

Think back to chapter five, where you encountered The Phoenix and met its founder, Scott Strode, now in substance abuse recovery for more than two decades. Scott's exercise-based model accomplishes what other treatments fail to provide: long-term support in a strong community setting.

DANA SMITH

TRANSFORMATION IS POSSIBLE

DANA SMITH IS REGIONAL DIRECTOR FOR THE PHOENIX. SHE STRUG-GLED WITH SUBSTANCE USE DISORDER FROM 2000 TO 2009.

There I stood in a Colorado alley, remembering how I got there. It's where my life took a radically different course. It was there that I realized I had finally found what I had been looking for. It was there that I found the strength and the community I needed to walk away from addiction forever.

Standing in that alley, I thought of everything that had brought me there. It started with some really bad choices I made when I was in high school. I craved excitement, which led me to drugs. What started with pills turned into heroin, then into dealing and arrests.

My thoughts turned to my last arrest. It came after I drove under the influence, drifted into oncoming traffic, and hit a man on a motorcycle. He never made it home to his wife and daughter.

I remembered walking into prison after my conviction. All I wanted to do was forget about what I'd done, but I couldn't. So I tried to distract myself in any way I could. The only thing that seemed to help was running. It was the only time I felt like I was worth anything. But I still felt alone.

From that alley, if I closed my eyes, I could still see the little plastic TV in my prison cell, all those years ago. There was a man on the screen, talking on CNN. His name was Scott Strode. He talked about his gym where they boxed and about going rock climbing, something called The Phoenix—a place where people who struggled with addiction were coming together to find a way to heal and let go of the shame. His words gave me hope that I could one day do the same.

I vividly recalled the promise I had made to myself that day watching Scott. I said I'd finish my sentence, complete my parole, and move to Colorado to be part of The Phoenix

Dana Smith broke free from drug and alcohol addiction while in prison. Now she's helping others do the same as a leader at The Phoenix. (Colorado Springs, 2019)

The Phoenix builds a community around each person that helps them recognize their unique potential and break free from addiction.

Scott Strode suffered from substance use disorder, which he beat through exercise combined with community. Now he's helping thousands of others do the same. (Colorado Springs, 2019)

The Phoenix is well over twice as effective as traditional addiction-recovery efforts. It shows a better way to end addiction—getting people to believe in themselves.

community. Four years later, that's exactly what I did.

I remembered the first time I walked into The Phoenix. Almost immediately, we got to boxing. I was so nervous. I didn't know what I was doing. But people welcomed me. And no one asked me what drugs I did. Instead, we talked about our families, our recovery, and how to throw a right hook. Hours later, I left happier than I'd been in years.

And that's how I found myself that night. In that alley.

I realized I was standing in the same spot where Scott stood in the video that I saw back in prison, with my hands on the same fence. On one side of the fence was The Phoenix. On the other side was the world that I'd come from years ago. I could still hear the words of hope that Scott had said on CNN. He said his goal was to bring people from the other side of the fence into The Phoenix community.

Everything I'd done up to that point was rushing through my head. I knew I could never give back what I'd taken from that family so many years ago. But what I could do was dedicate my life to doing for others what Scott had just done for me.

—DANA SMITH

Watch a video about the Phoenix's partnership with the Boston Red Sox at BelieveInPeopleBook.com/stories

The Phoenix is based on a philosophy of empowerment, viewing everyone as an individual, meeting them where they are, and helping them get to where they could be and *want* to be. Scott's approach to overcoming addiction is to believe in people.

This approach strongly contrasts with how society tends to address substance use disorder. For instance, with opioids, the default is to use medication-assisted treatment, or MAT for short. This includes methadone, a synthetic opioid that often comes with side effects and can itself be addictive.

Think what that means: we're swapping out one drug for another, instead of turning away from drugs altogether. While methadone can be lifesaving, it only treats symptoms. Rather than tapping into the intrinsic resiliency of the human spirit, it says, "This is the best we think you can do." This is common with attempts to help those who are struggling, and not just with substance abuse. It certainly isn't based on a belief in people.

The Phoenix takes the opposite approach, focusing on beating, not treating, addiction. And it works! As I mentioned in chapter five, after three months, a remarkable 80 percent of its members are still sober. To put that in perspective, the three-month relapse rate for traditional recovery methods is between 50 and 70 percent. For The Phoenix, it's 20 percent, making it well over twice as effective.

The Phoenix's peer-support approach is vital. It helps people learn what they're capable of in a nonjudgmental environment. Three out of four participants report having more confidence in themselves, a better ability to cope with stress, better self-esteem, and more purpose in their lives, as well as renewed connection to others. This directly affects their long-term success. More than half of The Phoenix's participants live in poverty, and a quarter are unemployed when they join. Studies show that as former substance abusers regain belief in themselves, upward mobility becomes much more likely.

This is huge. The Phoenix isn't just beating addiction—it's helping address the root causes of its participants' poverty.

Scott's work is inspirational, which is no small feat in an often bleak field. When people dealing with substance use disorder see the transformation in The Phoenix's participants, they realize they have the ability to break free too. Scott sets the tone, wearing a shirt emblazoned with the word "SOBER." You can't miss it. And you come to believe it's possible for you too.

Others are affected. Family members and friends regain hope for their loved ones. Members of the media and medical profession are also taking note.

Unsurprisingly, The Phoenix takes off everywhere it goes. Scott started small, in Colorado, with only one location. But he kept developing his model and his own abilities, allowing him to expand and help many more. Within a decade, he had grown The Phoenix to seven outposts across the country. Since we started working with Scott nearly four years ago, The Phoenix has grown to more than 50 locations, with further expansion on the horizon.

One of its most recent expansions was in Boston's "Methadone Mile." Named after the abundance of local methadone clinics, the area is also home to an open-air drug market. Addiction is its defining characteristic. Efforts to bring hope to its inhabitants fail no matter how much money or resources are thrown at it.

Enter The Phoenix.

The outpouring of interest and involvement has been extraordinary, with more than 1,500 people helped in Boston in 2019. The Phoenix now serves over 10,000 people nationwide, a number that is rising by leaps and bounds. Scott Strode's next milestone is to reach one million people, and he's well on his way. With more than 21 million currently in need of treatment for substance use disorder, this could be a tipping point in how our country thinks about addiction.[23]

CHANGED LIVES CHANGE MINDS

Just as The Phoenix relies on empowerment to solve addiction, Urban Specialists is doing the same to address gang violence and crime in cities. As you read in chapter five, Antong Lucky and Bishop Omar Jahwar come from communities where gangs are a major problem, which gives them a unique window on the solution. As a former gang leader, Antong in particular has special knowledge about what draws young men to that life and what can help them leave it.

Bishop Omar also knows the problem he's trying to solve. Like Antong, he grew up in South Dallas. But instead of founding a gang, he started a church and a community group. When violence hits his community, he is among the first on the scene. This was the case in 2016, when five police officers were killed by a sniper in retaliation for police violence, including the killing of black men in several cities.[24] Bishop Omar's insight and calming influence saved lives.

His experience as a pastor made him see that people could choose a better path. He began working in schools and prisons and was the first gang specialist hired in Texas to negotiate gang truces in incarcerated populations. In his prison work, he brought gangs together and, through furlough programs, brought people back to their neighborhoods to show that transformation is possible, even in the toughest environments.

Under Bishop Omar's leadership, and now in partnership with Antong Lucky, Urban Specialists has already mentored more than 18,000 people, transforming many lives. Nearly every school where it has a presence has experienced a culture change and a big drop in violence. Some had been designated by the State of Texas as "Improvement Required" schools, a label more than 90 percent overcame.

Now Urban Specialists has launched a new program called OGU— Original Gangsters United—to train a new generation of catalytic change agents. More than 100 OGs were trained in 2019, and that number should grow tenfold in 2020. And the number of kids the OGs mentor is expected to more than triple every year. For the record, when I say "mentor," Urban Specialists places OGs at bus stops to break up fights and mediate gang conflicts, among other courageous interventions.

OGs who come from other cities are taking the Urban Specialists model home with them and finding new ways to break the cycle of violence. The group has expanded into Atlanta and Baton Rouge, with more cities targeted. Urban Specialists has been able to successfully grow by remaining faithful to its model, drawing on the experiences and insights of people in its communities.

Progress will come as more people stop looking at the least fortunate as problems to be managed or controlled and start seeing them as individuals who have contributions to make.

And as with Café Momentum and The Phoenix, Urban Specialists' success has drawn attention from policymakers, reporters, educators, philanthropists, and many others. People see their transformative work and want to help them accomplish more.

A ROLE FOR EVERYONE

These inspiring examples show that we can make enormous progress on issues that seem intractable. I'm proud to work with many other partners to help them scale. But much more must be done. For a truly seismic shift, we need increasingly more effective and larger solutions to all the barriers holding people back. There needs to be a bevy of initiatives that empower people and inspire the nation.

If you have the ability and experience necessary to start something like Café Momentum, Urban Specialists, or The Phoenix, I applaud you. If you don't, don't give up—there are plenty of other things you can do.

Philanthropists can provide the funding to expand successful initiatives or get other promising local projects up and running. Businesses can partner with these efforts to help those who are struggling develop and apply their abilities. Activists can look for creative ways to help effective projects reach more people. Even if these options present too high of a bar, anyone can volunteer or otherwise provide support. When you encounter these incredible organizations, make their success known in your conversations or on your social media. Anyone can get involved in their own way.

Determining how you can get engaged begins with discovering the available opportunities. Think creatively, and you'll find quite a few. Now imagine helping to scale the other organizations I've mentioned, the many others I've been fortunate enough to support, or the countless others I'm unaware of. (You may already have some in mind.) Supporting effective ones and celebrating their successes can create a chain reaction.

Progress will come as more people stop looking at the least fortunate as problems to be managed or controlled and start seeing them as individuals who have contributions to make. It will come when we believe in those who are struggling and empower them—one at a time, then 10 at a time, multiplying and inspiring ever more people to participate in the transformation.

There's no going back once you start down this road. Once you see the injustices caused by control, you will do something about it. Once you see how many are being held back, you will work to break down the barriers that stand in their way. Once you recognize what people are capable of, you will see that it is possible to transform the institution of community to help every person rise.

7.
LIFELONG LEARNING

" To stimulate life,
leaving it free,
however, to unfold
itself, that is the first
duty of the educator. "
MARIA MONTESSORI[1]

Education has long been a passion of mine. In addition to devoting most of my time to reading, studying, and experimenting—both on the job and at home—I have long sought to help others discover and develop their aptitudes through learning and application, as I did mine. This began by responding to requests to speak on college campuses in my late twenties and quickly developed into providing support for educational initiatives, something I've done ever since.

When I think of education, I recall a young woman I met through Youth Entrepreneurs, a program my wife and I founded about 30 years ago in Wichita. We were at a banquet celebrating students who had submitted exceptional business plans. The story of the top winner, April, was unforgettable. She reinforced our view of how broken the education system is—and the path to fix it.

April told us of her troubled life growing up. She came from a dysfunctional family and lived in a dangerous neighborhood. Early in life, she resigned herself to a bleak future.

Education is supposed to be the great uplifter, the means by which even the least fortunate and most disadvantaged can find a path to success. Yet what April experienced at her school gave her little reason for hope. The rote courses and tests had little relevance to her life and failed to awaken her abilities. She quickly checked out in school, failing essentially everything.

One day, enrolling in her junior year, April heard about a class that offered her the opportunity to make some money. And so she signed up for Youth Entrepreneurs.

Liz and I started YE, as we call it, because we knew kids in Wichita who were in situations similar to April's. They mostly came from troubled neighborhoods, and while they clearly had potential, they struggled to find it in the typical classroom setting. To change that, we decided to invest in a program run by a national foundation based on core economic and entrepreneurial concepts. We adapted that core curriculum so it better resonated with students, which enabled it to show improved results. We started by supporting a single teacher—Matt Silverthorne—in one of Wichita's toughest schools. (Matt is still with the program to this day.)

The course allows students to lead the way. They engage in stock-market and trading games, with all the chaos that entails. They are encouraged to find what they enjoy most and to see if they can turn it into a business. "Market Day" is everyone's favorite. The school dedicates one lunch hour for the class to show their wares to the entire student body.

Then comes the hard part: writing a plan for a real business. When that's completed, it's up to the student to present it to the class. The plan that is voted best wins a choice of capital for a start-up or money to use toward the cost of college. The whole program gives students the freedom to develop their ideas and pursue their passions in a highly individualized setting.

This approach made all the difference for April, who had won the semester of the banquet. Initially motivated by the promise of seed capital, the rest was up to her. She needed to learn how to succeed in business, which in turn meant learning what she was good at and what she wasn't.

As she explained to the crowd of parents, teachers, and supporters at the banquet, she saw the value in learning specific skills. To write a business plan and pitch it to others, she needed to do well in English. To keep the books and turn a profit, she needed to learn math. She also learned the importance of treating customers with respect, causing a shift in her entire attitude toward those around her.

The more she learned, the more she came to chart her own course. Where once education had been imposed on her, now she was driving it herself—a chance that made all the difference. She told the banquet attendees that her failing grades turned into straight A's. By the time we met, she was well on her way to a life of contribution and fulfillment. I'm told that after college, she started her own consulting business.

I don't tell this story to tout Youth Entrepreneurs. The real takeaway is why it helped April—and why the current education system fails so many others.

THE IMPORTANCE OF EDUCATION

The goal of education is simple: self-actualization.

By helping students identify their gifts, develop them into valued skills, and apply them to benefit themselves and others, a good education enables people to have the best possible life and contribute to the creation of the best possible society. When students learn that the way to succeed is to create value for others, it changes the entire culture from one of conflict to one of mutual benefit.

This is true for all levels and kinds of education, including K–12, trade schools, universities, and beyond. Indeed, lifelong learning is essential to a good life, as I can attest, and as I hope this book demonstrates.

Yet if the goal really is to help students realize their potential, then American education is clearly falling short. It is an injustice holding back millions of people.

By high school graduation, many (if not most) students have little clue what gifts they have, what motivates them, and how they can succeed. They aren't contribution motivated. They're often not motivated at all. Only a third of students say they're "engaged" by the time they reach twelfth grade.[2]

LIZ KOCH

WHY WE STARTED YOUTH ENTREPRENEURS

LIZ AND I HAVE BEEN MARRIED FOR 48 YEARS. SHE LED THE FOUNDING OF YOUTH ENTREPRENEURS IN 1991.

The idea for Youth Entrepreneurs didn't come from a classroom or a teacher or a textbook or anything like that. It came out of Charles's and my desire to help our son, Chase, get to know a much more diverse group of kids than he was meeting at Collegiate, the private school he was attending.

So at age eight, we signed him up for the Salvation Army's Biddy Basketball program. He got on a team consisting largely of kids from tough neighborhoods who were very good players. As a result, Chase spent most of his time on the bench. But he became friends with several of his teammates, many of whom had obvious gifts beyond basketball.

We believed a number of them would benefit from attending Collegiate, so we tried to talk their parents into applying. We offered to arrange scholarships, but it was a tough sell, and we were only successful with a couple.

Nevertheless, the Salvation Army's program was beneficial. It helped keep the kids out of trouble. It helped them begin to believe they could succeed, learn to play by the rules, and develop relationships with others from very different backgrounds.

As a result, I went on the board of the local Salvation Army, after which I became chairman and led a major fundraiser. It was so successful that I was invited to join the national board. These experiences began to teach me what it took to enable someone growing up in a destructive environment to realize their potential, and they motivated me to do more.

Meanwhile, at Koch Industries, Charles was witnessing the good results of teaching people how to

As a high-school student in Youth Entrepreneurs, Toiya Smith learned problem-solving skills and now applies them to her passion for improving the criminal justice system. (2017, Texas)

Madison Jacques founded her school's first student-run coffee shop, a business she created as part of the Youth Entrepreneurs program. (Topeka, 2019)

unlock their talents and use them to help others through business.

Then it hit me: What if we created a course that combined the two, using the approach of the Salvation Army and the concepts and methods of Principled Entrepreneurship™?

I figured such a course could integrate theory and practice, show kids that they have talent, and be fun and rewarding at the same time. This led us to look for an inner-city public high school where we could start.

Our first course was at North High in Wichita, Kansas. Most of the kids who signed up came from troubled backgrounds. We got to know many of them, and I started to see why they struggled in school. Their classes didn't really help them discover who they were and what gifts they had, much less how to develop themselves.

Until they found Youth Entrepreneurs.

When they got to put their own plans into action, they felt empowered. They were free to create their own business plan and try to make it work. It made them see learning in a new light—one that was practical and tailored to their own talents and interests.

From the very start, YE was a big success, because the kids loved it and learned from it. For many, it was their first experience of being in control and trusted to chart their own course.

This is why Youth Entrepreneurs has grown. It has helped thousands, and soon, we hope, millions.

—LIZ KOCH

Learn more about how Youth Entrepreneurs empowers students at BelieveInPeopleBook.com/stories

Even fewer learn what they're being taught. The most recent federal data show that only 25 percent of twelfth-grade students are proficient at math.[3] The numbers are slightly better for reading, where 37 percent of students are proficient—still a far cry from success.[4]

Keep in mind: these numbers tell us nothing about students' unique abilities. It stands to reason that an even smaller percentage of students leave the K–12 system with any sense of their best path.

Sure enough, the early untaught lessons hold students back later in life. One recent study found that a quarter of college freshmen need remedial classes, meaning their previous schooling failed to prepare them.[5]

Within the graduation rate itself is another sign of the slide toward a two-tiered society. In the strongest communities, only 5 percent of people failed to graduate from high school. In troubled communities, that figure climbs to nearly 25 percent.[6] Even this doesn't begin to describe the disparity, as a high school diploma is no indication of a student's progress in self-actualizing.

It keeps getting worse. Higher education is hardly the solution to the problems that start in the K–12 system. The National Association of Colleges and Employers asked businesses to rank college graduates on eight measures of career readiness. In five categories, fewer than half of graduates were deemed ready for employment. In the best category, businesses felt that only 77 percent of graduates were adequately prepared to join the workforce.[7] It was the only passing grade among all eight categories—a C grade. Businesses spend billions each year helping new workers learn the basic skills they didn't get in school.[8]

Unsurprisingly, a growing number of people now wonder if higher education is worth it. One recent poll found that only half of Americans think a college education is very important, down from 70 percent in 2013.[9] Millions of students go to college every year, not because they see the benefit but because they've been programmed to think it's the single best next step, and that anything less is a failure.

Higher education is certainly a *costly* next step. Student debt in America currently totals more than $1.5 trillion—a staggering sum that's higher than credit card debt and auto loan debt—much of it owed by students who went to college without knowing why or to what end.[10] Considering that most graduates doubt the value of their college education, and that so many businesses have to retrain graduates, it seems obvious that most college students are not getting their money's worth—not even close.

Why does education fail for so many students and at essentially every level? The answer is that American education largely fails to meet students where they are and help them realize who they are. Instead, it pushes students to be something they're not.

The problems start early. Although there are some bright spots, the K–12 system is typically designed with the average student in mind. But the average student doesn't exist. No one makes this point better than educational innovator and Social Entrepreneur Todd Rose, author of *Dark Horse* and *The End of Average.*

Todd rightly points out that every student's aptitudes, interests, and abilities are different—often wildly so. This fact notwithstanding, our schools largely treat everyone as if they're more or less the same. They read the same books, solve the same problems, take the same tests, and tread the same dreary road as everyone else—day after day, week after week, month after month, year after year.

This is known as standardization, and it is a case study in how one-size-fits-all solutions are inherently harmful.

NO TWO STUDENTS ARE ALIKE

Standardization might make sense for manufacturing car parts or computers, but it does not work well for developing human beings. The educator Maria Montessori had it right when she declared that education ought to "stimulate life, leaving it free . . . to unfold itself." Standardization, on the other hand, directs students toward a predetermined end.

Standardization might make sense for manufacturing car parts or computers, but it does not work well for developing human beings.

It necessarily fails to tailor education to each student's unique aptitudes and needs. Instead of understanding how schooling can benefit them and allow them to experience the joy of learning, students rightly see it as a painful, boring exercise of little value. As April from Youth Entrepreneurs demonstrates, this discourages kids from applying themselves. It also prevents kids from becoming lifelong learners—a crucial factor for long-term success. Standardization is terribly counterproductive.

Standardization also pushes students into a zero-sum game. It ranks kids, putting some at "the top" while declaring that others are at "the bottom." This says nothing about their unique skills, only that some are better than others on an arbitrary scale. After spending so many years in this harmful system, students often adopt the same zero-sum mentality in life: for me to win, you must lose.

The standardized system is reinforced by policies and practices that stifle competition and innovation. These include caps and moratoriums on new kinds of schools. Another example is the teacher certification process, which forces would-be educators to go through their own process of standardization, limiting their ability to reach students, excel at their careers, and find fulfillment in their own lives.

Absurd outcomes can result. Consider one thought experiment: Does it make sense to you that until recently, Justice Sandra Day O'Connor, the first female justice on the U.S. Supreme Court, couldn't even teach civics at the high school named after her in her home state of Arizona without first going through the state's laborious certification process? Similarly, in nearly every state, is it right that Bill Gates can't teach computer science because he doesn't have the right degrees?[11] Not every teacher is going to be Sandra Day O'Connor or Bill Gates, but the lesson still stands: the hostility to the new cuts students off from the improved.

Nor are these issues relegated to K–12. Problems also abound in higher education. The concept of the university has hardly changed in a thousand years. The eleventh-century guild system is alive and well in the twenty-first.

One major problem is the accreditation system, which has morphed from its original intent of ensuring quality to a bureaucratic scheme that determines which schools qualify for federal funding. Without an accreditor's blessing, a university has little chance of attracting students or even staying in business.

Guess who sits on the accreditation boards? That's right—the existing universities. Why should accreditors certify innovative schools that would compete with their own employers? Why should colleges and universities experiment with new programs if it puts their accreditation at risk? The incentive is usually to stop a potentially better education in its tracks.

Of course, this is not to say that nothing has changed over the years. For instance, there are now more administrators than educators at the typical U.S. college.[12] (The same is true for K–12 schools, where the number of administrators grew eight times faster than the number of students between 1950 and 2009.[13]) There is no evidence that students benefit from this. There is evidence, however, that without the bureaucratic bloat since 1976, college tuition would be 20 percent cheaper.[14]

There are many other examples of how education fails students in both K–12 and higher ed. The common thread among all of them is protectionism.

If you recall, protectionism is a hostility to beneficial change. Whether it's standardization, teacher tenure, or accreditation, protectionism is harming all parties in the education system. It hurts the teachers and administrators who could find more fulfillment helping students succeed. It hurts parents whose kids aren't developing their abilities. And of course, it hurts millions of students, especially the most disadvantaged.

MORE OF THE STANDARDIZED SAME

Pretty much everyone agrees that American education isn't working. Only 19 percent of parents give the schooling system either an A or B grade.[15] Yet rather than propose or support meaningful changes, most everyone—reformers included—offers just a slight variation on the protectionist model. Instead of empowering students, they demand more control.

For example, many reformers want to increase standardization in the name of accountability and transparency, assuming it will help students succeed while addressing real concerns about the runaway cost of education. People often say that school choice advocates and teachers' unions want starkly different schooling systems, or that public and private schools have little in common, when in reality their visions for the classroom are remarkably similar.

Consider that standardization was the inspiration behind federal efforts such as No Child Left Behind in the early 2000s (under a Republican, George W. Bush) and Common Core State Standards (originally developed by private philanthropies) and Race to the Top (an Obama administration program) in the 2010s. They all significantly increased standardization in the K–12 system. Facing perpetually disheartening statistics of student achievements, we now hear calls for further standardization at public and charter schools, both from well-meaning government officials and private philanthropists.

There are also loud calls to increase funding for existing schools and models, despite their demonstrated failure to empower students. From 1970 to 2010, total K–12 spending on a per-student basis nearly tripled, with almost nothing to show for it. While fourth- and eighth-grade students saw small improvements in academic achievement, high school students saw none.[16] America has spent 150 percent more on schools in exchange for a near 0 percent improvement.[17] While some schools may indeed require more money, it makes no sense to spend ever-larger sums on the same failing model in the hope of a better outcome.

Elsewhere, philanthropists and policymakers alike are working to expand charter schools or provide public funding for private school alternatives. This is a source of intense controversy—should we invest in private schools, charter schools, or traditional public schools? But this is a false choice. Any of these options, if done well, will help students. Conversely, any, if done poorly, will harm them. The emphasis should be on what works, not the type of school.

When charter and private schools just replicate the standardized approach, as many do, then students will still struggle to discover who they are, or learn about their own individual strengths and weaknesses. Conversely, I've met students from good public schools whose teachers and administrators have been free to tailor their education based on each student's aptitudes—and they do fine. "School choice" is meaningless if the choices aren't that different from the status quo. When it comes to choices, parents should be at least as concerned about the quality as the quantity.

Similarly, the serious problems presented by higher education have led to many counterproductive solutions. Free college is a nice sound bite but a shortsighted policy. It would push more students into universities that already fail to prepare them for a lifetime of contribution, while making new and possibly better options less likely to emerge. In a classic example of protectionism, free college would prop up the current higher education model when a deeper transformation is needed.

Ditto student loan forgiveness. It skirts around a real problem—the often astounding cost of college tuition—but doesn't address it. Just the opposite: it encourages universities to continue raising tuition costs while assuming the government will swoop in when students can't pay. The schools get their money regardless of the quality of the education they provide and whether it leads to their students' long-term success, including the ability to pay back their loans. Thus protected from necessary change, student loan forgiveness would further break a broken system.

And yet the institution of education can be fixed—at every level. We don't have to settle for subpar schools and stagnant universities. Instead, we need education that helps every student unlock their potential.

The type of school, the school buildings, the lesson plans, the teacher credentials—none of it matters as much as each student's ability to learn in an individualized way.

PUTTING THE "I" IN EDUCATION

A better way is individualized education.

Most of society is moving toward individualization—in medicine, fashion, entertainment, and many other areas where products and services are tailored and curated for each individual. This is the age of Amazon, Apple, Netflix, and a thousand other companies that essentially let you choose your own adventure. It makes no sense that education is going in the opposite direction.

Given each person's unique talents, education should be among the most customized parts of life. It can be, but that won't happen by focusing on secondary concerns.

The type of school, the school buildings, the lesson plans, the teacher credentials—none of it matters as much as each student's ability to learn in an individualized way. When you start with the system, you tend to ignore the student. But when you start with the student, you can avoid rigid systems and pursue a dynamic range of options that meet each person's unique abilities and motivations. Instead of telling students what to learn and how to learn it, it's time to let them learn in the ways that are best for them.

Individualized education is the essence of bottom up. Rather than being dictated by experts on high, it empowers students, teachers, administrators, parents, and many others to work collaboratively. Likewise, instead of relentlessly focusing on protecting the current system, it adopts a mentality of openness, embracing the new and recognizing that the old way of doing things can always be improved. The principle of openness is always and everywhere essential to progress, and education is no exception.

Individualized education can happen in any learning setting—public or private, charter or district, parochial or secular, K–12 or collegiate, or vocational. It can also happen outside the traditional classroom. The focus is not on where the education happens but on what the education entails. Prioritizing the needs of each student instead of the type of school is far more likely to help students learn the values and skills necessary for a life of contribution and success.

Youth Entrepreneurs, the program I mentioned at the start of this chapter, is grounded in this philosophy. The whole point of YE is to let students apply themselves in a way that the typical classroom setting doesn't allow.

Individualized education is the essence of bottom up.

This approach clearly worked for April, and YE works for essentially everyone who participates, because each person's experience is tailored to their own interests and abilities. The program has now reached over 35,000 students, about 99 percent of whom graduate from high school. Their college graduation rate is 50 percent higher than the national average.

While some of the students' businesses have become successful in their own right, YE isn't about starting companies or making money. It's about introducing the concepts of contribution and lifelong learning. Students whose businesses don't succeed still see what it means to create value for others. They also learn valuable lessons about their abilities and interests.

Schools, students, and parents have taken interest in YE's outcomes. What started in a single public-school classroom in Kansas is now being used by almost 500 educators in 700 classrooms throughout 30 states. Most are in public schools. Wherever Youth Entrepreneurs takes root, students who were otherwise struggling find the kind of individualized education that puts them on a better trajectory.

But students aren't the only ones who benefit. So does basically everyone involved in the educational process. Frustrated teachers who were constrained by a one-size-fits-all curriculum can now apply their own innovative ideas to their classes, making them more effective educators and leaving them more fulfilled. Families are no longer left worrying that their kids aren't learning and aren't safe. Society benefits when students find where they can contribute.

This is how to transform education: by starting, finding, and growing the efforts that demonstrate the profound benefits of individualized education.

There are many other examples that prove this point, such as Narrative 4, based in New York City. Narrative 4's cofounder Colum McCann saw that students were being lectured at instead of given the freedom to exchange ideas and experiences with others. This left them frustrated, bored, lonely, and stressed, none of which is conducive to learning.

Narrative 4 overcomes this problem by going into classrooms with customized "story exchanges." A facilitator pairs students and asks them to share their stories with each other. The process teaches students active listening, self-reflection, and interpersonal skills, all while they learn to understand their peer's different perspective and life story. Far from rehashing the same old material, they are continually exposed to something new.

The Yale Center for Emotional Intelligence studied the effects of Narrative 4's story exchange and found that it causes students to feel fewer negative emotions while making them feel demonstrably more accepted, cheerful, confident, respected, and interested.[18] The kids who go through this program become more receptive to learning and more engaged in the classroom. They stand a better chance of discovering their abilities and where and how to start applying them.

These are only a few of the best examples of projects that provide options for students to pursue their interests and develop themselves. They have changed thousands of lives.

Yet more must be done. The goal should be to help millions of kids get similar life-changing experiences, no matter where—or even whether—they go to school.

If you're passionate about education, then you have a role to play in its transformation. The most important thing you can do is abandon the current us-versus-them mentality. Reformers vs. unions, teachers vs. parents, public vs. private, charter vs. district—none of it helps. In fact, the constant divisiveness hurts the students who need to discover their abilities. All of us need to work to empower all students.

Once you accept this mental shift (not an easy task), the road to institutional change has three parts: finding and supporting worthy causes, celebrating their success, and catalyzing widespread action.

FIND WHAT WORKS...

The first is finding and supporting efforts that individualize education.

For some, this may mean financial support. For others, it may mean volunteering. For still others, it may mean pushing to bring a worthwhile project to their kid's school. Maybe you're in a position to come together with other parents to start your own microschool (google it!). You could also try to educate your school board members about new options— failing that, elect a better school board—or work for policy changes at the local, state, or federal levels. Support can take many forms.

Individualized education doesn't mean changing everything a school does. Big benefits can accrue from local projects, as Narrative 4 and Youth Entrepreneurs show. But it does require constant experimentation. Far from one standardized solution, individualized education could potentially include as many methods as there are people.

Some solutions won't involve a traditional school at all. In some communities, groups of parents have pooled their resources to rent out space, hire good teachers (which may include parents), and build an educational setting that works for their kids and is based on their values. This works better for some students than the best public or private school in the area.

Whatever it may be, we all need to find more avenues for progress. My foundation recently partnered with the Walton Family Foundation to seed five hundred educational initiatives—everything from entire schools to specific programs.[19] Our rationale is simple: support teachers striving to enable millions of students to flourish in new and unexpected ways. Some won't pan out. But any one of them could help lead our country out of the current standardized system—and toward a more individualized, and beneficial, experience.

The same approach is needed in higher education. One of my longstanding goals has been to support faculty who work to expand the array of offerings at universities, thereby helping more students (and professors) discover their best individual path. Together with many other partners, we now support around one thousand professors and six hundred projects at more than three hundred universities.

One is the Political Theory Project at Brown University, led by Professor John Tomasi. In addition to boasting a diverse set of scholars, it runs the Janus Forum, which hosts debates between prominent academics on serious but controversial topics. The best part is that the students themselves run the forum—choosing the topics, picking the speakers, and so on. It's one big exercise in people with different perspectives working to achieve a common goal, fostering collaboration and respect. Students learn a lot from the forum speakers, but I bet they learn at least as much from the shared experience of putting the forum together.

While such efforts are necessary, they are not sufficient. Transforming higher education ultimately requires more than new classes, majors, and academic opportunities. The university system itself needs innovators to disrupt the usual four-year, debt-riddled, on-campus college experience. There is a great need for changes that simultaneously lower costs, expand options, and allow students to discover themselves in the truest sense.

Fortunately, many have taken on this task. Innovations like OpenStax, a project of Rice University, show that much of what we've taken for granted in higher ed is ripe for disruption.

OpenStax saw that textbooks lock in specific and limited teaching methods, while costing way too much. For some students, paying for books and supplies can raise the cost of community college by as much as 40 percent.[20] Its solution: free online modular textbooks that allow teachers to mix and match lessons based on what's best for their students. OpenStax has already saved students more than $800 million, while providing a higher-quality, more individualized experience for more people, including some who traditionally lack access to higher education.[21]

But this was just the beginning.

Now OpenStax is experimenting with machine adaptive learning, with the goal of giving each student a tailored educational experience that changes based on their individual aptitudes. This is a great example of harnessing technology to facilitate individualization, and it's potentially revolutionary given its ability to reduce costs and dramatically increase access to tailored learning.

Individualized education depends on a culture of openness and free expression, especially at the collegiate level. Students have the best chance of discovering and developing their gifts when they can debate different ideas and pursue unorthodox and even unpopular paths. The history of progress is the history of people pushing boundaries. Personal development follows the same course.

Groups like the Foundation for Individual Rights in Education (FIRE) are helping universities foster a culture of open inquiry and free speech. FIRE has found that American collegiate speech codes and related policies silence students' voices, whether by banning them from speaking, declaring that specific ideas are off-limits, or otherwise infringing on students' ability to experiment, discuss, and learn.

Such policies are destructive. When an educational environment stifles rather than stimulates students' discovery processes, it sends them into the world with minds that are closed, not open. This hurts both the student and society.

FIRE tackles this issue head-on. It works with students who have been silenced or stonewalled, telling their stories and sometimes suing on their behalf. The group has a success rate of 92 percent when defending student rights in court. FIRE has also worked with specific universities to repeal bad policies. By 2019, fewer than 25 percent of U.S. colleges maintained severely restrictive speech codes, down from nearly 75 percent in 2009. By 2020, thanks in large part to FIRE's work, nearly five million students were freed from speech restrictions.

Working with FIRE and others, dozens of colleges have also adopted strong policies based on the University of Chicago's "Chicago Statement."[22] It declares, unequivocally, that it "is not the proper role of the university to attempt to shield individuals from ideas and opinions they find unwelcome, disagreeable, or even deeply offensive." It continues: "Without a vibrant commitment to free and open inquiry, a university ceases to be a university."[23] To empower its students, an institution of higher learning must, at minimum, abide by these words.

We also need to recognize that higher education isn't for everyone.

It is widely assumed that every kid should aim for at least a bachelor's degree from a four-year college, yet university offerings can't meet every student's unique needs. Many young people have aptitudes that would be better developed in alternative settings. Trade and vocational schools, coding boot camps, and experiential learning programs are often scoffed at or overlooked, even though they provide a better learning environment for many, if not most, students. We shouldn't put college on a pedestal; alternative types of education must be made part of the answer.

Mike Rowe, the famous host of the TV show *Dirty Jobs*, has become the apostle of the skilled trades. A true Social Entrepreneur, he started a foundation to help people realize what our society misses when skilled labor is neglected. His work with plumbers, electricians, fishers, and others has introduced him to some of the happiest, most fulfilled people in the country—people who are doing better in life *because* they didn't follow the typical college track. Mike is working on several exciting projects to connect more people to these kinds of fulfilling careers. He's going to enable many thousands to realize their potential and make a bigger contribution.

As these examples show, there are many amazing initiatives that deserve support, and support can come in many different forms. Finding and helping worthy programs is the first step to transformation.

CELEBRATE SUCCESS . . .

The second step is to celebrate success. We have to help people see that it's possible to do better—that they don't have to settle for what they have now.

The beauty of individualized education is that it's leaps and bounds better than what's available at the majority of schools. And yet many people don't know about it. The best way to fix that is to find what works and get the word out.

When you see a program that gets results, tell your peers about it. When you see your kid or your neighbor's kid benefiting from a novel educational model, talk to other parents. Call attention to the best efforts however you can, wherever you can.

Celebration also shifts the conversation. So does cooperation. It takes the fire out of the us-versus-them mentality, redirecting the focus toward helping every student. Instead of getting lost in divisive debates, people unite.

One innovator who has united and inspired people is the president of Arizona State University, Michael Crow. When he took the helm, ASU was widely known as a party school.[24] The advice he received about how to change that was to cut freshman enrollment in half—as if the only way to improve educational quality is to restrict it to a smaller group of more elite kids. Not on his watch. Instead, he set out to change the school's performance by giving more, rather than fewer, students a more tailored, varied, and beneficial experience.

This learner-centric approach has been a game-changer for students. Under Michael's leadership, ASU has embraced online education, giving more students the opportunity to learn outside the classroom setting, which may better fit their needs, schedules, and wallets. ASU also engages high school students, letting them integrate with ASU education at an earlier age, when it's right for them.

One intriguing project is ASU's partnership with Starbucks. Starbucks pays for its employees to get a bachelor's degree through the university's online programs. This novel approach allows tens of thousands of people nationwide to pursue one of more than 80 degrees— whether or not they remain at Starbucks. It is another important move toward individualization, helping more people get a good education without forcing them into the standardized model.

ASU has now been ranked by *U.S. News & World Report* as the most innovative university in America for five years straight.[25] Since Michael Crow assumed the presidency in 2002, enrollment has increased from 55,000 to 110,000—a 100 percent increase—all while ensuring its student body more closely represents Arizona's demographics.[26] Other schools—and their students, professors, and parents—are taking note. They want to be more like ASU. And ASU is meeting more students where they are by opening branch campuses in cities outside Arizona.

This kind of public demand makes the third and final step possible: action that transforms the institution of education from the bottom up.

...TRANSFORM EDUCATION

As more people see what works and band together to support it, they become agents of change. They start calling for better educational opportunities in their local schools, their alma maters, and so on. They start demanding the kind of choices that can really make a difference: choices that recognize and reflect the uniqueness of every student and enable them to find their best path to success.

Once again, this will look different in different places.

For instance, parents and activists could band together to allow their school districts to give public school administrators more autonomy. Principals usually have authority over only 5 percent of their budgets, which prevents them from trying new things and tailoring their schools' offerings to students' varied aptitudes and interests.[27]

Research shows that empowered principals are much more thoughtful about allocating their resources. When given the flexibility, some choose to reduce the number of non-classroom employees and hire more teachers to work directly with students.[28] Other studies find a positive relationship between principal autonomy and student achievement.[29] The Progressive Policy Institute found that "students can achieve more if those who understand their needs best—principals and teachers, not the central office—make the decisions that affect their learning."

My foundation works with a high school principal in one of the poorest urban congressional districts in the country. She points out the difference between the decisions she gets to make and those that are still controlled by the central office. For example, the hallway clocks cannot be set by anyone but the central bureaucrats, but the school curriculum is up to the principal. This resulted in a clock stuck for more than two years at 2:15—you have to see it to believe it! But the rich curriculum is helping her students, some of the poorest in the country, accomplish incredible things despite their hardships.

The principal has incorporated a program from an organization I mentioned earlier, Narrative 4, with exceptional results. She has seen more of her students succeed precisely because they have experienced this measure of individualized education.

Another change worth pursuing is letting families choose the schools that are best suited to their kids—whether public or private. Arizona has adopted a version of this policy, known as "open enrollment." Assuming a public school or charter school has space, parents can enroll their kids there, even if they're not in the district.[30] West Virginia has implemented a similar policy.[31]

Other states allow families to use public funding to send their children to the schools that are best for them. Florida helps parents send their four- and five-year-olds to private, public, and highly specialized prekindergarten schools, paying up to $2,300 to the school of their choice.[32] This saves money—Florida spends about half the national average on preschool funding—and gives parents access to 6,200 pre-k options.[33] It's also hugely popular, with nearly 80 percent of families enrolling their children in the program. (If it works for four- and five-year-olds, why not do the same for six-year-olds, seven-year-olds, and, well, every student?)

The Sunshine State also offers an Empowerment Scholarship that gives some families more than $7,000 a year to spend on private school tuition.[34] In Arizona, some students can get an Education Savings Account of more than $12,500—about 90 percent of state funding per student—to spend on essentially any educational expense.[35] Parents love these programs, and the kids tend to get the education that's best for them.

As for higher education, a little experimentation will go a long way toward helping students find what's right for them. Student loans could also use more than a little disruption, as they are bankrupting students and making it easier for schools to hike tuition.

Purdue University recently introduced income-sharing agreements, which pay a student's way in exchange for a slice of their income in the decade after graduation (assuming they make above a minimum and pre-specified amount).[36] There's no crushing compound interest, and the payments rise only as students earn more, eventually reaching a cap. This gives the school an incentive to prepare students for the workforce, whereas student loans incentivize raising tuition without increasing the quality of the education. These arrangements may not work for everyone, so other financing options should also be explored.

One avenue that would affect both quality and cost is alternative credentialing. Instead of pursuing the traditional expensive four-year degree, students would pursue certificates focused on specific skills or a broader curriculum that covers less ground than a bachelor's degree. Some programs like this already exist, and the coursework is more focused on developing employable skills. Scheduling is also more flexible, enabling students to proceed at their own pace.

Some schools are already offering credentials designed in collaboration with specific industries (especially in Silicon Valley) to ensure that the education meets a specific economic need.[37] This gives students a quick "off-ramp" to employment when they are ready instead of making them spend a predetermined amount of time in a classroom.

Similarly, programs and technology that allow students to "stack" their credentials create "on-ramps" back into higher education.[38] As technology transforms the economy, people could quickly get up to speed, helping them become lifelong learners in the process. With more alternative credentialing, higher education could serve more people at a lower cost and a faster pace. What are we waiting for?

EDUCATION THAT EMPOWERS

These are important first steps on the road to individualized education. Many more will be necessary to create a truly innovative and supportive education system, one that helps every student discover their gifts and lead a life of contribution.

For that to happen, many more Social Entrepreneurs must emerge and increase their effectiveness. The successful models they create need to be promoted and celebrated so that individuals will see a better way and demand it for themselves and their families, which will spur even more bottom-up, individualized solutions to arise.

If you are passionate about education and want to empower students, ask yourself: Am I open to new methods, or am I perpetuating the status quo? Am I encouraging students to discover their gifts, or am I pushing them to follow a path that neither motivates them nor makes them successful? Teachers, administrations, parents, philanthropists, policymakers—these questions apply to everyone who wants to bring about an education system that empowers. Your answer will determine whether you help society move toward that goal.

There's no good reason not to transform education. New learning approaches are continually being unveiled. The tools of progress are all around us, making it easier than ever to design schools, products, and programs that treat students as distinct individuals, helping them unlock their aptitudes.

We can't possibly know what developments will arise or predict what methods and models will work best. But that's precisely the point.

Every person is unique, and every person deserves a unique education that challenges them to be the best version of themselves—lifelong learners who are motivated to contribute and realize their potential. That's what education is supposed to be. And that's the kind of educational system you can help create.

8.

AN ECONOMY FOR EVERYONE

---

66 Equal rights to all; special privileges to none. 99

THOMAS JEFFERSON (ATTRIBUTED)[1]

66 In the market economy, every owner is continuously obliged to justify, through service, his right to retain control of the resources he claims. 99

PAUL L. POIROT[2]

A few years ago, I gave a guest lecture at MIT's business school. I laid out my view that success in business begins by focusing on how you can create value for others, starting with your customers and employees.

One of the students immediately challenged this, which I welcomed. He said, "Isn't that naïve? In business, your focus needs to be on maximizing your profits."

I responded by asking, "What's more naïve, focusing on creating value for your customers, or expecting that they'll pay you if you're *not* creating value for them?" The conversation quickly changed.

This discussion is far from academic. Plenty of companies embrace the dangerous philosophy advocated by the student: profit by any means necessary. The result is injustice on a massive scale. It's harming millions of Americans—people like Melony Armstrong.

Melony decided in her mid-twenties that she wanted to pursue her passion for hair braiding.[3] Born in Ohio before moving to Mississippi, she acquired the skill by practicing on friends and family members. Demand for her services became so strong that she decided to make it a business. It wasn't long before she encountered the many obstacles built by companies that were willing to rig the system to maximize profit.

Melony had fallen victim to the scheme of "occupational licensing." Years before, Mississippi cosmetologists convinced the state government to create high barriers to entry into their industry. The reason: to stifle potential competitors and protect themselves—and their profits—from entrepreneurs like Melony. So they convinced the state that hair braiders should be required to get government approval before setting up shop, knowing full well that many, if not most, couldn't clear these hurdles. Politicians in Mississippi, like most other states, agreed to this injustice with little or no opposition.[4]

The state demanded that Melony take a "wigology" class, which had nothing to do with hair braiding, in which she was already proficient. The class itself took 300 hours, and only two schools in Mississippi offered it.[5] (By comparison, she would have needed only 120 hours of training to become an emergency medical technician—a job that quite literally deals with life and death.)

Since neither of the schools were in her hometown, it looked like Melony was out of options. She was ready to give up. Fortunately, a local cosmetologist agreed to teach her the class, keeping her dream alive.

That ordeal behind her, Melony finally opened her shop, Naturally Speaking, in Tupelo, Mississippi. Her plan was always to hire others and teach them the hair-braiding trade, yet that led to another, larger barrier. If she wanted to train and employ others, she would have to pay about $10,000 and take another 3,200 hours of schooling—a five-figure, three-year commitment.[6] Once again, none of the required "education" dealt with hair braiding.

This was devastating. Yes, Melony finally had her business, but she didn't have any legal way to expand it without jumping through another impossible hoop. Once again, the organized cosmetologist lobby had deliberately built a wall around their companies even though that meant hurting Melony and the people she might employ—not to mention the customers who valued her service.

Melony was going to train folks who might one day compete against *her*. For trying to empower others, she received a cease-and-desist letter. For trying to help people, she was held back.

It's difficult to overstate just how much occupational licensing punishes the least fortunate and those who start with nothing. Licenses cost money and time that most don't have. If you're already struggling to make ends meet, can you afford to take three years off to spend 3,200 hours in training? The system stifles those who merely want the opportunity to pursue their passions and contribute. (Don't worry, Melony persevered—stay tuned.)

GOOD PROFIT

Melony's story shows the danger of pursuing profits by any means necessary. It fundamentally misunderstands the role of business and the point of profits.

This was the topic of my earlier book *Good Profit*. For a business to succeed long-term, and deserve to, it must practice mutual benefit—a win-win philosophy. At their best, companies create the innovations that improve lives, delivering better products at lower prices for more people. Profit isn't the goal, it's the result. Specifically, it's the result of making a contribution to society. As Paul Poirot points out in the quote that frames this chapter, good profit is a measure of this contribution.

Good profit springs from businesses creating value for others. (This is what I call Principled Entrepreneurship™, if you recall from chapter three.) This concept requires listening and responding to changing needs and wants. To the extent that a company does this, it will deserve the money it makes, succeeding by enabling others to succeed. By contrast, ill-gotten gains—bad profit—come when businesses harm people to advantage themselves.

Customers depend on principled businesses, but not only them. So do employees. After formal education ends, business is the primary place where people discover, develop, and apply their gifts. Most folks work for most of their lives, as I have, and they need jobs that challenge and reward them for creating value for others. The best companies empower employees, helping them see that the more they serve customers, the more fulfillment and reward they'll receive. As I described in chapter three, this approach transformed Koch Industries.

To recap: as an institution, at its best, business does three things.

First, it empowers employees to self-actualize.

Second—and as a result of the first—it develops and supplies the products and services that others use to improve their lives.

Third, it helps create a culture of mutual benefit, in which people learn that success comes from contributing.

So, not only does business improve lives; it instills the mentality that is essential for societal success. At its best, business empowers people to contribute to progress.

But as Melony's story shows, that's not what many companies do. In certain key ways, the institution of business is breaking down. Instead of building a culture of mutual benefit, it is often pitting people against each other.

Why? Because of corporate welfare.

As you read in the introduction, corporate welfare is an insidious form of unequal treatment—which is to say, government-sponsored discrimination. It arises from collusion between businesses or other organizations (such as trade associations, unions, and nonprofits) and government. It allows the privileged to gain or keep power and wealth at the expense of everyone else. It takes the form of handouts, mandates, bailouts, and anticompetitive regulations, among many others, different examples of which I will cover shortly.

Whatever the name, corporate welfare is synonymous with a rigged economy, in which the politically connected climb higher by pushing the rest of society down. It's a dagger aimed at the heart of economic opportunity for all and a major reason why so many are skeptical of business—and rightfully so.

THE CORPORATE WELFARE CRISIS

Corporate welfare is never far from everyday life. As Melony's story demonstrates, the consequences may not be obvious, but they are significant and pervasive. Every American pays the price, and the price is bigger than anyone can see.

Occupational licensing illustrates this reality. Beyond Mississippi's unreasonable barriers for would-be hair braiders, roughly a quarter of U.S. workers—from barbers to interior designers to upholsterers to so many more—are now covered by these laws, which are mandated by cities and states.[7] This includes tens of millions of people in hundreds of different professions.[8]

While licensing differs by state, in almost every case, a profession is governed by a board. Eighty-five percent of these boards are controlled by—you guessed it—members of the licensed industry.[9] Their obvious interest is to restrict competition and protect their profits. If that sounds eerily similar to the protectionism in higher education discussed in chapter seven, it's because it is. And the result is the same—lower-quality products at higher prices.

While there are some legitimate public safety reasons for licensing—doctors, weapons manufacturers, and the like—many restrictions are patently absurd. For instance, you can't sell flowers in Louisiana without a license.[10] The established florists would prefer not to have you offering their customers better, less-expensive flowers. As a general rule, occupational licenses fail to improve health, safety, or quality, while they create other serious harms. So says about 90 percent of the economic research.[11]

By restricting competition, licenses hold back innovation and job creation, especially for the least fortunate. A 2018 study found that licensing prevents the creation of nearly two million jobs each year.[12] Another study found that occupational licenses lower business formation in low-income communities by more than 10 percent.[13] Corporate welfare is pushing down people who want to contribute and rise.

The businesses behind these destructive policies can also bilk the rest of us. Less competition generally means higher prices, and the annual cost of licensing is between $180 billion and $200 billion—money that Americans pay every year or fail to earn, lost to extra profit for protected industries.[14]

This puts the least fortunate at an even greater disadvantage. In addition to facing barriers to work, they also pay more at the register. They and their families are being squeezed from every angle. Minorities, people with criminal records, people for whom English is a second language, and military spouses are the hardest hit.[15]

It seems that only one group wins under occupational licensing: the companies behind the unjust system and their employees. Actually, they lose too.

Businesses that benefit from corporate welfare do so only in the short term. By turning their focus from serving the customer to securing their cartel, they lose sight of the innovation and value creation that would potentially transform them in the long run. Their focus on getting profit by any means today prevents the possibility of much more profit—*good* profit—tomorrow.

America's auto manufacturers are a case in point. In the 1980s, they opposed imported Japanese cars, fearing the competition and threat to their profits. They successfully obtained a "voluntary restraint agreement" that put caps on the number of Japanese auto imports.[16] American manufacturers benefited in the short term, keeping market share. But they lost in the long run by failing to adapt to customers' wishes or keep ahead of their competitors' innovations.

This ended up being catastrophic for the companies, millions of their employees, and hundreds of communities. Huge sections of the Rust Belt testify to the terrible cost of putting any profit ahead of good profit.

It's worth dwelling on the cost to workers. A business that doesn't innovate is holding back its workers. Their job may be protected for a while, and the pay may be good (also for a while), but the company isn't providing them with a platform to challenge and improve themselves and find new ways to satisfy customers and find fulfillment.

And when the jig is up—which always happens—the employees usually experience profound shock and struggle mightily. Workers laid off from the auto companies can attest to this. Their former employers failed to help them adjust and prepare for the future.

Another telling example is the taxicab industry. It colluded with government to protect itself, creating things like "medallion" rules that cap the number of cabs on the road, allowing for higher profits and captive markets.[17] Thus protected, the cab companies have stayed more or less the same for decades.

When rideshare companies entered the market, cabbies had spent so long stagnating that they couldn't catch up. The price of medallions plummeted—from $1.3 million to $160,000 in New York City and from $545,000 to $10,000 in Philadelphia—leaving cab companies with huge losses.[18] The rideshare revolution left taxis with fewer riders and lower profits. This outcome could have been avoided if they had pursued good profit.

These examples affect huge numbers of people. Yet they're only a fraction of the crisis. Monopoly grants, mandates, cash subsidies, bail-outs, tariffs, tax credits, loan guarantees, preferential and anticompetitive regulations, eminent domain abuse—they're all corporate welfare, and all destructive.[19]

Sometimes, businesses advocate for these policies with overtly self-interested arguments. Other times, they appeal to some higher concept, such as national security or jobs. (Which is why one of my patriotic father's favorite quotes was "Patriotism is the last refuge of a scoundrel."[20]) This certainly applies to tariffs, which I'll discuss in the pages ahead. While the arguments differ, the outcome is universal: long term, everyone is harmed.

The scale of this crisis is enormous. One way that companies—especially large ones—try to rig the system is by supporting complex and anticompetitive regulations. Why? Because they have large legal teams and can afford to comply, while the added costs will hurt smaller competitors and reduce start-ups.[21]

Hence, some big businesses cheer the growth of federal red tape, which ran to 23,000 pages in the Code of Federal Regulations in 1960 and nearly 190,000 pages in 2017.[22] (State regulations are even more numerous but difficult to count.) Meanwhile, from the mid-1970s to the mid-2010s, the percentage of U.S. companies that were under a year old fell by roughly half.[23] Regulation, much of it advocated by established business, is steadily stifling entrepreneurship and competition—often by design.

Elsewhere, the tax code contains $1.6 trillion in exemptions and other kinds of preferential treatment, benefiting a bewildering array of special interests.[24] Did you know that racehorse owners get a special tax break for their prize steeds? Or that major companies get subsidized for doing research they would have done anyway? There are plenty of handouts for the industries that Koch Industries is in—all of which we oppose. The tax code is so full of holes, it is like a sieve.

THE WRONG KIND OF COMPETITION

Companies have figured out the game. Instead of competing for customers' money through superior products and services, they compete for government-granted advantages using superior lobbying campaigns.

At the federal level, businesses employ armies of lobbyists whose sole job is to get special treatment for their clients. At the local level, they play cities and states against each other in search of the best "tax incentives," which is a fancy phrase for corporate welfare targeted to specific companies. The politicians who abet this are basically bribing companies with taxpayer money.

This is a massive scam, costing tens of billions of dollars.[25] When two scholars from Columbia and Princeton analyzed nearly 550 deals, they found that the cost extends far beyond the dollar amount.[26]

Tax incentives are usually sold as a quick way to get good jobs and spur widespread development. In reality, the overall employment bump is tiny—a few hundred extra jobs a year over a five-year period—and there's little evidence that the rest of the economy gets more jobs, higher wages, or any other benefit.[27] (Other research shows that as many as 98 percent of companies would have chosen the same location without subsidies, making the handouts essentially pointless.[28]) Moreover, the jobs themselves can cost up to $1 million apiece.[29] It may be the least-effective, highest-cost jobs program in history.

And surprise, surprise: politics often drives the giveaways. Elected officials support incentive programs because it means ribbon-cutting ceremonies, plant openings, and other good PR opportunities. They benefit even when the handouts have negative long-term consequences.

Which is how most tax incentives end up. Corporate welfare can cause firms to locate in the wrong cities for the wrong reasons. When companies make decisions based on corporate welfare, they undervalue much more important considerations, such as attractiveness to talent, proximity to customers and suppliers, transportation, supportive communities, and so on. They get a short-term boon but a long-term loss.

Amazon has fallen into this trap. The company pitted more than two hundred cities against one another to see which one would give it the most money for a second headquarters.[30] One of the winning bids, in Crystal City, Virginia, cost taxpayers at least $750 million.[31] The second winning bid, in New York City, came to more than $2.5 billion in handouts.[32] Amazon canceled its New York plans after citizens rightly revolted against this brazen corporate handout. The people of New York could tell you that tax breaks helped Amazon short term, and at the expense of everyone else.

CORPORATE WELFARE'S REAL COST

You may think, "So what?" Does corporate welfare really affect you? Absolutely.

To start, it worsens Americans' quality of life.

Consider the effects on public health. Most states have so-called certificate-of-need (CON) laws, which create government boards that determine whether medical facilities can expand, innovate, or even get off the ground.[33] The boards are usually stacked with representatives of hospitals and other healthcare providers—that is, the potential competitors of the new or improved facilities.[34] They have a clear incentive to deny CON applications, which happens all the time.

The result: studies show CON laws can reduce the number of hospitals in a given area by 30 percent.[35] And while CON laws are sold as a way to lower healthcare costs, they actually make healthcare more expensive. (It's no wonder that these were among the first laws to be waived in some states when the COVID-19 crisis hit. They made it harder for patients to get the care they needed.[36])

It's a similar story with other restrictive policies. Federal rules prevent doctors from practicing across state lines, which limits access to care—an absurdity in the age of telemedicine that only survives because state medical associations lobby for it. Similarly, state "scope of practice" laws restrict the services that nurses, physician assistants, and pharmacists can provide. This restriction benefits doctors but raises costs and limits access for those who can least afford it, which can lead to worse health outcomes.

Corporate welfare also hits Americans' wallets, in a big way.

The Mercatus Center has analyzed the price of some of these policies at the federal level. The researchers found that since 1980, regulations alone—huge numbers of which are anticompetitive—have made our country as much as 25 percent poorer than we otherwise would be. That's now a loss of at least $4 trillion annually, or more than $13,000 in lost income for each American per year.[37] This money could have improved lives, spurred innovations, and benefited people through higher wages, faster growth, and a litany of other social goods. And remember: this only pertains to one type of corporate welfare; many others exist.

Nor does corporate welfare impose a one-time cost. Its damages get worse over time, harming every American more and more, without us ever knowing what we're missing.

The cost isn't purely monetary or material, though. What's worse is the degeneration in the culture that this policy of discrimination brings about. Mutual benefit becomes an afterthought, if it's thought of at all. Society is corrupted from within.

To start, corporate welfare undermines the concept of equal rights. It causes businesses to think that consumers don't deserve the chance to choose for themselves, and that some companies and workers deserve different treatment than others. They think that they can, and should, help themselves without helping others—and indeed, at the expense of others. Corporate welfare pits people against each other.

Research shows that the executives of firms that benefit from corporate welfare are more likely to say that competition is "unfair" to business and less likely to say that customer focus is the most important factor to success. Instead, more are inclined to believe that government assistance and relationships with influential policymakers are more important. Interpretation: corporate welfare corrupts business leaders' whole approach.[38]

This helps explain why the public has increasingly lost confidence that business is a force for good.[39] As well they should! If people don't see companies creating value for them, then why should they trust them? For that matter, why should businesses even exist if they succeed without making their customers and communities better off?

Companies that advocate for corporate welfare are committing suicide, turning people against the institution of business itself. Society only accepts people getting wealthy if they earned it by improving people's lives. If collusion between business and government determines who gets rich, why do we need a middleman? Get rid of business altogether and let government do it directly. Is it any wonder that more and more Americans are attracted to socialism?[40]

Corporate welfare also corrupts individual attitudes, which has a ripple effect. When companies get ahead by cheating, the employees doing the cheating and the customers being cheated begin to get used to it and think that cheating is okay—not just in business, but in every aspect of life. So when business goes awry, it pits people against each other in ways that have nothing to do with business. For instance, when people see companies get ahead through special benefits rather than by creating value, they expect the same for themselves. The desire to contribute fades.

Finally, corporate welfare undermines the progress that benefits us all. Many businesses that focus on receiving it no longer help people succeed in a fast-changing world. Employees, like the companies they work for, stagnate. For example, they're not taught the skills needed to succeed in an increasingly automated, digital world. This is one of the primary contributors to a two-tiered society.

THE DISEASE AS CURE

To their credit, most Americans know that something is wrong: 68 percent think business and government collude, helping each other while hurting the rest of us; 76 percent think government should stop propping up specific firms and industries.[41]

Yet in response to public outcries, the opposite happens. Society gets more corporate welfare, not less—often at the insistence of well-meaning activists and politicians. This endless spiral compounds the damage enormously, holding back more people and slowing progress.

If people don't see companies creating value for them, then why should they trust them?

Look at the financial crisis of 2008. It was caused, in part, by corporate welfare for big banks. Policies encouraged these banks to sell financially unsound mortgages and then quickly pawn them off to Fannie Mae and Freddie Mac, giving them inflated profits and less risk.[42] While the banks profited from these loans, the people with the mortgages lost when the value of their homes plummeted.

When it all came crashing down, taking millions of jobs with it, people were outraged, as they should have been. They clamored for a response. They got one—and it was more corporate welfare.

First, the federal government bailed out the banks, using a $700 billion fund of taxpayer money. As far as corporate welfare goes, few examples are as clear-cut as bailouts.

Second, in 2010, Congress enacted the Dodd-Frank Act, wrapping big banks in more regulation that the banks themselves helped to write. Bank executives described these new rules as creating a "moat" around their businesses, making it harder for would-be competitors to challenge their dominance.[43] This turned into yet another fiasco, from which the big banks emerged the winners. Since the bailouts, the total number of banks has continued to decline, with no new charters since 2011.[44] Meanwhile, the 15 largest banks in the country control more than half of all assets in the banking industry.[45]

The regulatory burden from the Dodd-Frank bill is so severe that only big banks can afford it. Meanwhile, community banks have been decimated since the law's passage, with more than 1,700 closing their doors.[46] These are the smaller, specialized, and personalized companies that meet the needs of small businesses and families. Now they're disappearing.

As for the big banks, they now lobby to keep the parts of Dodd-Frank that benefit them.[47] The head of Goldman Sachs said in 2015 that his company was gaining market share because the law made it harder for small companies to compete.[48] Their gain is a loss for smaller competitors, the job creators those companies supported, and communities across America.

Another clear example of trying to cure a disease with the same disease is the reaction to tariffs. Tariffs are one of the most obvious, and destructive, forms of corporate welfare throughout history. They are protectionism, and protectionism is corporate welfare.

From our country's beginning, American industries have demanded tariffs to give them a leg up on foreign competitors. Recent examples include tariffs instituted on foreign steel and aluminum in 2018. Demanded by U.S. steel and aluminum producers, the tariffs were sold as a cost-free way to resuscitate key industries and communities.[49]

Yet the tariffs have huge costs. By making foreign metal more expensive, tariffs made the thousands of companies that use the metal less competitive, especially manufacturers. According to one leading estimate, steel tariffs increased the price of steel products by about 9 percent, costing consumers about $5.6 billion in just the first year.[50]

While the whole point of the tariffs was to save jobs at U.S. steel mills, tariffs caused other companies to cut jobs in response. Federal Reserve economists found that manufacturing lost jobs overall in response.[51] The government should have looked to history: the last round of steel tariffs in 2002 cost more jobs in other industries than it protected for steel companies.[52]

The damage wrought by tariffs became impossible to ignore. Yet what did the federal government do? More of the same. Instead of ending the tariffs, it began handing out exemptions to companies who petitioned the government. It's just another opportunity for favored businesses to game the system to their advantage and their competitors' disadvantage.

Within six months of the initial tariffs, the federal government granted more than 1,300 exemptions.[53] Many more followed.[54] Some exemptions were rejected after big steel companies pushed back.[55] Others were probably granted because of the political benefits, such as jobs in states that could influence an election.

Nor did it stop there. Many businesses saw their costs rise because steel tariffs made raw materials more expensive. In response, they sought tariffs for their own products. For example, American nail manufacturers got hammered by the steel tariffs, leading them to cut jobs and raise prices. The administration responded by giving at least one nail manufacturer an exclusion—another handout.[56] Then it slapped a new tariff on foreign-made nails, protecting the domestic manufacturers and raising costs for everyone.[57] If two wrongs don't make a right, then why would three?

The circus continued. Other businesses saw their markets fade as foreign nations instituted their own tariffs in response to America's. For example, America's tariffs on China caused China to slap tariffs on American soybeans. The federal government then set up a $28 billion subsidy scheme to keep farmers afloat.[58] Once instituted, corporate welfare spreads like cancer.

And families and communities suffer the consequences. Corporate welfare encourages firms to focus on wooing bureaucrats rather than innovating and creating value for customers and society. Entire industries become obsessed with lobbying for favors, so the damage keeps mounting.

BUILDING BETTER BUSINESSES

Corporate welfare is so ingrained in the economy and the business community that it seems difficult, if not impossible, to eradicate. But we must eradicate it if we are to have a just and prosperous society.

If we do, more people will be able to find jobs that match their abilities. More businesses will focus on helping their employees flourish and contribute, spurring innovation and progress. If we eliminate corporate welfare, we can begin building a culture of mutual benefit and an economy that works for all.

So, where should a Social Entrepreneur start? What can you do to transform the institution of business? What is a better way, and how can you help bring it about?

We need CEOs who practice Principled Entrepreneurship™— the practice of doing well by doing good.

The first thing we need are business leaders to take a stand. We need CEOs who practice Principled Entrepreneurship™—the practice of doing well by doing good.

This means building a company that empowers employees and contributes to communities. I know many CEOs who feel this way.

And we strive to do this at Koch Industries by applying Market-Based Management®. Other companies have begun applying MBM, and for many, it has made a real difference.

Whatever management or business framework you use, or whether you use one, I encourage business leaders to focus relentlessly on creating an environment where people can self-actualize. No company will succeed in the long run if its team members don't first succeed by contributing.

If a culture of contribution is essential, then corporate welfare cannot be tolerated. The best advocates against it are business leaders who don't want it. This is a bigger pool than you might think: 84 percent of the leaders at companies that don't benefit from such favoritism logically oppose it.[59] If this describes you, one practical thing you can do is to publicly criticize corporate welfare and explain why. Don't stay quiet.

We're doing our part at Koch Industries. We participate in industries where subsidies, mandates, and favoritism are part of the legally mandated system and can't be avoided. We nonetheless oppose corporate welfare in all its forms and lobby against it. We know that ending it will help us more in the long term. What is true for us is true for every business, no matter how much its owners or managers think they need special treatment to survive.

Corporate welfare has been around since well before I returned to the company, and I made an early point to oppose it. In 1971, Richard Nixon's Committee to Re-elect the President—aptly nicknamed CREEP—asked our company for an illegal donation. The implication was clear: support us, and you'll get favors; don't, and you'll get the opposite. I immediately turned down Nixon's agents. Other business-people succumbed, and suffered the legal consequences.

Of course, most corporate welfare isn't illegal, although it is always wrong and harmful to its recipients and to society. Here are two examples of where we vocally oppose such policies in our own industries.

Our company is one of America's largest producers of ethanol, a substance with a wide range of uses, including as fuel. Ethanol is essential to innovation on better fuel economy, which is part of why we are in the industry. Yet that doesn't mean ethanol should be propped up. Unfortunately, over the years, other ethanol producers successfully lobbied for federal ethanol mandates and subsidies—blatant handouts that we fought tooth and nail.

In 2011, we helped persuade the federal government to end direct ethanol subsidies. While this hurt our bottom line in the short term, it was the right thing to do, and it contributed to a better business environment in the long term.

We continue to oppose other ethanol policies that act as special favors to producers, such as the Renewable Fuel Standard, which mandates the blending of ethanol into gasoline. Like the subsidies, the current policy benefits Koch short term—ensuring that we always have a market for our product—but it hurts us long term, along with everyone else.

Policymakers recognize these issues yet are unwilling to abandon the RFS mandate. The reason is easy to discern: corn farmers in Iowa—the first state in the presidential primary process—support it.[60] Politicians sometimes try to have it both ways, preserving the mandate while giving exemptions to other companies and certain refiners. This is just one more handout. We remain convinced that ethanol can succeed and improve people's lives without government support. And so Koch will continue advocating an end to the RFS.

Another example of egregious corporate welfare that we vigorously and successfully opposed was the so-called border-adjustment tax in the 2017 federal tax reform bill. This provision would have created a new taxation system designed to benefit select U.S. companies, including manufacturers like us. It would have done so on the backs of the American people.

Koch Industries would have profited handsomely from the BAT. For example, while one of our refineries would have been subject to higher-priced imports from Canada, our refinery in Texas would have gained a big advantage on our competitors because we purchase our raw materials domestically. Another Koch company, Georgia-Pacific, primarily uses domestic southern pine trees to produce paper products, while its primary competitors rely on imports. In both cases, the BAT would have allowed us to raise our prices on consumers and capture a much bigger profit and market share. We opposed it anyway.

If it would make us money in the short term, why would we reject this policy? Because harming your customer is an excellent way to go out of business. Sure, the BAT would have given us potentially billions of dollars in profit, but consumers would have paid more than a trillion dollars in higher costs on imported goods. We would have made plenty of profits short-term, but in the long run, it would have made those who could least afford it poorer.

That is no recipe for long-term success. A company that disrespects customers will lose its customers. Either people will turn against it or creative destruction will overtake it. The better path is to strive to supply what customers value, giving them better products at better prices and rejecting mandates, subsidies, and measures to handicap competitors.

Are you a business leader? Do you know one? You can advocate against corporate welfare too. I have a colleague who calls it "being the skunk at the garden party." When the city council proposes a tax credit for companies that move to or expand in your community, go to the council meeting and object. Tell them the handout corrupts business, which should only profit by creating value for, not harming, others. Let your local member of Congress know that your support depends on whether they treat all businesses equally—and the best way to lose your support is to offer you a subsidy. If you don't, who will?

ART CIOCCA

A STORY OF BOTTOM-UP BUSINESS

ART CIOCCA IS FOUNDER OF THE WINE GROUP, WHICH HE GREW INTO THE WORLD'S SECOND-LARGEST WINE COMPANY. THROUGH HIS PHILANTHROPY, HE HAS HELPED ESTABLISH THREE UNIVERSITY CENTERS FOCUSED ON PRINCIPLED ENTREPRENEURSHIP™.

When I got back from the Catholic University of America, I knew we were really onto something. The faculty got it. They saw the connection that I did between our faith and empowering people through business. They shared my almost visceral aversion to corporate welfare.

I made my largest philanthropic contribution in partnership with Charles soon after. The Ciocca Center at Catholic University is helping future business leaders see the importance of virtue in business— and the danger of abandoning it. It helps future entrepreneurs understand the importance of doing right by others.

This was a lesson I had learned many times in my career, like the time an employee told me, "This is stupid. I'm ready to quit."

These words came from a line supervisor, and she was furious. She held nothing back, which was good, because I'd asked for her honest thoughts.

"We're wasting time, we're wasting money, and it's making me crazy. It's making my whole team crazy. We know how to fix this, but no one's listening."

We were standing next to a high-speed production line. It was sputtering, and the labeler was jammed, idling the line and the 15-person line crew. The expression on their faces told me they were depressed and demotivated. This was a stark contrast to the rest of the bottling room, which was alive with whirring, clicking, clanking.

I was there because we had a problem. I'd been going over the numbers and found that production was falling and costs were rising. For a small business like ours that operated on very thin margins, trends like that could be a death knell. We had to stay nimble to compete with the big boys.

When I got there that day, the bottling room manager said I had to meet someone who was about ready to walk off the job. A few minutes later, I found myself face-to-face with the line supervisor in front of Line #8.

Over the next few minutes, she laid out a very real problem.

She pointed out that there were issues with the brand management team's new bottle label. The label was beautiful, she said, but it was an unusual shape on a thick paper stock that the labeler simply wasn't designed to handle. No wonder the labeler was breaking and production was slowing, she told me.

I empathized with her, and I thanked her for flagging this problem. Then I asked if she had any solutions. She smiled. No one had ever asked her that. And she had a damn good answer.

As Line #8 bumped along next to us, she laid out some small but substantive changes to the label shape and paper stock. They were brilliant. After some arm wrestling with brand management, we introduced a new label that was cheaper and easier to apply but didn't compromise on aesthetics or anything else marketing was trying to accomplish. It was a win-win.

That single change allowed us to make an extra 600,000 bottles of wine a year, at no extra cost. We recognized and rewarded the line supervisor for her honesty and creativity. We celebrated her success and showcased her as a winner.

But more important than the improved line efficiency was the culture change this event caused. Suddenly our people knew that if they spoke out, someone would listen. Our entire bottling team became motivated to make the business better, and that attitude soon spread to others.

In the history of our company, it was a real turning point. Empowering our employees has been a huge part of our success, and it's a principle I'm working hard to share with as many future business leaders as I can.

—ART CIOCCA

Find more stories of
principled entrepreneurs at
BelieveInPeopleBook.com/stories

STAND UP, SPEAK OUT

This leads to the second action you can take: celebrate principled businesses. Equally important, celebrate the principled role of business in society.

Because of corporate welfare, a growing number of Americans no longer believe that business is benefiting them, and they're right. This is a big reason why socialism is gaining ground, particularly among young people.

The Harvard economist Edward Glaeser has persuasively argued that decades of corporate welfare have pushed jobs, homes, and bright futures out of reach of the rising generation. He points the finger at industries and interest groups across the spectrum, from corporations to unions to retirees to homeowners. All have created an economic system that benefits them at the expense of younger generations.[61]

No wonder huge majorities of young Americans reject business as a force for good; they haven't seen it do much good for them. They correctly think the economy is rigged against them.

While their concerns are justified, their solutions are misguided. Socialism means government ownership or control of the means of production, such that all economic decisions will be made by government officials. The people who benefit—in addition to the government officials—will be those who can curry the most favor with them.

This turns everything into a system of government-granted privilege. Seen through this lens, socialism is not the answer to corporate welfare, but rather its fullest expression.

We shouldn't expect those who support socialism to change their minds until they see that business is truly dedicated to succeeding by creating value for others. It's up to the business community to begin operating with a philosophy of mutual benefit, making a contribution and serving customers, and ultimately society. That requires rejecting the very idea of corporate welfare.

In addition to celebrating business done right, we all need to single out business gone wrong. This is something anyone can do.

I learned early on how hard it is to get this institution to stay on track. In the late 1970s, Milton Friedman helped me form a group named BLAST—Business Leaders Against Subsidies and Tariffs. We were persuaded to tone down our rhetoric, so we changed the name to Council for a Competitive Economy. But our mistake wasn't changing the name, it was our strategy.

Only a handful of fellow business leaders joined. The typical response to the hundreds of letters I sent can be summed up in one that I'll never forget. It reads, "I love what you and Milton are doing, but it won't work in my industry. My company makes blue jeans, and if we go out of business, who will make our boys' uniforms in time of war?" Such hypocrisy is unbelievable!

This experience made me realize that businesses will only change when they are pressured to do so. That pressure can only come from the bottom up—from you and me and many others.

You may not own a business, but your life is deeply influenced by what businesses do. Everyone has the right to expose and work to eliminate corporate welfare.

Employees also need to speak out. Talk to your peers or supervisors about why special treatment for the business is both wrong and harmful. Show that they are committing long-term suicide. If their practices are hurting rather than helping customers and society, they are harming their employees—and thus it's not a good place to work.

Customers can also make a difference. Don't like that the airline you fly lobbies for rules that limit their competitors? Fly a different airline and explain why on Twitter. Don't like your car manufacturer supporting tariffs? Buy from someone else. Make the injustice known—letters to the editor, stockholder meetings, social media—and get others to do the same.

Find and show corporate welfare's true human cost. Highlight its victims, tell their stories, and shame the businesses that hurt them. Companies respond to public pressure. So do the policymakers who aid and abet bad business practices. They all need to know that people demand better. The more of us who speak out, the sooner we'll be able to transform the institution of business and reap the benefits it has to offer.

TRANSFORMING BUSINESS

Melony Armstrong shows the way. Her story didn't end at the barriers built by Mississippi's cosmetologist lobby and lawmakers.

Melony became so upset by the absurdity of the obstacles she faced that she dedicated herself to removing them. She talked to anyone who would listen, informing them about the injustice. She spent seven years writing letters, lobbying lawmakers, and building support.

Melony Armstrong was prevented from starting a business because of the rules erected by established businesses to block new competition. She fought back and was able to open her hair-braiding boutique, Naturally Speaking, in Tupelo, Mississippi.

Many people never knew the licensing system existed; others thought it would be too difficult to end. They were wrong.

Melony persevered, mobilizing a movement of concerned citizens, aspiring hair braiders, and civil rights advocates. After drawing enough attention—including filing a federal lawsuit—she persuaded the Mississippi legislature to free hair braiders from the licensing racket. The new cost to be a hair braider? A registration fee of 25 bucks.[62]

Her stand against corporate welfare made an immediate difference. The day after the law was signed, four hundred Mississippians became hair braiders.[63] The number has since grown to more than four thousand. She stood for the principle of equal rights, and won.

And what started with hair braiding didn't stop there. After winning her first victory, Melony kept pushing for occupational licensing reform to help people in other industries. Following a second reform bill in 2017, Mississippi now requires licensing boards to demonstrate a concrete public harm before passing a new occupational license requirement.[64] And it must ensure that any rule passed is the least burdensome to prevent the harm.

Similar and even more complete reforms have spread to other states, including Nebraska and Ohio, covering more than two million current workers.[65] Countless future entrepreneurs and jobseekers will benefit. There's also a growing national consensus that occupational licensing needs to be rethought.[66] Melony helped catalyze a movement, transforming business from the bottom up. She is self-actualizing by pursuing her passion and empowering more people than she ever imagined.

You can too. I have never been more optimistic about the possibility of eradicating corporate welfare. Americans overwhelmingly see the problem, which means the solution's time has come. The mounting dissatisfaction with the economic status quo shows that the country is hungry for a better way. One that opens doors of opportunity instead of closing them off for all but the fortunate few.

Social Entrepreneurs can bring that day about. We can build an economy where each person has a fair shot, where businesses continually transform, benefiting themselves by empowering their employees and creating value for society. This vision of an economy that works for everyone is closer than it seems.

9.
UP FROM PARTISANSHIP

" I would unite with anybody to do right; and with nobody to do wrong. "

FREDERICK DOUGLASS[1]

What does injustice look like? For Weldon Angelos, that was a question he thought he'd be contemplating for 55 years.[2] Weldon had a bright future in music. He started a hip-hop label, Extravagant Records, and caught the attention of some of the biggest names in the industry, including Snoop Dogg and Tupac Shakur. Weldon was on track to do well for himself.

Unfortunately, Weldon made a poor decision to finance his music career: selling drugs. In the early 2000s, as the War on Drugs was raging, he sold a small amount of marijuana to a confidential informant on three occasions, allegedly carrying but not brandishing a gun for one of them. The local police swooped in to catch their criminal.

Weldon Angelos made a mistake. He broke the law. But if we want laws to be respected, then laws must be respectable. And the law in this case was anything but.

The prosecutor convinced a grand jury to indict Weldon on 20 counts. More important than the number of charges was the length of prison sentence they required. The indictments dealt with crimes covered by "mandatory minimums," which set minimum prison terms. This lets ambitious prosecutors "stack" penalties, ensuring that a possible sentence skyrockets as charges are added.

At the trial's end, Weldon Angelos was convicted of 13 of the 20 charges. Even though he was a first-time, nonviolent offender, he was handed a non-negotiable prison sentence of 55 to 63 years.

Before the sentencing, nearly 30 former prosecutors and judges wrote a letter condemning Weldon's treatment. The judge who handed down the sentence called it "unjust, cruel, and irrational"—a demonstrably true statement, given that Weldon would have spent less time in prison for committing rape or an act of terrorism. But the law tied the judge's hands and forced him to bind Weldon's hands for more than half a century.

Fortunately, Weldon's story didn't end there. A growing chorus of voices, including mine, spoke out against his treatment, leading the same prosecutor who originally went after Weldon to have a change of heart. He helped persuade the federal courts to release Weldon from prison in 2016, just in time for his eldest son's high school graduation. His sons were only six and four years old when he went to prison. His daughter was an infant. They spent 12 long years without their father in their lives. Now they have him back.

Weldon's reprieve was more than overdue. Yet his case is the exception. The criminal justice system is still rife with barriers that injure those in prison, their families, and, ultimately, society. It exemplifies the kind of injustice that arises when government policy goes awry.

GOVERNMENT'S VITAL ROLE

One of government's responsibilities is keeping us safe from crime. The police and the military are responsible for protecting us from violent threats. Criminal justice is such an important part of government's role that fully five of the 10 amendments in the Bill of Rights deal with police powers and the criminal justice system.

This makes sense. Government, at its best, fosters the rules of just conduct that enable individual success and societal well-being. As the institution with the legal monopoly on the use of force in a given geographic area, it is the only institution in a position to protect equal rights, set and enforce laws, and restrain those who threaten our person and property.

The Declaration of Independence articulates the vision of a just government: one that secures to all the inalienable rights of "life, liberty, and the pursuit of happiness." Insofar as America has pursued this vision, our country has made incredible progress.

To realize this vision, government upholds the rule of law and uses force only in those areas where force works better than voluntary cooperation and competition. It gives the other institutions the space they need to fulfill their roles while fostering a system of mutual benefit. This provides people with an environment in which to flourish, enabling everyone to discover, develop, and apply their gifts. Without a beneficial government, individual and societal success is impossible.

Yet beneficial government is not what most Americans believe our country has. A mere 17 percent trust government to do what's right.[3] Overwhelming majorities of Republicans, Democrats, and Independents hold these views. How did we get to a place where close to everyone agrees that government is broken?

I submit that the problem isn't government by itself. As with all our institutions, the source of the problem is what we as a society expect it to accomplish, and how we use it. Too often when we see a problem, our first impulse is to look to government to solve it. Rather than finding cooperative solutions grounded in individual empowerment, we separate into camps to fight over how government can best address our problems. Instead of starting from a point of unity, we start from a place of division.

TWO TRIBES

Welcome to the crisis of partisanship.

More than two hundred years ago, George Washington declared that political parties are likely "to become potent engines by which cunning, ambitious, and unprincipled men will be enabled to subvert the power of the people and to usurp for themselves the reins of government."[4] Time has proven our first president correct.

Whether at the local, state, or federal level, politics is almost always divided between two warring sides, both of which constantly try to damage and defeat the other. They try to arrange policy and politics to their maximum advantage, and to their opponents' maximum disadvantage. The focus is not on public policies that empower people and improve their lives; it's on political victory at any cost.

Partisanship is a form of tribalism, which is exactly what it sounds like: different tribes duking it out for supremacy. Where once the tribes used weapons of war, now they use television ads and microtargeting. The motivation remains the same, however: to ensure that your tribe comes out on top—and, equally important, that the other comes out on the bottom. This isn't just zero-sum, it's *negative*-sum.

Tribalism makes it very difficult to get good things done in government. It shifts attention from policy to politics, from empowering people to beating up the other side. Instead of working together, people and parties focus on staying in control, propping up allies, and punishing or scapegoating opponents.

Tribalism also makes it harder for Social Entrepreneurs to break down barriers. The way that politics works means that before attempting to solve problems, people must first try to hamstring their opponents. Mutual benefit is a foreign concept. Pitting people against each other is the name of the game. And I use the word "game" because that's how so many treat it, as a contest to win by any means.

DUMB ON CRIME: A CASE STUDY

What does this have to do with Weldon Angelos? Everything.

Tribalism led politicians on both sides of the aisle to misuse government power for their advantage. On criminal justice, they found that bad public policy made good party politics.

Have you ever heard the phrase "tough on crime"? Politicians of both parties have used this phrase to sell dangerous and destructive policies for many decades. They come out looking like the defenders of public safety while casting their opponents as "soft on crime." Yet their victory comes as a loss, not only for their political adversaries but also for people like Weldon and their communities (more on that later).

It has worked this way since at least the late 1960s. Perhaps the most infamous example of this style of politics was the "Willie Horton" ad that ran in the 1988 election. George H. W. Bush was able to convince voters that Michael Dukakis was weak because a man committed a heinous crime when he was released from prison through a weekend furlough program.

Tribalism led politicians on both sides of the aisle to misuse government power for their advantage.

The lesson for politicians: you'll get blamed for the bad things that happen as a result of the policies you pass, overshadowing any credit you get for the good things that happen from those same policies—even if the good far outweighs the bad.

From that moment on, any politician who considered reforming the criminal justice system was warned by political consultants, "If you do that, you'll get Willie Hortoned."[5] And instead of focusing on public safety and making the criminal justice system more just, politicians have made it more unjust in the rush to seem tough on crime.

Hence we have a criminal justice system that defies logic and ruins lives. Incarceration has exploded in recent decades. More than two million people are now behind bars in this country—four times more than in 1980.[6] While the United States contains 5 percent of the world's population, the fact that it has 20 percent of the world's prison population is a national disgrace.[7] Moreover, the fact that justice is not applied equally, with communities of color suffering disproportionately from the system's inequities, is a national tragedy.[8]

In the early 1980s, the federal criminal code contained 3,000 offenses.[9] Nearly 40 years later, after endless partisan one-upmanship, a definitive count can no longer be determined.[10] The best guess is that the number of federal criminal laws is somewhere north of 4,400.[11] Additionally, there are now more than 300,000 federal regulations with criminal penalties.[12]

Legal expert Harvey Silverglate wrote a book titled *Three Felonies a Day*, which refers to the number of felony crimes committed daily and unwittingly by the average person.[13] In their zeal to be tough on crime and defeat their opponents, partisans on both sides of the aisle have criminalized a vast swath of regular life.

Many of these laws contain the sort of mandatory minimum requirements that nearly destroyed Weldon Angelos's life. Most mandatory minimums were instituted in the 1980s and 1990s, and many were created even after violent crime rates had already started falling.[14] Far from being a needed policy tool, they were more a political tool to show that lawmakers were "doing something."[15]

Whatever the reason, currently around 90,000 federal inmates— more than half the federal prison population—are serving sentences controlled by mandatory minimums.[16] States have enacted mandatory minimums of their own, which helps explain why state prison populations soared by more than 220 percent between 1980 and 2010.[17]

Prosecutors like mandatory minimums because they get more leverage. If someone feels like they are destined to spend a long time behind bars, then a plea bargain that admits guilt for a lighter sentence is much more appealing. Even an innocent person may be inclined to take that deal, given the possible alternative of a lifetime in prison. This explains why 97 percent of federal criminal cases (and 94 percent of state cases) end in plea bargains rather than a trial and a chance to defend oneself in court.[18] It's not how the system is supposed to work.

By imprisoning so many people for so long, we've made it harder for them to develop skills and find employment after their release—controlling, rather than empowering, or at least rehabilitating, them.

About 95 percent of those who are incarcerated will be released, and it's in everyone's interest that they be able to succeed, rather than blocked from contributing.[19] But various laws and policies limit their post-release options in at least 44,000 ways, more than two-thirds of which make it harder to find a job.[20] Within a year of obtaining freedom, more than half still lack any employment, often because businesses won't or can't hire people with criminal records.[21] Those who find jobs make an average income of only $9,000—well below the poverty line.[22]

This creates a new cycle of despair and crime. Cut off from the ladder of opportunity, many feel that they have no good option but to break the law again. More than three-quarters of those who leave state prisons will be arrested again; the same is true for almost half of federal inmates.[23] This removes people, especially men, from their neighborhoods and families.[24] A staggering 2.7 million children have a parent behind bars, devastating a generation of kids during their most formative years.[25] The consequences will be felt for the rest of their lives and across all of society.

For all this, the criminal justice system leaves many people less safe. While crime rates overall have been declining for decades, some well-meaning policies have led to more crime.[26]

This is true for low- and moderate-risk defendants who are jailed for a time before trial. Their time behind bars often causes them to lose jobs and harms their families, pushing them toward crime to make up for whatever they lost.[27] More broadly, multiple studies have found that incarceration doesn't deter crime and may increase it, compared to alternative punishments.[28] To put it simply, the criminal justice system creates repeat offenders and at least as many problems as it prevents.

Partisan tribalism helped build these barriers. It also makes them harder to knock down. The problems with the criminal justice system have become obvious to many, yet partisan and ideological divides have made people hesitant to collaborate and hostile toward each other. Social Entrepreneurs have struggled to make progress.

Small-government conservatives generally look at the justice system and see all the hallmarks of the failure of "big government." They criticize the massive increase in the criminal code, as well as the rise of offenses that don't require the lawbreaker to have criminal intent. These two developments have correctly convinced many right-of-center reformers that criminal law is out of control and needs to be scaled back.

While conservatives look at injustice in the laws, liberals look at injustice in their application. They see gross racial disparities, such as how African Americans comprise 13 percent of the U.S. population but 33 percent of the prison population.[29] They also see different standards for the rich and the poor. The former can afford well-connected attorneys and often get off easy, while the latter typically get hit hard. They too rightly demand a better, fairer system.

I've always felt that both sides were right. Starting in the 1970s, I supported work that pointed out the inequities in criminal law enforcement. I began to ramp up my support for groups like the National Association of Criminal Defense Lawyers, typically thought of as a left-of-center group, in the early 2000s. I also backed groups like Right on Crime that urged right-of-center organizations to get engaged on this issue.

But rather than work together, the left and right often attacked each other's motives—conservatives saying liberals hate the police, liberals saying conservatives only want to help corporations. Such tribal sniping stood in the way of progress. The criminal justice system, meanwhile, kept ruining lives, creating new problems for communities and holding many people back.

Tribalism also held back progress in politics. I doubt that any politician set out to ruin lives, but a shocking number don't seem to mind what's happening. Republicans and Democrats usually don't see how better policies would help them win the next election. So they let the problem fester, despite its terrible human cost. The parties allow the continuation of a criminal justice system that doesn't deserve the name.

BIG PROBLEMS GET WORSE

The same sad story plays out across politics. On issue after issue, partisanship prevents the two parties from working together to do the right thing. They define themselves in tribal opposition to each other, and the very concept of cooperation cuts against that paradigm. The political incentive is to let injustices worsen, lest a solution hurt them or help their opponent.

Is it any wonder that America's biggest problems keep getting worse?

On foreign policy, the country is embroiled in endless war, costing thousands of promising young lives, wasting trillions of dollars, and making America less safe and the world more chaotic.

On healthcare, people are getting priced out of the treatments they need, while quality care keeps getting harder to find, despite decades of policies meant to solve these problems.[30]

Government spending continues to set records, year after year, even though the country can't pay for it. Thanks to spending sprees by both parties, the national debt is already more than $26 trillion and will, on present course, add significantly more than a trillion dollars every year until kingdom come—an unsustainable trajectory.[31]

ALICE JOHNSON

I AM BUT ONE PERSON

ALICE MARIE JOHNSON WAS SENTENCED TO LIFE WITHOUT PAROLE IN 1996 FOR PASSING ALONG MESSAGES TO COCAINE DEALERS— A NONVIOLENT FIRST-TIME OFFENSE. AFTER HER SENTENCE WAS COMMUTED IN 2018, SHE PARTNERED WITH STAND TOGETHER TO SUPPORT CRIMINAL JUSTICE REFORM.

When I entered prison, my paperwork reflected that my projected release date would be death. I was told that the only way I would ever be reunited with my family would be as a corpse.

No parole board would ever hear of my remorse for being involved in criminal activities. In federal prison, life means life. There would be absolutely no opportunity for redemption.

These were all the ingredients of a hopeless situation. But my faith in God allowed me to see beyond bars, to hear beyond words, to dream beyond doubt.

My incarceration affected more than just my freedom. It had a domino effect. Because when a person goes to prison, their entire family goes with them. Their entire community goes with them. There is no measure or analysis of the true effect that incarceration has on society. Yet we see it and feel it.

I've been asked how I was able to find purpose in prison. But actually, my purpose found and embraced me.

When I looked around and saw so many hurting and dejected people, it awakened in me a passion to make a difference.

It is so heartbreaking to see women who are in hospice care in prison, dying alone in a lonely place. It somehow takes away the last bit of dignity a person has. I became a hospice certified volunteer so I could care for and offer companionship to women so they would not die alone. I could make a difference in someone's life.

Alice Johnson transformed her life while serving a life sentence in prison for a nonviolent first-time offense. Just months after her sentence was commuted, she was advocating for criminal justice reform at a Stand Together summit. (Palm Springs, 2019)

While in prison, I met a woman whose legs had been amputated from the knees down. She told me the thing she missed most was the ability to dance. So I helped coordinate the first Special Olympics in prison for women with mental and physical challenges. For this work, I received a Special Events Coordinator of the Year award in 2011. At the awards ceremony, the woman with no legs was able to dance to a song that I choreographed for her called "Never Give Up."

I found women who were hungry for someone to believe in them and see that there was something they could do. So I started mentoring women in theatrical productions. One of my good friends, Christie, was under my mentorship for four years. When I met her, she was a shy woman who couldn't even look you in the eyes and kept her head down. She later produced an original play that had four productions in a single year.

The day I left prison will forever be etched in my mind. When the announcement came across the loudspeaker—"Alice Marie Johnson, report to Receiving and Discharge with all of your properties"—there was a deafening cry that went up in the building.

As I walked out of the door, women were in every single window, beating on the bars and screaming my name. As I left the prison, I passed by a low-security camp. Every one of the 250 women, and all the officers and guards, were standing outside waving and crying and rejoicing to see me released from my life sentence.

Now I'm fighting for those women and men who have been left behind in our country's prisons. I promised I would not forget about them. I have not. I never will.

I am but one person. You are but one person. But together, we are many. And we can make a difference.

—ALICE JOHNSON

Watch Alice's presentation to the Stand Together community at BelieveInPeopleBook.com/stories

Corporate welfare, including protectionism, is growing in size and destructiveness.[32] The economy is more rigged by the day.

And on immigration, a broken system stays broken, condemning people who want to come to America and contribute. The plight of the Dreamers—the million-plus undocumented immigrants who were brought here as children—is especially urgent. Those who are, or will be, contributing are held back by the fact that they could be deported at any time.

More than 80 percent of Americans want the Dreamers to stay.[33] Leaders of both parties say they want the same. And yet both sides see the Dreamers as a rallying point for their political base and so are content to do nothing but demonize the other side. Meanwhile, good people who are already making our country better are suffering. It's unjust and counterproductive.

There are many other pressing issues I could name that Americans want and need solved. The us-versus-them mentality dominating politics all but assures that nothing positive will happen. The incentive with partisanship is to use problems as weapons to beat the opposing team instead of empowering people. In many cases, our leaders use people's suffering to score political points. What's good for the parties today is usually the opposite of what's good for Americans.

Can America survive as a country if our citizens despise each other?

Worse, partisanship is pushing the parties toward extremes, including ideologies and policies that are demonstrably destructive. It is also convincing people to hate their fellow Americans. About half of the members of each party already think the members of the other party are "ignorant" and "spiteful." More than a fifth of each party views the other as "evil."[34] Can America survive as a country if our citizens despise each other?

PARTISANSHIP DOESN'T WORK. I SHOULD KNOW.

For me, this question is far from academic. In my own work as a Social Entrepreneur, I have tested the proposition that partisan politics can cure what ails society. My conclusion: partisanship doesn't work.

I avoided partisan politics like the plague from the 1960s to the 2010 election cycle. The "Congress Critters" and presidential candidates who often came calling seemed like nice enough people—some of the time—but I didn't see the point of engaging with them. Koch Industries has never been in the business of asking for favors, and outside of the company, my focus was mostly on education.

With time, however, it became clear that helping people required more than educational efforts in schools, universities, and think tanks. We also needed to change the policies holding millions back. So the philanthropic community that I founded got involved in electoral politics. We bet on the "team" that seemed to have more policies that would enable people to improve their lives. You only get two choices in our system, so we chose the red team.

We should have recognized right from the start that this was far too limiting. The "team approach" means that to get the policies that you think will help the country, you have to take all the other policies your team is offering, even if you disagree with many (or most) of them.

Your options winnow further once your team tries to make the other team look bad. You oppose the other party's policies, no matter how good or bad they are, simply on the grounds that they're the other party's policies.

Even if your team wins the election and gains power, it's usually not a victory from a policy perspective. You've already narrowed the list of things that are possible. With the other team still fighting you at every step, many of those policies are pushed out of reach. By that point, you've spent so long fighting the other team that the idea of collaboration seems like a sick joke.

Meaningful achievements—policies that enable more people to flourish—become difficult and rare in this environment. Your team has an incentive to build barriers instead of knocking them down. The whole system pushes beneficial government out of reach.

The quick version is that partisan politics prevented us from achieving the thing that motivated us to get involved in politics in the first place—helping people by removing barriers. I was slow to react to this fact, letting us head down the wrong road for the better part of a decade.

Boy, did we screw up. What a mess!

Once this became clear, we changed our approach. Far from withdrawing from politics, we decided to get more involved. But instead of picking a team and figuring out who would work with us to get good policy passed, we decided to skip the first step and do a better job of the second. We now work with people on the red team, the blue team, or no team at all! We now go issue by issue and work with anyone, regardless of political party.

In short, we abandoned partisanship and chose *partnership* instead. This simple distinction has made all the difference. It is key to transforming government, so it is key to helping every person rise. In matters of public policy, partnership is a better way.

In short, we abandoned partisanship and chose *partnership* instead. This simple distinction has made all the difference.

GRATITUDE, ALWAYS

ONE OF THE MOST painful periods of my life was also one of the longest. It ripped our family apart and nearly destroyed the family business.

It all started in 1980, when two of my brothers and another stockholder tried to take over the company and steer it in an entirely different direction. My brother David, I, and a sixth shareholder disagreed and blocked the attempt. They sued, which led to our buying their stock. It looked like a win-win—they'd get the money they wanted, and we'd continue to run the business the way we believed was right.

Unfortunately, they filed many more lawsuits, the story of which has already been told many times. Mercifully, the onslaught finally ended in 2001—21 years after it started.

For many years, I took the lawsuits in stride, but that got more difficult as their main suit approached trial in Topeka in 1998. I became completely absorbed with preparing for it. So did a growing number of our executives, leading to increasingly bad business decisions in the company.

By the time of the trial, I was in a deep depression. I could barely function. Although we were confident we did nothing wrong, I could see that there was a risk they could spin these complicated events in a way that might convince a jury. Ultimately, the jury ruled in our favor—we won. After the trial, the judge wrote that if he had known earlier how little the other side had, he would've thrown the whole case out. But my depression continued for at least another six months.

Recovery from this kind of depression is never easy. It required refocusing my mind by working hard to get the company back on track, daily exercise, and a supportive community, especially Liz and our children.

It also helped to reflect on what I'd learned from the Stoics years before. Those Greek and Roman philosophers believed that we should be grateful for everything—our mistakes, our struggles, even our adversaries.

The difficulties we face ultimately make us who we are. Even the most painful parts of our life can cause us to realize what matters and recognize where to go next. That helped me realize that my brothers had done us an enormous favor. We didn't share vision and values, so if they had stayed in, the company could have been forever crippled. We never would have been able to accomplish a fraction of what we have.

I look at my experience with partisan politics through the same prism.

As far as mistakes go, it was a big one. And the vitriol that came with it is hard to describe. But without the pain of that experience, without the benefit of the lessons learned, I wouldn't be as passionate as I am now about our current path. I wouldn't have the same appreciation for the need to partner with such a wide diversity of truly inspiring people.

As with the rest of my life, I'm grateful for everything and everyone who enabled me to get where I am today, whatever part they played.

—CHARLES KOCH

This concept applies to every Social Entrepreneur. At its most basic level, partnership is what Frederick Douglass meant when he said, "I would unite with anybody to do right; and with nobody to do wrong." It means adopting an attitude of mutual benefit and working with others to achieve policies that will empower people. You may disagree with someone on 99 percent of issues, but that 1 percent offers you the chance to join forces. Instead of demanding all or nothing, partnership treats people with the respect they deserve and recognizes that, whatever our differences, we always have things in common.

The hardcore partisan will tell you that partnership is impossible— a feel-good, naïve pipe dream. Their argument boils down to a simple assertion: help their preferred party win, and society's problems can be fixed. No cooperation necessary. Yet decades of evidence prove this doesn't work. Einstein had a word for this: insanity! You should ask those who advocate for business as usual in politics: Why should we expect things to be different after the next election?

THE PEOPLE KNOW BETTER

Here, as in many cases that we'll see in the next chapter, the American people are way ahead of the political class. A growing number of Americans are rejecting what they're selling.

The data show that partisanship no longer appeals to the American people. Over the past three decades, both Republicans and Democrats have gone from net favorable views to net unfavorable views among the wider population. Three in five Americans feel that neither party represents them. A whopping 83 percent of Americans say tribal divisiveness is a "big problem." More than 90 percent want to stop it and find some way to bring people together.[35]

For that matter, many politicians are sick of the partisan B.S. This may sound crazy, but I don't think politicians are bad people—with perhaps some notable exceptions. I think most of them ran for office because they wanted to help others. They're just as beat down by pressure to get reelected and bickering brawls as the rest of us. I can't tell you the number of times I've heard a politician say, "This isn't why I ran for office" or "This isn't why I came to Washington."

Clearly, Americans want a better way. So do the leaders we elect. They continue to double down on partisanship because they think that's all there is. Politicians honestly believe their only option is to beat the other side, and voters are left to decide which is the lesser of two evils. Yet if the recent past proves anything, more partisanship will only further divide people and turn them off while leading to less individual empowerment and societal progress. The only sure thing that happens when you fight fire with fire is that you burn the house to the ground.

So instead of constantly raising the tribal temperature, maybe it's time to cool things down. Partnership does that, helping any Social Entrepreneur become more effective.

The lie of tribalism is that your gain must come at my political expense. It is inherently exclusionary, a project of division. Partnership, by contrast, is naturally inclusive, encompassing more and more people from different backgrounds. It's a project of addition. It means we can all win together—and the bigger the "we," the bigger the win.

This is the essence of bottom-up transformation. When people unite, they prove to each other that we can all be much more effective together. It makes people wonder why they fought in the first place.

Politicians react in turn. They're nothing if not attuned to what their constituents are saying, and so their incentives shift under public pressure. When they see their constituents unite, they realize that they need to do the same. Instead of running toward the extremes and competing for who can propose the worst policies, they begin to see that good policy can make good politics—that empowerment is an electoral winner. Then they work with their supposed opponents to get things passed.

PARTNERSHIP IN ACTION

I know this is true because I've seen it happen. I have participated in these kinds of bottom-up movements, achieving policy victories that once seemed impossible.

In 2018, Republicans and Democrats worked together to pass a historic bill that eliminated some of the worst injustices in the federal criminal justice system. The First Step Act makes it possible for thousands of people with criminal records to rejoin society and start to realize their potential.[36] Among other important reforms, it stops horrific practices like shackling pregnant women to the bed while they give birth and eliminates the possibility that prosecutors will "stack" mandatory minimums for first-time offenders, as happened to Weldon Angelos.[37]

How did this happen amid the partisan impasses I described earlier? Tribalism was overcome, replaced by partnership and mutual benefit.

The federal reform marked the culmination of a years-long process. It began when small groups of people realized they shared similar views, despite their differences on other issues. It started in the most unlikely of places (in this case, Texas) and spread from there. The beauty of bottom-up progress is that it can start anywhere, with anyone—and quickly gain steam.

The coalition that began to form included people who had no reason to work together under the tribal mentality—businesses and non-profits, prosecutors and public defenders, small-government conservatives and progressive activists, religious groups from many faiths, and many others. They came from think tanks, academia, grassroots organizations, and communities that had suffered from the criminal justice system's flaws. Together, we made the case for change.

Crucially, we also committed to watch each other's backs when the politics of tribalism came after any one of us. And that's what we did— we stuck together.

The first signs of progress occurred at the state level. Confronted with a movement grounded in mutual benefit, lawmakers (both Republican and Democrat) began to abandon the tribal mentality, making positive action possible.

With the help of this emerging coalition, from the mid-2000s to the mid-2010s, 35 states passed empowerment-based reforms of one kind or another.[38] Some slashed the lengthy sentences (mandatory minimums) that locked people away for longer than appropriate. Some expanded judicial discretion on sentencing, rolling back the one-size-fits-all approach that failed to account for individual circumstances.

To tackle high levels of recidivism, some states implemented programs and partnered with private organizations to teach incarcerated individuals the values and skills necessary for success when they returned to society. These programs have been shown to reduce recidivism by an average of 13 percentage points.[39] One such effort, Hudson Link, has reported recidivism rates in the low single digits, compared to about 40 percent in New York State, where the group is based, and closer to 70 percent nationally.[40] These state-based efforts relied on science and data, not the tribal politics and fear of the tough-on-crime mentality. The list goes on.

Over that same decade, state incarceration rates fell by 6.5 percent, and the federal rate by 8.3 percent.[41] America experienced double-digit declines in both violent and property crime, demonstrating that less incarceration does not mean less public safety.[42] Another benefit was the money it saved taxpayers. Best of all, people who had been locked away got second chances (or in some cases, the first chance they ever got), giving them a better shot at developing their skills and contributing to their communities.

As these numbers demonstrate, smart-on-crime is more effective than tough-on-crime.

The movement grew larger and louder, until Congress couldn't ignore it. After decades of bad actions or inaction, the First Step Act passed in late 2018 by overwhelming majorities of both parties, with a vote of 87–12 in the U.S. Senate during a time that has been described as one of the most divisive in our country's political history.[43] People called the approach naïve and said it couldn't be done just days before the law passed. They were wrong.

Partnership and empowerment carried the day. Behind this victory was a diverse coalition that continually grew in size and effectiveness. Such partnerships—and there were countless—turned criminal justice reform from an impossibility to an inevitability.

A FLUKE? FAR FROM IT

Nor was criminal justice reform a one-off. At the time, critics said it couldn't happen again. Yet that same year, the country saw similar progress on other important issues.

Veterans' healthcare is one. In the mid-2010s, the Department of Veterans Affairs healthcare system was overrun with scandal. The government-run hospitals were found to have secret lists meant to

Matt Bellina was diagnosed with ALS in 2014. At a Stand Together summit, Matt and his wife Caitlin gave a heartfelt testimonial about the difference one person can make. Their courage inspires us all. (Colorado Springs, 2018)

cover up how long veterans waited for care. In 2015, more than two hundred veterans died on wait lists in Phoenix alone.[44] Across the whole VA system, more than 100,000 veterans were forced to wait too long for treatment.[45] It was later found that, between 2010 and 2014, as many as 49,000 veterans may have died before the VA processed their applications for medical treatment.[46]

The crisis was real, but tribalism pushed a solution out of reach. Republicans and Democrats attacked each other instead of uniting to give veterans the care they had earned. But while the politicians did nothing, regular people and veterans demanded better. Folks from across the political spectrum began working together to make transformative change a reality.

It worked. As more people demanded change, politicians put aside their differences to make it happen. Two major pieces of legislation passed with bipartisan support. The first brought accountability to the VA, allowing for the quicker firing of staff who mistreat veterans.[47] The second brought real choice to veterans' healthcare.[48] America's

Matt and Caitlin sent me this note in 2018 thanking the Stand Together community for its role in passing the Right to Try law.

veterans are now empowered to choose the healthcare provider that's best for them, public or private. Partnership, not partisanship, made these achievements possible.

The same is true with another healthcare policy, what became known as the Right to Try.

Most people will never hear about this issue, but for some, it's a matter of life and death. Imagine your spouse or, god forbid, one of

After the federal Right to Try law, Matt was able to access an experimental treatment to extend his life, and, in 2019, it gave him a limited ability to stand again.

your children is diagnosed with a terminal illness. A doctor looks you in the eye and says they only have a few months or a few years to live. Their disease has no known cure.

But there may be another option. Innovative companies are developing new treatments and potential cures all the time. They have passed safety tests, and some show promise during clinical trials but are still years or even decades away from final approval. For someone with only months to live, that's too long. The treatments could literally save their life. And yet the law prevents them from accessing what could be their last hope.

About 70 percent of Americans agree that terminally ill patients should have the freedom to try these experimental treatments that could save their life.[49] Even so, for many years, partisanship prevented action. Democrats didn't want to give Republicans a policy win, and Republicans benefited from the gridlock.

That changed once the American people got involved. One way they did was through the story of a man named Matt Bellina, a U.S. Navy pilot with a young family.[50] He was diagnosed with ALS, which gradually robbed him of his ability to move, eat, speak, and breathe. His only chance to survive and stay with his family beyond a few years was to get access to promising treatments still under development. Our philanthropic community helped tell Matt's story—a clear example of the injustice that resulted from extreme partisanship.

As more Americans learned of the issue and spoke up, politicians took note. Where previously inaction was in their interest, this bottom-up pressure showed elected officials that they needed to act. The groundswell of support pushed long-stalled legislation across the finish line in mid-2018.[51] It empowered people like Matt Bellina in a major way.

The final law bore Matt's name. Matt and his wife, Caitlin, wrote me a note that I'll never forget. They said, "We know the right to try law would never have succeeded without your involvement. We are forever grateful for the hope you have given our family and all Americans." As I write this, he is undergoing experimental treatment that may yet extend his life.[52]

Kicking off Stand Together's semi-annual summit. These events bring together hundreds of business leaders, philanthropists, and social entrepreneurs. (2017, Colorado)

TRANSFORMING GOVERNMENT

Look closely at these three examples—criminal justice reform, veterans' healthcare reform, and Right to Try—and you'll see a road map to bottom-up transformation. They are the same three steps you've encountered in the previous three chapters. If you're a Social Entrepreneur who's passionate about public policy, this is where you'll find a better way.

First, find what works and support it.

In this context, that means finding people who share your passion and are willing to work with you, even if you disagree on other issues. Have their backs when the partisans attack and ask them to have yours. If you choose your partners based on the "R" or "D" next to their name, you're limiting your chances of success. Remember Frederick Douglass's wise advice to "unite with anybody to do right."

Second, celebrate success.

Partnership unites people who, under a tribal mentality, would be enemies instead of allies. This is progress by itself. Highlighting how your differences don't prevent you from uniting will inspire others to do the same. They see that they can work together even with those they greatly disagree with on other issues.

Remember Frederick Douglass's wise advice to "unite with anybody to do right."

Finally, topple the barriers.

The more people get involved, the more others will want to get involved, and the more politicians will rise to the occasion. Elected officials in both parties will realize that voters want results, not more partisan wrangling, and that doing the right thing will help them politically. Their electoral interests will finally align with the interests of the American people. When good policy becomes good politics, we can expect politicians to finally do the right thing and empower people instead of holding them back.

Transforming the institution of government isn't that far off. Every policy victory that comes from partnership will help shift the parties themselves. Right now, the parties are inclined toward ever-worse extremism and control. They will continue down that path until enough people demand a different approach on more and more societal problems.

No problem is intractable. No injustice is impossible to end. Is there a destructive policy that motivates you? A wrong you want to right, people you want to help? You can try to do so by pulling others down in a tribal, partisan way, even though that approach is already tearing America apart. Or you can give partnership a go. You'll be amazed at the allies you attract, what you accomplish, the people you empower. And, like me, you'll wish you'd taken this path all along.

In the build-up to criminal justice reform, my philanthropic community worked with a man named Van Jones. A former political appointee under President Obama, Van once organized a protest outside a conference I hosted. He disagreed—and still does—with many of the causes I support. I'm critical of his point of view on a number of issues.

As we came to see, none of our disagreements were as important as the area where we agreed. We shared a desire to remove the injustices in the criminal justice system. Once we realized this, we began working together.

After the First Step Act passed, Van participated in a video with Mark Holden, Koch Industries' longtime general counsel and a committed leader for criminal justice reform. Standing side-by-side with Mark, Van said, "You got awesome people, and beautiful people, on both sides who don't know what to do together, and if we start working on that, a lot of this stuff is going to get better."[53]

Then he said words I will never forget: "We started working together to get some other people free, but the reality is, those of us who worked on this, we got some freedom." That freedom, he says, should enable us all "to see the country differently and do more good." Van's words ring true. I intend to keep following this wisdom. For the sake of America, I hope you do too.

10.

MOVEMENTS OF MILLIONS

" The ultimate measure of a [person] is not where he stands in moments of comfort and convenience, but where he stands at times of challenge and controversy. "

MARTIN LUTHER KING JR.[1]

I don't know what injustice you want to see ended. I don't know what motivates you, or what your passion is. But I do know that whatever it is, none of us can do it on our own. Big changes come when diverse voices sound together. If we want to make a difference, we need to be as effective as possible and demonstrate that there's a better way so we can build massive movements. To make all this happen, you've got an important role to play.

How do I know this? Because that's how Social Entrepreneurs have tackled society's biggest problems since before America's Founding.

The stories of movements fill our history books. The American independence movement gave rise to the first nation in history whose founding document—the Declaration of Independence—offered the promise of equal rights to all, not just those born to nobility. Decades later, the abolition movement got America to begin taking this promise seriously, ultimately ending the evil of slavery.

Throughout the nineteenth century, and especially after the turn of the twentieth century, the women's rights movement shifted our country further in the right direction, although the progress was slow and painful and continues to this day. It transformed women's ability to participate and contribute. Since then, there have been many more movements that have brought our country closer to America's Founding ideals, making our country far better, from civil rights to antiwar activism to marriage equality and many others. We still have a long way to go, but the progress is undeniable.

We remember and celebrate these movements for good reason: they ended some of the worst injustices of their day, breaking down the barriers that prevented so many from rising. They empowered millions, bringing to life the promise of America, by practicing the principles of individual dignity, equal rights, and openness—that is, by recognizing the essential conditions for a society based on mutual benefit, where every person can realize their potential.

While each movement has been different, they have all followed a similar course. They were all built from the bottom up, starting in relative obscurity, with a small number of people, or in different and disparate places with little to connect them. Success was never assured, sometimes unlikely or seemingly impossible, as all faced strong opposition.

Yet in all of them, what started small became bigger and more effective with time. They suffered defeats, then won small victories, which led to bigger victories, which led to the transformation of our country. They succeeded because they motivated millions to demand change that empowered millions more to participate in society and contribute to its success.

THE WOMEN'S RIGHTS MOVEMENT

The women's rights movement is instructive. Not long after the Declaration of Independence and the Founding of America, courageous women began to demand that their rights be respected. They saw that their treatment was both unjust and harmful to society. They were not content to be written off as second-class citizens or merely their husband's helper.

Can you imagine taking up that cause at the turn of the nineteenth century? Women were ignored, ridiculed, punished for their so-called insolence, or worse. Their demands for justice were often met with more injustice, a vicious cycle. But the leaders among them—Social Entrepreneurs all—refused to back down.

The process was slow and uneven, but it steadily moved forward. In 1842, Maryland gave married women the right to earn and keep their own money instead of forcing them to give their earnings to their husband. Other states followed suit.[2] In 1848, New York and Pennsylvania granted married women the right to own property. Others, once again, took similar action.[3]

More victories began to accumulate. In 1850, Tennessee banned violence against women.[4] Other states began allowing women to hold trade licenses. California ratified a state constitution in 1879 banning employment discrimination based on gender.[5] While many of these laws were far from perfect, they nonetheless represented big steps in the right direction.

In 1890, Wyoming became the first state in America to give women the right to vote and hold elected office. The territory of Wyoming had allowed women to vote since 1869. When Congress tried to get the territory to restrict the vote to men as a condition of statehood, the state legislature responded with a telegram: "We will stay out of the Union a hundred years rather than come in without our women." Congress backed down.[6]

Women made progress in other institutions too. Before the nineteenth century, women were generally banned from attending college. The assumption was that they didn't need higher education, if they needed any education at all. Then, in 1837, Oberlin College admitted four women—a revolutionary move. The first woman to graduate from medical school did so in 1849.[7] Slowly but surely, new colleges for women began to open, and existing schools stopped admitting only men. (Shamefully, many elite universities continued to discriminate against women until the 1970s.[8])

Behind each of these victories was a diverse group of principled people demanding justice. What started with women inspired men to join the cause. Their actions in some states spurred similar action in others. The women's rights movement snowballed until it achieved what was then the greatest victory. Come 1920, the nation as a whole recognized women's right to vote with the Nineteenth Amendment.

RICH TAFEL

ON THE FRONT LINES

RICH TAFEL IS A PASTOR, AN EARLY AIDS ACTIVIST, AND FOUNDER OF LOG CABIN REPUBLICANS. THROUGH HIS DECADES OF LEADERSHIP RICH HELPED PAVE THE WAY FOR THE VICTORY OF MARRIAGE EQUALITY IN 2015.

We all have our own moments of courage. We often don't recognize them at the time, but they become clear in retrospect.

My own happened in the 1980s. That's when I came out as gay, even though I risked losing friends, family, and my career. As I watched a generation of mostly gay men dying in Boston, I became an "AIDS Buddy," which meant visiting a person with AIDS weekly. Nothing taught me more about sacrifice, love, compassion, death, and the importance of civil rights.

Those two decisions helped me find my life's work. I wanted to devote myself to the fight for inclusion, tolerance, and love. Having graduated from Harvard Divinity School, where I served a stint as assistant minister at the Harvard Memorial Church, I began to speak out, from whatever pulpit or podium I could.

In the years that followed, I founded the Log Cabin Republicans, an organization to give voice to gay and lesbian members of the GOP. I knew it would be an uphill battle, but I had no idea what I was in for.

I spent the better part of a decade debating the religious right. You'd have thought that would endear me to the progressive left. Nope. They only saw a Republican—too interested in "straight institutions" like religion and marriage. But slowly, surely, we were building a movement that would soon attract people from all different perspectives and walks of life.

There are many moments that stand out in our struggle. None

As part of Rich Tafel's tireless advocacy for equal rights, he testified before Congress in 1995.

as vivid as a sequence of events in 1998 during what would come to be known as the "summer of hate."

Those were dark days. The gay and lesbian community was reeling. We were losing battles at the ballot box. We were losing legislative fights.

Jim Lehrer asked me on national television: Will the gay issue ever be resolved? I said yes, we would win. But words have consequences, I told him, as I looked across the table at the representatives of the so-called moral majority who had come on his show to debate me. It was their bigoted words in particular that I was referring to.

Three months later, Matthew Shepard—a gay 21-year-old student in Wyoming—was tortured and brutally murdered. His death would come to signify one of the lowest points in our movement's struggle for equality.

Such was the atmosphere we were living in. But amid it all, the growing group of activists who were beginning to join forces didn't lose hope. They embodied courage. I saw it firsthand in Fort Worth, Texas, during that horrible summer.

One day in particular will stay with me as long as I live. It was 100 degrees outside, and the men in front of me were boiling with rage. About 30 or 40 of them had been brought in on buses by an anti-gay group. They were screaming as loud as they could.

They were trying to shut down a rally being held by the Texas chapter of Log Cabin Republicans. A few days earlier, the chapter had been banned from participating in the state party's convention. Texas had turned into the frontline of our struggle. So I got on a plane and flew down to help them hold a rally.

None of us expected the counter-protesters.

Looking out at that crowd, the words of the local sheriff were still fresh in my mind: "A lot of people carry guns around here. My men can't protect you. We would not advise you to continue."

Sure enough, when yelling didn't work, the protesters tried to rush the stage. We blocked them. The longer we went, the angrier and more aggressive they got. But their rage only strengthened our resolve.

My turn came to take the stage. I was planning to give a prepared speech, one I'd given a dozen times before. But in the heat of the moment, I threw it away. I spoke straight from the heart.

As I came to the close, I drew on my faith and spoke with all the conviction that I had.

"We know that when we fight for the voiceless, when we fight for people who want to love each other, when we fight for people to be honest, we know that our cause is just, we know that God is on our side. And we know something very powerful. They may have more numbers, but numerical strength never, never will beat moral strength. We will win this battle. We will win this struggle!"

In the years that followed, we never gave up. We made our case, showed people the justice of our cause, that we shared values with them—whether straight or gay, Democrat or Republican. Our shared commitment to love and inclusion was far more important than the areas on which we disagreed.

As we reached more people, our movement swelled—and then, we hit a tipping point. All of a sudden, people who just a few years before had kept quiet, or worse, found their own courage to stand with us and speak out.

First we changed the culture. And now marriage equality is the law of the land.

—RICH TAFEL

Discover more stories of activists tackling injustice at BelieveInPeopleBook.com/stories

The struggle continues, but from that point on, there was no question that discrimination against women is wrong and unacceptable, and that progress on this issue is non-negotiable. We are all better off for it.

Securing the right to vote for women took the better part of a century. But progress can also happen much faster. Less than 20 years elapsed between the passage of the discriminatory Defense of Marriage Act in 1996 and the enactment of marriage equality in 2015. The marriage equality movement transformed America for the better at an unprecedented speed, driven in large part by principled Social Entrepreneurs.

THE MECHANICS OF MOVEMENTS

Of course, the challenges we face today differ greatly from the injustices of the past. They are not as brutal as slavery or as blanket as a prohibition on women voting. They nonetheless ruin individual lives and injure society. They will continue to do so until enough people unite to overcome them.

As you have seen in the last few chapters, if we are to go beyond fighting injustice one person at a time, then the core institutions of community, education, business, and government must be transformed. Each one must consistently empower people to find their own unique ways to contribute and succeed. That won't happen until enough people demand better and then combine to make it happen, changing how our country thinks about, talks about, and tackles the biggest challenges we face.

But a movement? That still sounds like a tall order, even for the most talented Social Entrepreneur. How can you, as a single individual, help galvanize a massive number of people to take action on a specific issue? How can you possibly make a difference given the size and strength and sheer number of the barriers around us?

If we are to go beyond fighting injustice one person at a time, then the core institutions of community, education, business, and government must be transformed.

For the answer, look to the lessons of history. Think back to Frederick Douglass. Think back to all the remarkable people you've met in this book. They, along with my decades of study and experience, have taught me three main things about building movements. Each applies to every Social Entrepreneur, regardless of your passion or project.

The first lesson is the most important. It's simple: you can't manufacture a movement. The movements that will succeed have already begun. They're already there, hiding beneath the surface. They just need help in coalescing and aiming toward a common goal.

One of the great lies in America today is that nobody agrees on anything. False. On the biggest issues of our time, there is often clear common ground.

Take immigration, a perennially unsolved crisis.

If you recall from chapter nine, most Americans support finding a way for Dreamers to stay, and a remarkable 76 percent think immigration is good—an all-time high.[9] This historic level of agreement comes at a time when most would think of immigration as one of the most, if not *the* most, divisive issues of the day. Yet the vast majority of people reject the idea that we must choose between welcoming new immigrants and securing our borders. Americans know we can have both, even though the groups on the fringes (fewer than 15 percent of people) say we can't.[10] The extremes are drowning out the majority.

Or consider education. Only 19 percent of parents give America's schools an A or B grade.[11] That means at least 81 percent of families know we can do better at teaching our kids.

On poverty, over 75 percent of Americans are unsatisfied with how our society helps the least fortunate.[12] They know—they *see*—that the current approach continually fails tens of millions of people.

One of the great lies in America today is that nobody agrees on anything. False. On the biggest issues of our time, there is often clear common ground.

More than two-thirds of our fellow citizens realize that the economy is rigged, as we discussed in chapter eight. A stunning 84 percent say politicians have too much power in the economy, picking who wins and who loses.[13]

The same trend holds on issue after issue. More than 60 percent of Americans—and more than 70 percent of veterans—want to end the war in Afghanistan.[14] When it comes to America's role in the world, a plurality of citizens reject the false choice between isolationism and being the world's policeman.[15] They know we can choose to have a more realistic foreign policy, which starts by ending the primacy of the military option (aka bomb first, ask questions later).

And when it comes to the two major political parties, at any given time, anywhere from one-third to nearly one-half of Americans don't identify with either.[16] Moreover, about 60 percent say they don't feel represented by either party.[17] People see what's happening to our country. They know that partisanship is tearing us apart.

Each of these numbers should give us great hope. The American people are much wiser than they are often given credit for being. Our country is ripe for major change. People want societal transformation.

So why don't we see this broad agreement turn into action?

The answer involves a phenomenon that social scientists call "preference falsification," a concept pioneered by Duke economist Timur Kuran.[18] It simply means that people are reluctant to publicly speak out about their true beliefs when they feel that few others agree with them.

Research by Gallup and Todd Rose, the author mentioned in chapter seven and founder of Harvard University's Laboratory for the Science of Individuality, has shown that about two-thirds of people think that most others see the world through a zero-sum lens. They also overwhelmingly assume that most people believe that one person's success means another person's loss. Yet when you ask Americans how *they* see success, 90 percent say they want personal fulfillment more than they want to be better than others, and that each person's success can benefit those around them.[19]

What an enormous mismatch! The data say that the great majority of people are contribution motivated. Most folks just assume they're the only ones. This colors how they approach issue after issue. They don't speak up for fear of being the only one, but if they realized that they are not alone, they would be much more likely to voice their true beliefs. And as experience shows, when people do so *en masse*, the result can be progress, quickly and on a momentous scale.

Think back to the marriage equality movement. It turned out that most Americans already agreed with its aims and calls for equality before those goals were realized.[20] They just assumed that no one else felt the same way, so they didn't say anything. Neither did their friends and neighbors, who probably shared their views. Things began to change when people realized that many others felt the same way they did and began to speak up.

By giving people the permission to say what they already believed, a huge pent-up demand for change was unleashed. America went from a situation where none of the mainstream candidates for president dared advocate for marriage equality in 2008 to a celebration that lit up the White House in the rainbow colors of the movement for equality in 2015.[21]

Similar movements are possible today. Look for the issues on which the majority of people disagree with how things are but keep that disagreement under wraps out of concern that few feel the same way. That's where you'll find the quiet but widespread desire for change. Something, someone must turn that silent sentiment into action.

SHOW A BETTER WAY

Which brings us to the second lesson I have learned: as a Social Entrepreneur, you need to show people a better way.

This gets to the heart of the latter half of this book. To transform society for the better, we must believe that we can do better. We have to show what's possible. People will choose bad ideas if that's all that's on offer. Remember the choice between the lesser of two evils in chapter nine?

As history shows, the best way to beat a bad idea is with a better idea. Successful movements don't just criticize what's wrong. They elevate and celebrate what's right.

The beauty of a better way is that once you see it, you never forget it. It's so obviously superior that you want it for yourself, your family, your friends, your community, your country. You can't go to sleep until you see it happen. You can't stand the sight or thought of the old way of doing things, because it's so demonstrably wrong. Its very existence is offensive. You know what could be, what *should* be, and you're willing to sacrifice to achieve it for yourself and those you care about.

This lesson holds across progress of every kind. When people were first introduced to the automobile, it wasn't long before settling for a horse and buggy was unacceptable. The first people to hold an iPhone never wanted to pick up a landline again. (This change happened fast. Indeed, you may be reading this and thinking, "What's a landline?") In so many cases, the advantage is so apparent that change can sweep society in what seems like the blink of an eye.

Successful movements don't just criticize what's wrong. They elevate and celebrate what's right.

Similarly, with social progress, change happens when something is so obviously superior that it's unimaginable that a person would settle for what they have now.

This is not to say that it will be easy. America's Founders experienced freedom, so they demanded to be released from British rule. They succeeded, but only after fighting a brutal war for independence. As women claimed more of their rights, people saw how much they added to our society, but it took most of a century of struggle to make this a reality. As leaders like Frederick Douglass revealed what all people were capable of, a growing number of Americans demanded the end of slavery. It took the Civil War to make that happen.

Additionally, shameful periods like Jim Crow show that progress is anything but inevitable. The defenders of the status quo, no matter how unjust, will often try to stop progress, sometimes with violence. Others may oppose change simply because it makes them uncomfortable.

None of this is insurmountable. So long as courageous people stand for something better—for justice over injustice—there will always be momentum, however slow it may seem. The struggle for empowerment is never-ending. We can expect to make meaningful progress, but our work is never done. Perseverance is a necessary virtue for every Social Entrepreneur.

Think back to the last few chapters. In each one, you saw a better way.

We can fix communities not by controlling people but by liberating and empowering them, and by supporting Social Entrepreneurs closest to the problem as they implement their own bottom-up solutions.

We can ensure that every student has access to a world-class education by abandoning a rigid one-size-fits-all system for an open, individualized approach.

We can transform business into a powerful force for good by showing that creating value for others is far superior to taking from others through corporate welfare.

Finally, we can move government toward mutual benefit and partnership and away from partisanship, opening untold doors for policy progress.

In each case, there are people and projects that show the way forward. These Social Entrepreneurs are helping millions and growing their effectiveness exponentially.

Ask Scott Strode. Ask Antong Lucky. Ask Michael Crow. Ask Melony Armstrong. Ask Van Jones. They will all tell you that they aren't settling for the way everyone else does things. They've chosen a different path, one that makes transformational change a reality. Their actions demonstrate that they believe in people. If you do the same, anything is possible.

UNITE WITH ANYBODY TO DO RIGHT

The third and final lesson follows from the first two. If people are demanding change, and if a solution to the problem is clear, then the movement can succeed. But only if it unites a diversity of voices.

Let's unpack this further. A movement can't gain the momentum required to transform society if it consists of only one type of person, one homogenous group, or one set of people who hold the same views. Instead, they must bring together many who respect each other's differences and see the bigger picture.

Truly successful movements are inclusive, uniting people with varied perspectives and complementary abilities. Each person has a distinctive and vital role to play. Each person makes the movement stronger. As Abraham Maslow said, "The best way to help the society [is to] first find out what you can do best and then offer yourself to do that."[22] The more who do, the better the outcome for everyone.

> # This means Social Entrepreneurs need to go out of their way to find a diversity of allies and get them engaged.

Practically speaking, this means Social Entrepreneurs need to go out of their way to find a diversity of allies and get them engaged. So what if you disagree with someone on this, that, or the other thing? You agree on the need to defeat at least one injustice, and by uniting, you'll be able to make real progress.

By contrast, the agree-with-me-on-everything approach means movements shrink, not grow. Instead of movements of millions, you'll get movements of me, myself, and I. After all, you can always find a reason to disagree with someone. No two people agree on everything.

Imagine if Frederick Douglass had refused to work with Abraham Lincoln because they disagreed about the right time to abolish slavery. (That was the case.[23]) Or imagine if Elizabeth Cady Stanton and Susan B. Anthony divided the women's rights movement over their views on religion. (They disagreed.[24]) In every movement, you'll find plenty of people who had plenty of quarrels. But they didn't let their differences stand in the way of ending an injustice.

When you think of a movement, it's easy to think about one group winning over another. Yet there's a fundamental difference between a movement that unites people to achieve change and one that divides people in pursuit of the same end. Even if a divisive approach succeeds in the short term, it will likely fail in the long term. Bowling over your opponents will sow the seeds of resentment, which will bear ugly fruit long after you've "won."

We become what we do. If your means are exclusive, controlling, and hurtful, then you can expect your ends to reflect that. But if you act in an inclusive manner, treating everyone with respect, welcoming all comers who share a vision for overcoming injustice, then you will achieve an inclusive society. Not despite your differences, but because of them!

Successful movements also invite people not only to join together but to act together. Consider the story of civil rights. For years, African American communities struggled to break the barriers that stood in their way. The vile system of "separate but equal" seemed impervious, despite the obvious injustice that accompanied it. It was so oppressive and pervasive that its victims often felt powerless.

Martin Luther King Jr. proved the opposite was true—that the people held the true power. He inspired Americans to forsake "comfort and convenience" and lend their voices to "challenge and controversy." He convinced millions that their daily actions were essential to progress, and that together they could break monstrous barriers.

Dr. King's nonviolent vision inspired thousands of people to boycott the buses in Montgomery, Alabama. It caused four college students in Greensboro, North Carolina, to sit at a lunch counter at a local department store, spurring other sit-ins across the South.[25] Whereas once people assumed that separate-but-equal could not be broken, now they came to see that *they* could break it through countless individual actions, united by a deep belief in people. And so they did.

What started small grew larger and more successful with every passing week. Restaurants and department stores began to desegregate, until segregation became unthinkable.[26] The combination of individual actions fundamentally changed how the institution of business operated, ending a major barrier and chipping away at a larger injustice.

Meanwhile, the campaign for equality continued to pick up speed, such that it could no longer be ignored in the halls of government. When landmark legislation like the Civil Rights Act and the Voting Rights Act passed, it was because millions of individual people—especially those who had suffered—found a way to use their talents in the fight for justice. As they improved lives, they inspired others to stand with them, empowering still others.

The movements we need today must also give people the chance to act in concert and contribute based on what they have to offer. Not everyone can be a Dr. King, but anyone can spend a day doing the equivalent of a sit-in at a lunch counter. Everyone has a part to play in bottom-up social change.

Maybe it means working with fellow parents in your neighborhood to enact changes at your kid's school. Maybe it's uniting customers to boycott a business that advocates for corporate welfare. Maybe it's sharing on social media the success of a community organization that empowers people to overcome poverty. There are plenty of options. As more people come together, they'll find more ways to move the ball forward. You'll be part of a growing movement. It will take you further than you think.

Remember the multifaceted movement behind criminal justice reform? Since the First Step Act passed in 2018, its members continued to push for even better reforms at every level of government. We're building toward more transformative victories in the near future.

And success begets success. The cynic will say that criminal justice reform was one in a million—a unicorn accomplishment, never to be seen again. They couldn't be more wrong. Many of the same people who participated in the coalition to reform the criminal justice system are now working together on immigration. Similar coalitions are forming to improve K–12 education, foreign policy, and other major issues.

I've never been more excited at the prospect of real progress on the issues that matter most, or more optimistic about transforming every institution to end injustices and empower people across the country.

The demand for change is there, on every issue. A better way exists, in every case. And across the nation, people of every belief and background are willing and able to unite to do right.

It's up to you and me and all of us to make it happen, uniting and forging the movements that will empower people and fulfill the promise of America. When you get engaged in a cause larger than yourself, you will find the kind of fulfillment that most people spend a lifetime yearning for—the kind that comes from truly contributing to an unlimited future for our country and all who call it home.

A LIFE WELL LIVED

――――――

“ What one can be,
one must be. ”
ABRAHAM MASLOW[1]

――――――

W hen I told my wife I wanted to write another book, she looked at me like I was crazy. Then she *told* me I was crazy. Her exact words were, "Your next book will be with your next wife."

Typical Liz humor. As usual, her hyperbole carried a deeper meaning. Having watched me write a second book in the early to mid-2010s, Liz dreaded my becoming completely absorbed in the project, taking months, if not years, to complete it. (She was right.) Since I still have a day job, she knew it would occupy my evenings and weekends, leaving little time for her and the things we do together.

I'm 85 years old. Instead of drafting another tome, I could have spent more time with Liz, enjoying my kids and grandkids, traveling, or just retired like a normal person. At the very least, I could have taken better control of my calendar, office hours, evenings, and weekends.

But I didn't. (And for the record, Liz didn't want me to! She knew I had to do it.) Instead, I put pen to paper, quibbling over every word, and did it over and over again, because the efforts described in these pages are my life's work. This is my latest attempt to share what enabled me to have a wonderful life—the last piece in the transformation that has enabled me to achieve and contribute more than I ever imagined possible.

Even though I didn't recognize it at the time, empowering people has been my driving motivation since my twenties. Following that epiphany in 1963—when I saw that we can have an unlimited future if everyone has the chance to realize their potential—I have developed and applied my own narrow talents to do my best to bring that vision about.

A bumpy journey, to put it mildly. My life has been one long story of trial and error, ups and downs, two steps forward and one step back. If we learn from our mistakes, then according to Liz, I should be a wizard by now. Yet the application of the principles in this book has ensured that even when I went in the wrong direction, what I learned set the stage for future success. My life is its own story of transformation. Yours can be too.

My life is its own story of transformation. Yours can be too.

I spent my early years thinking I was destined for a career in engineering. At MIT, it became clear that I would be a lousy engineer. So I focused my studies on what I was good at—the abstract concepts on which engineering is based. I was very lucky to have discovered this before I wasted any more time. This turned out to be a powerful way to develop my specific aptitude, which later enabled me to be an effective business and Social Entrepreneur.

MY GREATEST INFLUENCES

Along the way, I have absorbed concepts from more individuals and books than I can count. I approached each with the intent of learning everything I could and applying those lessons in every aspect of my life.

Besides my parents, six people in particular have had the greatest influence on my values, life, and success. I divide them into three groups.

The first includes those I've known personally, starting with Sterling Varner, since our relationship began earliest—70 years ago. As you read in chapter three, he may have started life in a Texas oil field tent as a mule driver's stammering son, but he retired as president of Koch Industries and taught me much about mutual benefit, entrepreneurship, and motivating people. He fit my definition of the ideal partner, as we shared a vision and values and had complementary capabilities.

But the partner who has done the most to transform my life is my wife, Liz. We have been together for more than 50 years. She is good at everything I'm not, leading us to celebrate our differences and dedicate ourselves to helping each other self-actualize. She is loyal, loving, supportive, smart, insightful, courageous, and a constant source of joy, despite—or, more likely, because of—her constantly challenging my foibles. If I searched the world over, I could not have found a better mate.

The next group is authors. Out of the thousands I have read, the two who have had the most influence on me are probably Abraham Maslow and Friedrich Hayek.

From Maslow I learned that to have a happy, fulfilling life, you must be "everything [you] are capable of becoming"[2]—you must self-actualize. Those who do are essential to the success of any organization or society.

From Hayek I learned that human well-being and progress come through a spontaneous order of cooperation and competition, guided "only by abstract rules of conduct," and that the attempt to succeed by controlling and dominating people is a "fatal conceit" that will end in failure.

Finally, there are two role models who have inspired me to become a Social Entrepreneur. Each represents the possibility of self-actualizing under the most dire conditions.

Frederick Douglass (chapter five) was able to self-actualize first by realizing he was a worthy human being, then by finding ways to contribute even while still in slavery, and finally, when free, by applying his gift to end that worst of all injustices, as well as others.

Viktor Frankl (chapter one) survived the Nazi death camps by focusing on saving others, rather than just saving himself. This was his highest purpose, and afterward he dedicated his life to helping people find their own North Star, saying, "Ever more people today have the means to live, but no meaning to live for."[3]

Such is the power of self-actualizing, for the Social Entrepreneur as much as anyone else. When you identify your abilities and use them to benefit others, you find the highest fulfillment. When you continually apply yourself in the pursuit of noble ends, you help people beyond your expectations. When you forge partnerships in pursuit of common goals, you enormously increase your effectiveness.

MY PROMISE TO YOU

That is the story of human progress—economic, cultural, spiritual, and every other dimension. The greatest advances in history ultimately came down to principled men and women applying their gifts, empowering others, and transforming society from the bottom up. They became the best versions of themselves, making the world a better place for us all.

What they began, we must continue. Your success, as mine, depends on how we live our lives—the choices we make, the principles we follow, the barriers we break. The concepts you have read in these pages—mutual benefit, openness, equal rights, partnership, and many others—should help your efforts to end the injustices holding millions back. Believe in people, and you will empower them.

I wake up every morning looking for ways to apply these principles to make a bigger difference. It has become automatic. Even at the age of 85, I want nothing more than to contribute and empower others.

My North Star remains a society in which every person can realize their potential—a society of mutual benefit, in which individuals succeed by creating value for others. It would be a more just, inclusive, prosperous, and peaceful society than any yet seen. Such a future is within our reach, if all of us play our part—if all of us believe in people.

My North Star remains a society in which every person can realize their potential.

I will strive to achieve this vision until I no longer can. I take comfort in the knowledge that, when that day arrives, countless people from all walks of life will carry on, empowering others and elevating all. For your own happiness, and for that of everyone else, I hope that you will be among them.

APPENDIX

KOCH INDUSTRIES' GUIDING PRINCIPLES

1. ### INTEGRITY
    Have the courage to always act with integrity.

2. ### STEWARDSHIP AND COMPLIANCE
    Act with proper regard for the rights of others. Put safety first. Drive environmental excellence and comply with all laws and regulations. Stop, think, and ask.

3. ### PRINCIPLED ENTREPRENEURSHIP™
    Practice a philosophy of mutual benefit. Create superior value for the company by doing so for our customers and society. Help make Koch the preferred partner of customers, employees, suppliers, communities, and other important constituencies.

4. ### TRANSFORMATION
    Transform yourself and the company. Seek, develop, and utilize the visions, strategies, methods, and products that will enable us to create the greatest value.

5. ### KNOWLEDGE
    Acquire the best knowledge from any and all sources that will enable you to improve your performance. Share your knowledge proactively. Provide and solicit challenge consistently and respectfully.

6. **HUMILITY**

Be humble, intellectually honest, and deal with reality constructively. Develop an accurate sense of self-worth based on your strengths, limitations, and contributions. Hold yourself and others accountable to these standards.

7. **RESPECT**

Treat everyone with honesty, dignity, respect, and sensitivity. Embrace different perspectives, experiences, aptitudes, knowledge, and skills in order to leverage the power of diversity.

8. **SELF-ACTUALIZATION**

Be a lifelong learner and realize your potential, which is essential for fulfillment. As you become increasingly self-actualized, you will better deal with reality, face the unknown, creatively solve problems, and help others succeed.

SELECTED BIBLIOGRAPHY
AND RECOMMENDED READING

CLARK ALDRICH

Unschooling Rules: 55 Ways to Unlearn What We Know about Schools and Rediscover Education (2011)

ANDREW J. BACEVICH

America's War for the Greater Middle East: A Military History (2016)

FRÉDÉRIC BASTIAT

The Law (1850)

TIMOTHY P. CARNEY

Alienated America: Why Some Places Thrive While Others Collapse (2019)

RICHARD C. CORNUELLE

Reclaiming the American Dream: The Role of Private Individuals and Voluntary Associations (1965)

FREDERICK DOUGLASS

Narrative of the Life of Frederick Douglass, an American Slave (1845); *My Bondage and My Freedom* (1855); *Life and Times of Frederick Douglass* (1881)

WILLIAM EASTERLY

The Tyranny of Experts: Economists, Dictators, and the Forgotten Poor (2014)

VIKTOR E. FRANKL

Man's Search for Meaning (1946)

MILTON AND ROSE FRIEDMAN

Free to Choose: A Personal Statement (1980)

HOWARD GARDNER

Frames of Mind: The Theory of Multiple Intelligences (1983)

JONATHAN HAIDT

The Happiness Hypothesis: Finding Modern Truth in Ancient Wisdom (2006); *The Coddling of the American Mind: How Good Intentions and Bad Ideas Are Setting Up a Generation for Failure* (with Greg Lukianoff, 2018)

FRIEDRICH AUGUST VON HAYEK

"Competition as a Discovery Procedure" (1968); "The Use of Knowledge in Society" (1945); *The Fatal Conceit: The Errors of Socialism* (1988); *Law, Legislation, and Liberty* (1973); *The Constitution of Liberty* (1960)

ROBERT HIGGS

Crisis and Leviathan: Critical Episodes in the Growth of American Government (1987)

THOMAS S. KUHN

The Structure of Scientific Revolutions (1962)

DON LAVOIE

National Economic Planning: What Is Left? (1985)

JOHN LOCKE

The Second Treatise on Civil Government (1689)

ABRAHAM MASLOW

Eupsychian Management (1965) *aka Maslow on Management* (1998); *Toward a Psychology of Being* (1962)

DEIRDRE MCCLOSKEY

The Bourgeois Era trilogy (2006)

MAURICIO L. MILLER

The Alternative: Most of What You Believe about Poverty Is Wrong (2017)

LUDWIG VON MISES

Human Action (1949); *Theory and History: An Interpretation of Social and Economic Evolution* (1957)

CHARLES MURRAY

In Pursuit: Of Happiness and Good Government (1988)

MICHAEL POLANYI

"The Republic of Science: Its Political and Economic Theory" (1962); *Personal Knowledge: Towards a Post-Critical Philosophy* (1958)

KARL POPPER

"Science as Falsification" (1963)

MATT RIDLEY

The Evolution of Everything: How New Ideas Emerge (2015); *The Rational Optimist: How Prosperity Evolves* (2010)

TODD ROSE

The End of Average: How We Succeed in a World That Values Sameness (2016); *Dark Horse: Achieving Success Through the Pursuit of Fulfillment* (2018)

NATHAN ROSENBERG AND L.E. BIRDZELL JR.

How the West Grew Rich: The Economic Transformation of the Industrial World (1986)

JOSEPH SCHUMPETER

Capitalism, Socialism and Democracy (1942)

THOMAS SOWELL

A Conflict of Visions: Ideological Origins of Political Struggles (1987); *Knowledge and Decisions* (1980)

ADAM THIERER

Permissionless Innovation: The Continuing Case for Comprehensive Technological Freedom (2014)

PAUL WEAVER

The Suicidal Corporation (1988)

NOTES

Preface

1 Shawn Boburg, Robert O' Harrow Jr, Neena Satija, and Amy Goldstein, "Inside the coronavirus testing failure: Alarm and dismay among the scientists who sought to help," *The Washington Post*, April 3, 2020, https://www.washingtonpost.com/investigations /2020/04/03/coronavirus-cdc-test-kits-public-health-labs/?arc404=true; Matthew D. Mitchell, "First, Do No Harm: Three Ways That Policymakers Can Make It Easier for Healthcare Professionals to Do Their Jobs," Mercatus Center at George Mason University (2020), accessed May 26, 2020, https://www.mercatus.org/publications/covid-19-crisis -response/first-do-no-harm-three-ways-policymakers-can-make-it-easier; Edward J Timmons, Ethan Bayne, Conor Norris, "A Primer on Emergency Occupational Licensing Reforms for Combatting Covid-19," Mercatus Center at George Mason University (2020), accessed May 26, 2020, https://www.mercatus.org/publications /covid-19-policy-brief-series/primer-emergency-occupational-licensing -reforms-combating.

2 Jonathan Rothwell, "Official jobless figures will miss the economic pain of the pandemic," Brookings Institution (2020), accessed May 26, 2020, https://www.brookings.edu/blog/up-front/2020/04/03/ official-jobless-figures-will-miss-the-economic-pain-of-the-pandemic/.

3 Taylor Telford and Kimberly Kindy, "As they rushed to maintain U.S. meat supply, big processors saw plants become covid-19 hot spots, worker illnesses spike," *The Washington Post*, April 25, 2020, https://www.washingtonpost.com/business/2020/04/25 /meat-workers-safety-jbs-smithfield-tyson/; Billy Binion, "Michigan Bans 'All Public and Private Gatherings,' Will Still Allow Lottery Sales," Reason, April 13, 2020, https://reason. com/2020/04/13/michigan-gretchen-whitmer-bans-all-public-and-private-gatherings -will-still-allow-lottery-sales/.

4 Lisa Baertlein, "U.S. grocers add plexiglass sneeze guards to protect cashiers from coronavirus," Reuters, March 3, 2020, https://www.reuters.com/article/us-health -coronavirus-kroger/u-s-grocers-add-plexiglass-sneeze-guards-to-protect -cashiers-from-coronavirus-idUSKBN21H3G1; Aaron Kassraie, "Supermarkets Offer Special Hours for Older Shoppers," *AARP*, April 22, 2020, https:// www.aarp.org/home-family/your-home/info-2020/coronavirus-supermarkets.html; Austen Hufford and Bob Tita, "Coronavirus Pushes Factories to Stagger Shifts, Separate

Workers," The Wall Street Journal, March 17, 2020, https://www.wsj.com /articles/u-s-factories-work-around-coronavirus-impact-11584447707.

5   Thomas Kuhn, *The Structure of Scientific Revolutions*, 3rd ed. (Chicago: University of Chicago Press, 1996), 10.

6   Thomas Kuhn, *The Structure of Scientific Revolutions*, 3rd ed. (Chicago: University of Chicago Press, 1996), 92.

7   Thomas Kuhn, *The Structure of Scientific Revolutions*, 3rd ed. (Chicago: University of Chicago Press, 1996), 79.

8   Thomas Kuhn, *The Structure of Scientific Revolutions*, 3rd ed. (Chicago, University of Chicago Press, 1996), 122.

Introduction

1   Gilbert Farrar, *Typography of Advertisements That Pay* (New York: D. Appleton and Company, 1917), epigraph.

2   Richard V. Reeves and Katherine Guyot, "Fewer Americans Are Making More Than Their Parents Did—Especially If They Grew Up in the Middle Class," Brookings Institution (2018), accessed April 20, 2020, https://www.brookings.edu/blog/up-front/2018/07/25 /fewer-americans-are-making-more-than-their-parents-did-especially-if-they-grew-up -in-the-middle-class/.

3   Holly Hedegaard, Sally C. Curtin, and Margaret Warner, "Increase in Suicide Mortality in the United States, 1999–2018," National Center for Health Statistics (2020), accessed April 20, 2020, https://www.cdc.gov/nchs/data/databriefs/db362-h.pdf; Holly Hedegaard, Arialdi M. Miniño, and Margaret Warner, "Drug Overdose Deaths in the United States, 1999–2018," National Center for Health Statistics (2020), accessed April 20, 2020, https:// www.cdc.gov/nchs/data/databriefs/db356-h.pdf; "Nationwide Trends," National Institute on Drug Abuse (2015), accessed April 18, 2020, https://www.drugabuse.gov/publications /drugfacts/nationwide-trends.

4   "Mortality Trends in the United States, 1900–2017," National Center for Health Statistics, accessed April 18, 2020, https://www.cdc.gov/nchs/data-visualization /mortality-trends/#dashboard.

5   Jessica Semega, et al., "Income and Poverty in the United States: 2018," U.S. Census Bureau (2019), accessed April 17, 2020, 1, https://www.census.gov/content/dam/Census/library /publications/2019/demo/p60-266.pdf.

Chapter One

1 Bob Dylan, "It's Alright, Ma (I'm Only Bleeding)," track 10 on Bringing It All Back Home, Columbia Records, 1965.

2 Luke 12:48 KJV.

3 Samuel Barber, *Hudibras* (Reprint, London: John Murray, 1835), Vol. I, Part II, Canto I, line 844, https://archive.org/details/hudibraswithnot00hudigoog/. Likely a paraphrase of "He that spareth his rod hateth his son: but he that loveth him chasteneth him betimes" (Proverbs 13:24 KJV).

4 Antonio Terracciano, Paul T. Costa Jr., and Robert R. McCrae, "Personality Plasticity after Age 30," *Personality & Social Psychology Bulletin* 32, no. 8 (2006): 999–1009, https://doi.org/10.1177/0146167206288599.

5 Aristotle, *Nicomachean Ethics*, trans. C. D. C. Reeve (Indianapolis: Hackett Publishing Company, Inc., 2014), 10.

6 Howard Gardner, *Frames of Mind: The Theory of Multiple Intelligences*, 3rd ed. (New York: Basic Books, 2011), xxix, 3–12, 63-76.

7 Alexis de Tocqueville, *Democracy in America*, Vol. 2, trans. Henry Reeve (New York: J. & H. G. Langley, 1840). Reprinted with introduction and notes by Phillips Bradley (New York: Alfred A. Knopf, 1945), 122.

8 Abraham Maslow, "A Theory of Human Motivation," *Psychological Review* 50, no. 4 (1943), 370–96.

9 Abraham Maslow. *Eupsychian Management: A Journal* (Homewood, IL: Richard D. Irwin, Inc. and The Dorsey Press, 1965), 20.

10 Viktor E. Frankl, *Man's Search for Meaning* (Massachusetts: Beacon Press, 2014), 92.

11 Viktor E. Frankl, *Man's Search for Meaning* (Massachusetts: Beacon Press, 2014), 78.

Chapter Two

1 F.A. Hayek, *Law, Legislation and Liberty*, Vol. 2 (Chicago: University of Chicago Press, 1978), 136.

2 Richard Rumbold, "The Last Speech of Coll. Richard Rumbold, with Several Things That Passed at His Tryal, 26 June, 1685," (aka "Speech on the Scaffold") in *The last words of Coll. Richard Rumbold, Mad. Alicia Lisle, Alderman Henry Cornish, and Mr. Richard Nelthrop who were executed in England and Scotland for high treason in the year 1685*, https://quod.lib.umich.edu/e/eebo/A57890.0001.001/1:1.1?rgn=div2;view=fulltext.

3 This section benefited from many excellent works, including: Deirdre McCloskey, "The Bourgeois Era" trilogy: *The Bourgeois Virtues: Ethics for an Age of Commerce*, Vol. 1

(Chicago: University of Chicago Press, 2006); *Bourgeois Dignity: Why Economics Can't Explain the Modern World*, Vol. 2 (Chicago: University of Chicago Press, 2010); *Bourgeois Equality: How Ideas, Not Capital or Institutions, Enriched the World*, Vol. 3 (Chicago: University of Chicago Press, 2016); Matt Ridley, *The Rational Optimist: How Prosperity Evolves* (New York: Harper, 2010); *The Evolution of Everything: How Ideas Emerge* (New York: Harper, 2015); Joel Mokyr, *A Culture of Growth: The Origins of the Modern Economy* (Princeton, NJ: Princeton University Press, 2017); Johan Norberg, *Progress: Ten Reasons to Look Forward to the Future* (London: Oneworld Publications, 2017).

4   Max Roser, "Economic Growth," Our World in Data, accessed April 18, 2020, https://ourworldindata.org/economic-growth.

5   Max Roser, Esteban Ortiz-Ospina, and Hannah Ritchie, "Life Expectancy," Our World in Data, accessed April 18, 2020, https://ourworldindata.org/life-expectancy#life-expectancy-has-improved-globally.

6   Deirdre McCloskey, *Bourgeois Equality: How Ideas, Not Capital or Institutions, Enriched the World*, Vol. 3 (Chicago: University of Chicago Press, 2016), 10–11.

7   Deirdre McCloskey, *Bourgeois Equality: How Ideas, Not Capital or Institutions, Enriched the World*, Vol. 3 (Chicago: University of Chicago Press, 2016), 6; "Real Gross Domestic Product per Capita," Federal Reserve Bank of St. Louis, accessed April 18, 2020, https://fred.stlouisfed.org/series/A939RX0Q048SBEA.

8   "We Can End Poverty: Millennium Development Goals and Beyond 2015," United Nations, accessed April 18, 2020, https://www.un.org/millenniumgoals/poverty.shtml.

9   Johan Norberg, *Progress: Ten Reasons to Look Forward to the Future* (London: Oneworld Publications, 2017), 11.

10   Joseph Loconte, "How Martin Luther Advanced Freedom," *Wall Street Journal*, October 26, 2017, https://www.wsj.com/articles/how-martin-luther-advanced-freedom-1509059066.

11   Eric Metaxas, *Martin Luther: The Man Who Rediscovered God and Changed the World* (New York: Viking, 2017), 348–49, 640-43.

12   David Daniell, *William Tyndale: A Biography* (New Haven: Yale University Press, 1994), 1–2.

13   Stillman Drake, "Galileo's Explorations in Science," *Dalhousie Review* 61, no. 2 (1981): 219, https://dalspace.library.dal.ca/bitstream/handle/10222/60308/dalrev_vol61_iss2_pp217_232.pdf?sequence=1&isAllowed=y.

14   Freeman J. Dyson, *The Scientist as Rebel* (New York: New York Review Books, 2006), 196.

15   David Brewster, "Letter to Robert Hooke, February 5, 1675–6," in *Memoirs of the Life, Writings, and Discoveries of Sir Isaac Newton*, Vol. 1 (Edinburgh: 1855), 142, http://www.newtonproject.ox.ac.uk/view/texts/normalized/OTHE00101.

16   This history of the Dutch Golden Age benefited from many sources, including: Deirdre
      McCloskey, "The Bourgeois Era" trilogy: *The Bourgeois Virtues: Ethics for an Age of
      Commerce,* Vol. 1 (Chicago: University of Chicago Press, 2006); *Bourgeois Dignity: Why
      Economics Can't Explain the Modern World,* Vol. 2 (Chicago: University of Chicago Press,
      2010); *Bourgeois Equality: How Ideas, Not Capital or Institutions, Enriched the World,* Vol. 3
      (Chicago: University of Chicago Press, 2016); Simon Schama, *The Embarrassment of Riches:
      An Interpretation of Dutch Culture in the Golden Age* (Berkeley: University of California
      Press, 1988). Jan De Vries and Ad van der Woude, *The First Modern Economy: Success,
      Failure, and Perseverance of the Dutch Economy, 1500–1815* (Cambridge: Cambridge
      University Press, 2000); Maarten Prak, *The Dutch Republic in the Seventeenth Century,*
      trans. Diane Webb (New York: Cambridge University Press, 2005).

17   Thomas Jefferson, "Letter to John Holmes, April 22, 1820," Library of Congress, accessed
      April 18, 2020, https://www.loc.gov/exhibits/jefferson/159.html.

18   Thomas Jefferson, *Notes on the State of Virginia* (Boston: Lilly and Wait, 1832), 170.

Chapter Three

1   Karl Marx, "Theses on Feuerbach," *Marx/Engels Selected Works,* Vol. 1 (Moscow: Progress
      Publishers, 1969), 15. Quoted in Marxists Internet Archive, "Theses on Feuerbach," accessed
      April 22, 2020, https://www.marxists.org/archive/marx/works/1845/theses/theses.htm.

2   "Full Transcript of Charles Koch's Interview with Fortune," *Fortune,* July 12, 2016, https://
      fortune.com/2016/07/12/transcript-charles-koch-fortune/.

3   Koch Newsroom, "Driving Transformation with Laser-Guided Autonomous
      Vehicles," October 30, 2018, https://news.kochind.com/news/2018/
      laser-guided-autonomous-vehicles-safety-transforma.

4   Frank Lewis Dyer and Thomas Commerford Martin, *Edison: His Life and Inventions,* Vol. 2
      (New York: Harper & Brothers, 1910), 616.

Chapter Four

1   John F. Kennedy, "Address in the Assembly Hall at the Paulskirche, Frankfurt, 25 June 1963,"
      accessed April 18, 2020, https://www.jfklibrary.org/asset-viewer/archives/JFKPOF/045
      /JFKPOF-045-023.

2   "The Future of Work in America," McKinsey Global Institute (2019), accessed April 17,
      2020, 16, https://www.mckinsey.com/~/media/mckinsey/featured insights
      /future of organizations/the future of work in america people and places today and tomor-
      row/the-future-of-work-in-america-full-report.ashx.

3   "From Great Recession to Great Reshuffling: Charting a Decade of Change across American Communities," Economic Innovation Group (2018), accessed April 17, 2020, 4, https://eig.org/wp-content/uploads/2018/10/2018-DCI.pdf.

4   Megan Brenan, "Americans More Optimistic about Future of Next Generation," Gallup (2018), accessed April 17, 2020, https://news.gallup.com/poll/232076/americans-optimistic-future-next-generation.aspx.

5   Raj Chetty, et al., "The Fading American Dream: Trends in Absolute Income Mobility Since 1940," National Bureau of Economic Research (2016), accessed April 10, 2020, 2, https://opportunityinsights.org/wp-content/uploads/2018/03/abs_mobility_paper.pdf.

6   Mark Murray, "'Wrong Track': Public Sours on Nation's Direction after Shutdown," *NBC News*, January 27, 2019, https://www.nbcnews.com/politics/meet-the-press/wrong-track-public-sours-nation-s-direction-after-shutdown-n963051; Kim Parker, Rich Moran, and Juliana Henasce Horowitz, "Looking to the Future, Public Sees an America in Decline on Many Fronts," Pew Research Center (2019), accessed April 17, 2020, https://www.pewsocialtrends.org/2019/03/21/public-sees-an-america-in-decline-on-many-fronts/.

7   Chelsea White, "U.S. Suicide Rate at Its Highest Since the End of the Second World War," *New Scientist*, June 20, 2019, https://www.newscientist.com/article/2207007-us-suicide-rate-at-its-highest-since-the-end-of-the-second-world-war/.

8   Holly Hedegaard, Arialdi M. Miniño, and Margaret Warner, "Drug Overdose Deaths in the United States, 1999–2018," National Center for Health Statistics (2020), accessed April 17, 2020, https://www.cdc.gov/nchs/data/databriefs/db356-h.pdf.

9   Aaron M. White, et al., "Using Death Certificates to Explore Changes in Alcohol-Related Mortality in the United States, 1999 to 2017," *Alcoholism: Clinical and Experimental Research* 44, no. 1 (2020), https://onlinelibrary.wiley.com/doi/abs/10.1111/acer.14239.

10 Anne Case and Angus Deaton, "Mortality and Morbidity in the 21st Century," *Brookings Papers on Economic Activity* 47, no. 1 (2017): 397–443.

11 "Mortality Trends in the United States, 1900–2017," National Center for Health Statistics, accessed April 18, 2020, https://www.cdc.gov/nchs/data-visualization/mortality-trends/#dashboard.

12 "Death Rates and Life Expectancy at Birth," Data.CDC.gov, accessed April 24, 2020, https://data.cdc.gov/NCHS/NCHS-Death-rates-and-life-expectancy-at-birth/w9j2-ggv5/data; Lenny Bernstein, "U.S. Life Expectancy Declines Again, a Dismal Trend Not Seen Since World War I," *Washington Post*, November 29, 2018, https://www.washingtonpost.com/national/health-science/us-life-expectancy-declines-again-a-dismal-trend-not-seen-since-world-war-i/2018/11/28/ae58bc8c-f28c-11e8-bc79-68604ed88993_story.html.

13   "National Vital Statistics System," National Center for Health Statistics (2020), accessed
      April 17, 2020, https://www.cdc.gov/nchs/data/factsheets/factsheet_NVSS.pdf.

14   Quoctrung Bui, "Map: The Most Common* Job in Every State," *NPR*, February 5, 2015,
      https://www.npr.org/sections/money/2015/02/05/382664837/map-the-most-common
      -job-in-every-state; Robert Allison, "What Are the Most Common Occupations in Each US
      State?," *SAS Learning Post*, August 17, 2018, https://blogs.sas.com/content
      /sastraining/2018/08/17/what-are-the-most-common-occupations-in-each-us-state/.

15   "Employee Tenure in 2018," Bureau of Labor Statistics (2018), accessed April 10, 2020,
      https://www.bls.gov/news.release/tenure.nr0.htm.

Chapter Five

1   Abraham Maslow, *Maslow on Management* (New York: John Wiley & Sons, Inc., 1998), 282.

2   Many excellent works informed my understanding of Douglass's life. First and foremost
      are his autobiographies and speeches. Of immense help were also: David Blight, *Frederick
      Douglass: Prophet of Freedom* (New York: Simon & Schuster, 2018); John Stauffer and
      Henry Louis Gates Jr., *The Portable Frederick Douglass* (New York: Penguin Classics, 2016);
      Nicholas Buccula, *The Political Thought of Frederick Douglass: In Pursuit of American
      Liberty* (New York: New York University Press, 2012).

3   Frederick Douglass, *The Speeches of Frederick Douglass: A Critical Edition*, ed. John R.
      McKivigan, Julie Husband, and Heather L. Kaufman (New Haven and London: Yale
      University Press, 2018), 62.

4   Frederick Douglass, *The Life and Times of Frederick Douglass: From 1817-1882, written
      by himself; with an Introduction by the Right Hon. John Bright*, ed. John Lobb (London:
      Christian Age Office, 1882), 52, http://oll.libertyfund.org/titles
      /douglass-the-life-and-times-of-frederick-douglass-from-1817-1882.

5   David Blight, *Frederick Douglass: Prophet of Freedom* (New York: Simon & Schuster, 2018),
      43–47.

6   Frederick Douglass, *My Bondage and My Freedom*, ed. David W. Blight (New Haven: Yale
      University Press, 2014), 161.

7   Frederick Douglass, *The Life and Times of Frederick Douglass: From 1817-1882, written
      by himself; with an Introduction by the Right Hon. John Bright*, ed. John Lobb (London:
      Christian Age Office, 1882), 87, http://oll.libertyfund.org/titles
      /douglass-the-life-and-times-of-frederick-douglass-from-1817-1882.

8   Frederick Douglass, *The Life and Times of Frederick Douglass: From 1817-1882, written
      by himself; with an Introduction by the Right Hon. John Bright*, ed. John Lobb (London:

Christian Age Office, 1882), 177, http://oll.libertyfund.org/titles
/douglass-the-life-and-times-of-frederick-douglass-from-1817-1882.

9   Frederick Douglass, "Our Composite Nationality: An Address Delivered in Boston,
     Massachusetts, on 7 December 1869," in *The Frederick Douglass Papers Speeches, Debates,
     and Interviews*, Vol. 4, 1864–80, ed. John W. Blassingame and John R. McKivigan (New
     Haven: Yale University Press, 1992), 253.

10   "Key Substance Use and Mental Health Indicators in the United States: Results from
     the 2018 National Survey on Drug Use and Health," Substance Abuse and Mental Health
     Services Administration (2019), accessed April 20, 2020, 50–51, https://www.samhsa.gov/
     data/sites/default/files/cbhsq-reports/NSDUHNationalFindingsReport2018
     /NSDUHNationalFindingsReport2018.pdf.

11   Based on a study conducted by The Phoenix, less than 20 percent of survey respondents
     relapsed during the first three months. Researchers reviewing the effectiveness of other
     programs find a range of 50–70 percent relapse rates for the same period. See: Nicholas
     Guenzel and Dennis McChargue, "Addiction Relapse Prevention," *StatPearls* (2019),
     https://www.ncbi.nlm.nih.gov/books/NBK551500/; Rajita Sinha, "New Findings on
     Biological Factors Predicting Addiction Relapse Vulnerability," *Current Psychiatry Reports*
     13 (2011), https://www.ncbi.nlm.nih.gov/pmc/articles/PMC3674771/

Chapter Six

1   Richard Cornuelle, *Healing America* (New York: G.P. Putnam and Sons, 1983), 196. Quoted
     in Robert F. Garnett Jr., Paul Lewis, and Lenore Ealy, *Commerce and Community: Ecologies
     of Social Cooperation* (London & New York:: Routledge, 2014), 5–6.

2   "America's Addiction to Juvenile Incarceration: State by State," American Civil Liberties
     Union, accessed April 10, 2020, https://www.aclu.org/issues/juvenile-justice
     /youth-incarceration/americas-addiction-juvenile-incarceration-state-state.

3   Sarah Mimms and Stephanie Stamm, "2 Million Kids Are Arrested in the U.S. Every Year.
     Congress Is Trying to Change That," *The Atlantic*, May 2, 2014, https://www.theatlantic.
     com/politics/archive/2014/05/2-million-kids-are-arrested-in-the-us-every-year
     -congress-is-trying-to-change-that/450522/.

4   Howard N. Snyder and Melissa Sickmund, "Juvenile Offenders and Victims: 2006 National
     Report," National Center for Juvenile Justice (2006), accessed April 20, 2020, 234, https://
     www.ojjdp.gov/ojstatbb/nr2006/downloads/NR2006.pdf.

5   Tim Carney, *Alienated America: Why Some Places Thrive While Others Collapse* (New York:
     HarperCollins, 2019).

6   "Loneliness and the Workplace: 2020 U.S. Report," Cigna (2020), https://www.cigna.com
    /static/www-cigna-com/docs/about-us/newsroom/studies-and-reports/combatting
    -loneliness/cigna-2020-loneliness-report.pdf.

7   Anne Case and Angus Deaton, "Mortality and Morbidity in the 21st Century," *Brookings
    Papers on Economic Activity* 47, no. 1 (2017): 429-39.

8   Tim Carney, *Alienated America: Why Some Places Thrive While Others Collapse* (New York:
    HarperCollins, 2019), 27–30.

9   Lyndon B. Johnson, "Annual Message to the Congress on the State of the Union," January 8,
    1964, https://www.presidency.ucsb.edu/documents/annual-message-the-congress-the
    -state-the-union-25.

10 This is largely based on the government's official poverty rate, which finds only a 5 percent
    decrease in poverty since 1964. Alternative measures taking government transfers into
    account find more substantial decreases, but many programs only serve as short-term
    bridges that fail to empower people to build a future for themselves and their families. Ajay
    Chaudry, et al., "Poverty in the United States: 50-Year Trends and Safety Net Impacts,"
    U.S. Department of Health and Human Services (2016), accessed April 18, 2020, 8, https://
    aspe.hhs.gov/system/files/pdf/154286/50YearTrends.pdf.; Bruce D. Meyer and James
    X. Sullivan, "Winning the War: Poverty from the Great Society to the Great Recession,"
    Brookings Papers on Economic Activity 42, no. 2 (2012): 136; Nicholas Eberstadt, "The Great
    Society at Fifty: The Triumph and the Tragedy," American Enterprise Institute (2014),
    accessed April 18, 2020, 20–21, https://www.aei.org/wp-content/uploads/2014/05/-the
    -great-society-at-fifty-the-triumph-and-the-tragedy_102730423054.pdf; "Opportunity,
    Responsibility, and Security: A Consensus Plan for Reducing Poverty and Restoring the
    American Dream," American Enterprise Institute and Brookings Institution (2015),
    accessed April 18, 2020, 18–19, https://www.brookings.edu/wp-content/uploads/2016/07
    /Full-Report.pdf.

11 "Poor America; Poverty in America," *The Economist*, September 26, 2019, https://www.
    economist.com/special-report/2019/09/26/the-best-way-to-eradicate-poverty
    -in-america-is-to-focus-on-children.

12 Michael Tanner, "The American Welfare State: How We Spend Nearly $1 Trillion a Year
    Fighting Poverty—and Fail," Cato Institute (2012), accessed April 18, 2020, 2, https://
    www.cato.org/sites/cato.org/files/pubs/pdf/PA694.pdf.

13 Charity Navigator, "Giving Statistics," accessed April 11, 2020, https://
    www.charitynavigator.org/index.cfm?bay=content.view&cpid=42.

14 William Easterly, *The Tyranny of Experts* (New York: Basic Books, 2013).

15 Mauricio Miller, *The Alternative: Most of What You Believe about Poverty Is Wrong* (self-pub. (Morrisville: Lulu Publishing Services, 2017), 9–10.

16 Emily Ekins, "What Americans Think about Poverty, Wealth, and Work," *Cato Institute 2019 Welfare, Work, and Wealth National Survey*, Cato Institute (2019), accessed April 18, 2020, https://www.cato.org/publications/survey-reports /what-americans-think-about-poverty-wealth-work#overview.

17 Mauricio Miller, *The Alternative: Most of What You Believe about Poverty Is Wrong* (self-pub. (Morrisville: Lulu Publishing Services, 2017).

18 DallasObserver.com, "The 100 Best Dallas Restaurants of 2020: Café Momentum," *Dallas Observer*, accessed April 18, 2020, https://www.dallasobserver.com/top-100-dallas -restaurants/cafe-momentum-7617179.

19 CBS.com, "'We Want to Provide Hope': LA Rams, Café Momentum Host Pop-up Dinner to Help At-Risk Youth," *CBS Los Angeles*, September 23, 2019, https://losangeles.cbslocal .com/2019/09/23/la-rams-cafe-momentum-reentry/.

20 "The AFCARS Report," U.S. Department of Health and Human Services, Administration for Children and Families, Administration on Children, Youth and Families, Children's Bureau (2019), accessed April 18, 2020, 1, https://www.acf.hhs.gov/sites/default/files/cb /afcarsreport26.pdf.

21 Mark E. Courtney, et al., "Midwest Evaluation of the Adult Functioning of Former Foster Youth Outcomes at Age 26," Chapin Hall at the University of Chicago (2011), accessed April 18, 2020, 113, https://www.chapinhall.org/wp-content/uploads/Midwest-Eval-Outcomes-at-Age-26.pdf; Tina Polihronakis, "Mental Health Care Issues of Children and Youth in Foster Care," National Resource Center for Family-Centered Practice and Permanency Planning at the Hunter College School of Social Work (2008), accessed April 18, 2020, 3, http://www.hunter.cuny.edu/socwork/nrcfcpp/downloads/information_packets /Mental_Health.pdf.

22 "The AFCARS Report," U.S. Department of Health and Human Services, Administration for Children and Families, Administration on Children, Youth and Families, Children's Bureau (2019), accessed April 18, 2020, 3, https://www.acf.hhs.gov/sites/default/files/cb /afcarsreport26.pdf.

23 "Key Substance Use and Mental Health Indicators in the United States: Results from the 2018 National Survey on Drug Use and Health," Substance Abuse and Mental Health Services Administration (2019), accessed April 18, 2020, 50–51, https://www.samhsa.gov /data/sites/default/files/cbhsq-reports/NSDUHNationalFindingsReport2018 /NSDUHNationalFindingsReport2018.pdf.

24   Manny Fernandez, Richard Pérez-Peña, and Jonah Engel Bromwich, "Five Dallas Officers Were Killed as Payback, Police Chief Says," *New York Times*, July 8, 2016.

Chapter Seven

1   Maria Montessori, *The Discovery of the Child* (Delhi: Aakbar Books, 2004), 141.

2   Valerie J. Calderon and Daniela Yu, "Student Enthusiasm Falls as High School Graduation Nears," Gallup (2017), accessed April 18, 2020, https://news.gallup.com/opinion /gallup/211631/student-enthusiasm-falls-high-school-graduation-nears.aspx.

3   Joel McFarland, et al., "The Condition of Education 2019," National Center for Education Statistics (2019), accessed April 18, 2020, 103, https://nces.ed.gov/pubs2019/2019144.pdf.

4   Joel McFarland, et al., "The Condition of Education 2019," National Center for Education Statistics (2019), accessed April 18, 2020, 91, https://nces.ed.gov/pubs2019/2019144.pdf.

5   Mary Nguyen Barry and Michael Dannenberg, "Out of Pocket: The High Cost of Inadequate High Schools and High School Student Achievement on College Affordability," Education Reform Now (2016), accessed April 18, 2020, 5, https://edreformnow.org/wp-content /uploads/2016/04/EdReformNow-O-O-P-Embargoed-Final.pdf.

6   "From Great Recession to Great Reshuffling: Charting a Decade of Change across American Communities," Economic Innovation Group (2018), accessed April 18, 2020, 22–23, https://eig.org/wp-content/uploads/2018/10/2018-DCI.pdf.

7   Jeremy Bauer-Wolf, "Overconfident Students, Dubious Employers," Inside Higher Ed, February 23, 2018, https://www.insidehighered.com/news/2018/02/23 /study-students-believe-they-are-prepared-workplace-employers-disagree.

8   Nan Stone, "Does Business Have Any Business in Education?," *Harvard Business Review*, March–April 1991, https://hbr.org/1991/03/does-business-have-any-business-in -education; Sam Dillon, "What Corporate America Can't Build: A Sentence," *New York Times*, December 7, 2004, https://www.nytimes.com/2004/12/07/business/what -corporate-america-cant-build-a-sentence.html.

9   Stephanie Marken, "Half in U.S. Now Consider College Very Important," Gallup, December 30, 2019, https://www.gallup.com/education/272228/half-consider-college-education -important.aspx.

10   Center for Microeconomic Data, "Quarterly Report on Household Debt and Credit 2019 Q4," Federal Reserve Bank of New York Research and Statistics Group (2020), accessed April 18, 2020, https://www.newyorkfed.org/medialibrary/interactives/householdcredit /data/pdf/hhdc_2019q4.pdf.

11   Western Governors University, "Teacher Licensure State Requirements," accessed April 17,

2020, https://www.wgu.edu/online-teaching-degrees/state-licensure.html#close.

12   Richard Vedder, "'Kill All the Administrators' (Not Really)," *Forbes*, March 10, 2018, https://
www.forbes.com/sites/richardvedder/2018/05/10/kill-alll-the-administrators
-not-really/#e74d2056210a.

13   Benjamin Scafidi, "The Dismal Productivity Trend for K–12 Public Schools and How to
Improve It," *Cato Journal* 36, no. 1 (2016): 122–23, https://www.cato.org/sites/cato.org
/files/serials/files/cato-journal/2016/2/cato-journal-v36n1-9.pdf.

14   Richard K. Vedder, *Restoring the Promise: Higher Education in America* (Oakland, CA:
Independent Institute, 2019), chap. 10, para. 5, Kindle edition.

15   "Frustration in the Schools," *Kappan Magazine*, August 26, 2019, K21, https://
kappanonline.org/wp-content/uploads/2019/08/pdk_101_1_PollSupplement.pdf.

16   Neal McCluskey, "Show Me the (Education) Money!," *Cato at Liberty*, April 20, 2018,
https://www.cato.org/blog/show-me-education-money; "Long-Term Trends in Reading
and Mathematics Achievement," National Center for Education Statistics, accessed April
17, 2020, https://nces.ed.gov/fastfacts/display.asp?id=38.

17   There has been near-zero percent improvement in 12th-grade reading and math scores;
furthermore, math and reading scores for all students have flatlined over the last decade.
"Data: Breaking Down the Where and Why of K-12 Spending," *Education Week*, September
24, 2019, https://www.edweek.org/ew/section/multimedia/the-where-and-why-of-k-12
-spending.html; "Long-Term Trends in Reading and Mathematics Achievement," National
Center for Education Statistics, accessed April 17, 2020, https://nces.ed.gov/fastfacts
/display.asp?id=38.

18   "Our Work," Narrative 4, accessed April 13, 2020, https://narrative4.com/about/our-work/.

19   Walton Family Foundation Press Release, "4.0 Launches $15M Fund to Grow the Field of
Education Entrepreneurs and Expand Innovative Approaches to New Schools," June 21,
2019, https://www.waltonfamilyfoundation.org/about-us/newsroom/4-0-launches-15m
-fund-to-grow-the-field-of-education-entrepreneurs-and-expand-innovative-approaches
-to-new-schools.

20   College Board, "Trends in College Pricing, 2019," *Trends in Higher Education Series*,
November 2019, 9–10, https://research.collegeboard.org/pdf/trends-college-pricing-2019
-full-report.pdf.

21   OpenStax Website, accessed April 16, 2020, https://openstax.org/impact.

22   FIRE Website, "Chicago Statement: University and Faculty Support," February 6,
2020, accessed April 18, 2020, https://www.thefire.org/get-involved/student-network/
take-action/adopting-the-chicago-statement/.

23   "Report on the Committee of Freedom of Expression," accessed on April 16, 2020,
      https://provost.uchicago.edu/sites/default/files/documents/reports/FOECommittee
      Report.pdf.

24   Rachel Leingang, "How Michael Crow Took ASU from a Party School to the Nation's Most
      Innovative University," *AZ Central*, April 3, 2019, https://www.azcentral.com/in-depth
      /news/local/arizona-education/2019/02/28/michael-crow-changing-arizona-state
      -university-reputation-party-school-asu-innovation-global-brand/2670463002/.

25   "Most Innovative Schools," *U.S. News and World Report*, accessed April 10, 2020, https://
      www.usnews.com/best-colleges/rankings/national-universities/innovative.

26   "Enrollment History: Headcount / FTE / SCH, 1970 to Present," Arizona State
      University Office of Institutional Analysis, accessed April 10, 2020, https://uoia.asu.edu/;
      CollegeFactual, "Ethnic Diversity," accessed April 10, 2020, https://www.collegefactual.com/.

27   Student Based Allocation 101, "Edunomics Lab" (2015), https://edunomicslab.org
      /wp-content/uploads/2015/01/SBA101.pdf.

28   William G. Ouchi, "Accept No Substitutes for Real Decentralization," *Education Week*,
      October 30, 2009, https://www.edweek.org/ew/articles/2009/11/04/10ouchi_ep.h29.html.

29   David Osborne and Emily Langhorne, "Can Urban Districts Get Charter-Like Performance
      with Charter-Lite Schools?," Progressive Policy Institute (2018), accessed April 20, 2020,
      2–3, https://www.progressivepolicy.org/publications/can-urban-districts-get
      -charter-like-performance-with-charter-lite-schools/.

30   "Open Enrollment Policies: State Profile—Arizona," Education Commission of the States
      (2018), accessed April 18, 2020, http://ecs.force.com/mbdata/mbstprofile?rep
      =OE18ST&st=Arizona.

31   West Virginia Legislature, House, "An Act to amend and reenact §5-16-2 and §5-16-22 of
      the Code of West Virginia, 1931, as amended," HB 206, 2019 First Extraordinary Session,
      https://www.wvlegislature.gov/Bill_Text_HTML/2019_SESSIONS/1X/bills/HB206%20
      ENR.pdf.

32   Travis Pillow, "Putting Florida's Preschool Programs in Perspective," RedefinED (2015),
      accessed April 17, 2020, https://www.redefinedonline.org/2015/05
      /putting-floridas-preschool-programs-in-perspective/.

33   Allison H. Friedman-Krauss, "The State of Preschool 2018," National Institute for Early
      Education Research (2019), accessed April 18, 2020, 68–69, http://nieer.org/wp
      -content/uploads/2019/08/YB2018_Full-ReportR3wAppendices.pdf; "About Voluntary
      Prekindergarten," Florida Department of Education, accessed April 17, 2020, http://
      www.floridaearlylearning.com/vpk/floridas-vpk-program.

34   "Florida—Family Empowerment Scholarship Program," EdChoice, accessed April 17, 2020,
      https://www.edchoice.org/school-choice/programs/florida-family-empowerment
      -scholarship-program/.

35   "Arizona—Empowerment Scholarship Accounts," EdChoice, accessed April 17, 2020,
      https://www.edchoice.org/school-choice/programs/arizona-empowerment
      -scholarship-accounts/.

36   Scott Cohn, "Forget Taking Out a Student Loan. Purdue University Has Come Up with a
      New Way to Pay for College," cnbc.com, last updated February 15, 2019, accessed April 18,
      2020, https://www.cnbc.com/2019/02/08/purdue-university-introduces-first
      -income-sharing-agreement-for-students-.html.

37   Carla Otto, "Tackling the Skills Gap with a Technical School Partnership," *IndustryWeek*,
      April 23, 2019, https://www.industryweek.com/talent/article/22027494/tackling
      -the-skills-gap-with-a-technical-school-partnership; Julia Freeland Fisher, "As Cities Axe
      Summer Youth Work Programs, Here Are Alternatives to Consider," EdSurge, April 14,
      2020, https://www.edsurge.com/news/2020-04-14-as-cities-axe-summer-youth-work
      -programs-here-are-alternatives-to-consider; Hallie Busta, "Why Western Governors U
      Thinks Microcredentials Are the Path to Degrees," *Education Dive*, September 24, 2019,
      https://www.educationdive.com/news/why-western-governors-u-thinks-microcredentials
      -are-the-path-to-degrees/563454/; Natalie Schwartz, "Google to Expand IT Certificate to
      100 Community Colleges," *Education Dive*, October 4, 2019, https://www.educationdive
      .com/news/google-to-expand-it-certificate-to-100-community-colleges/564410/.

38   Paul Fain, "On-Ramps and Off-Ramps: Alternative Credentials and Emerging Pathways
      between Education and Work," An Inside Higher Ed Special Report (2018), accessed April
      18, 2020, https://www.insidehighered.com/sites/default/server_files/media/IHE
      -On-Ramps-and-Off-Ramps-Alternative-Credentials-Preview.pdf.

Chapter Eight

1   Quote is attributed to Jefferson by William Jennings Bryan. See William Jennings Bryan,
     "Imperialism," Voices of Democracy: U.S. Oratory Project, accessed April 18, 2020, para. 5,
     https://voicesofdemocracy.umd.edu/william-jennings-bryan-imperialism-speech-text/.

2   Paul L. Poirot, "Ownership as a Social Function," in *Toward Liberty: Essays in Honor of
     Ludwig von Mises on the Occasion of his 90th Birthday, September 29, 1971*, Vol. 2, ed. F.A.
     Hayek, Henry Hazlitt, Leonard R. Read, Gustavo Velasco, and F.A. Harper (Menlo Park:
     Institute for Humane Studies, 1971), 296.

3   Dick M. Carpenter and John K. Ross, "The Power of One Entrepreneur: Melony Armstrong,

African Hairbraider," Institute for Justice (2009), accessed April 18, 2020, https://ij.org
/wp-content/uploads/2015/03/powerofone-armstrong.pdf.

4   Paul Avelar and Nick Sibilla, "Untangling Regulations: Natural Hair Braiders Fight against
      Irrational Licensing," A Report by the Institute for Justice (2014), accessed April 18, 2020,
      https://ij.org/wp-content/uploads/2015/03/untangling-regulations.pdf.

5   Dick M. Carpenter and John K. Ross, "The Power of One Entrepreneur: Melony Armstrong,
      African Hairbraider," Institute for Justice (2009), accessed April 18, 2020, 11–12, https://
      ij.org/wp-content/uploads/2015/03/powerofone-armstrong.pdf.

6   Dick M. Carpenter and John K. Ross, "The Power of One Entrepreneur: Melony Armstrong,
      African Hairbraider," Institute for Justice (2009), accessed April 18, 2020, 11–12, https://
      ij.org/wp-content/uploads/2015/03/powerofone-armstrong.pdf.

7   Evan Cunningham, "Professional Certifications and Occupational Licenses: Evidence from
      the Current Population Survey," Bureau of Labor Statistics (2019), accessed April 18, 2020,
      https://www.bls.gov/opub/mlr/2019/article/professional-certifications-and
      -occupational-licenses.htm.

8   U.S. Bureau of Labor Statistics, "Professional Certifications and Occupational Licenses:
      Evidence from the Current Population Survey," *Monthly Labor Review* (2019), accessed
      April 18, 2020, https://www.bls.gov/opub/mlr/2019/article/professional
      -certifications-and-occupational-licenses.htm.

9   Rebecca Haw Allensworth, "Foxes at the Henhouse: Occupational Licensing Boards Up
      Close," *California Law Review* 105, no. 6 (2017): 1570.

10   Dick M. Carpenter II, et al., "License to Work: A National Study of Burdens from Occupational
      Licensing, 2nd Edition," Institute for Justice (2017), accessed April 18, 2020, 80, https://ij.org
      /wp-content/themes/ijorg/images/ltw2/License_to_Work_2nd_Edition.pdf.

11   Matthew D. Mitchell, "Ohio Occupational Licensure and Universal Recognition,"
      Mercatus Center at George Mason University (2020), accessed April 20, 2020,
      4–5, https://www.mercatus.org/system/files/mitchell_-_testimony_-_ohio
      _occupational_licensure_and_universal_recognition_-_v1.pdf.

12   Morris M. Kleiner and Evgeny S. Vorotnikov, "At What Cost?: State and National Estimates
      of the Economic Costs of Occupational Licensing," Institute for Justice (2018), accessed
      April 20, 2020, 5, https://ij.org/wp-content/uploads/2018/11/Licensure_Report_WEB.pdf.

13   Stephen Slivinski, "Bootstraps Tangled in Red Tape: How State Occupational Licensing
      Hinders Low-Income Entrepreneurship," Goldwater Institute (2015), accessed April 20,
      2020, 1, https://goldwaterinstitute.org/wp.content/uploads/cms_page_media/2015/4/15
      /OccLicensingKauffman.pdf.

14   Morris M. Kleiner and Evgeny S. Vorotnikov, "At What Cost?: State and National Estimates of the Economic Costs of Occupational Licensing," Institute for Justice (2018), accessed April 20, 2020, 5, https://ij.org/wp-content/uploads/2018/11/Licensure_Report_WEB.pdf.

15   Matthew D. Mitchell, "Occupational Licensing and the Poor and Disadvantaged," Mercatus Center at George Mason University (2017), accessed April 20, 2020, 2, https:// www.mercatus.org/publications/corporate-welfare/occupational-licensing-and -poor-and-disadvantaged.

16   Douglas R. Nelson, "The Political Economy of U.S. Automobile Protection," *National Bureau of Economic Research* (January 1996): 126–146, https://www.nber.org/chapters /c8705.pdf?new_window=1.

17   Anna Barlett and Yesim Yilmaz, "Taxicab Medallions—a Review of Experiences in Other Cities," Government of the District of Columbia, Office of the Chief Financial Officer, Office of Revenue Analysis Briefing Note (2011), accessed April 20, 2020, http://cfo.dc.gov/sites /default/files/dc/sites/ocfo/publication/attachments/ocfo_taxicab_briefing_note.pdf.

18   Sam Harnett, "Cities Made Millions Selling Taxi Medallions, Now Drivers Are Paying the Price," *NPR*, October 15, 2018, https://www.npr.org/2018/10/15/656595597 /cities-made-millions-selling-taxi-medallions-now-drivers-are-paying-the-price.

19   Matthew D. Mitchell, *The Pathology of Privilege: The Economic Consequences of Government Favoritism* (Arlington, VA: Mercatus Center at George Mason University, 2014), 3-14; Bruce L. Benson and Matthew Brown, "Eminent Domain for Private Use: Is It Justified by Market Failure or an Example of Government Failure," in *Property Rights: Eminent Domain and Regulatory Takings Re-Examined*, ed. Bruce L. Benson (New York: Palgrave Macmillan, 2010), 149–72.

20   James Boswell, *The Life of Samuel Johnson, L. L. D.: Complete and Unabridged with Notes* (New York: Modern Library, 1957), 525.

21   David T. Scheffman and Richard S. Higgins, "Twenty Years of Raising Rivals' Costs: History, Assessment, and Future," *George Mason Law Review* 12, no. 2 (2004).

22   "Code of Federal Regulations Total Pages 1938-1949, and Total Volumes and Pages 1950– 2019," National Archives and Records Administration, accessed April 14, 2020, https:// www.federalregister.gov/reader-aids/understanding-the-federal-register /federal-register-statistics.

23   "Dynamism in Retreat: Consequences for Regions, Markets, and Workers," Economic Innovation Group (2017), accessed April 20, 2020, 8, https://eig.org/wp-content /uploads/2017/07/Dynamism-in-Retreat-A.pdf.

24   "An Update to the Budget and Economic Outlook: 2019 to 2029," Congressional Budget

Office (2019), accessed April 20, 2020, 26, https://www.cbo.gov/system/files /2019-08/55551-CBO-outlook-update_0.pdf.

25   Tad DeHaven, "Corporate Welfare in the Federal Budget," Cato Institute (2012), accessed April 20, 2020, https://www.cato.org/sites/cato.org/files/pubs/pdf/PA703.pdf; Cailin R. Slattery and Owen M. Zidar, "Evaluating State and Local Tax Incentives," National Bureau of Economic Research (2020), accessed April 20, 2020, 1, https://scholar.princeton.edu /sites/default/files/zidar/files/slattery-zidar-taxincentives-2020.pdf.

26   Cailin R. Slattery and Owen M. Zidar, "Evaluating State and Local Tax Incentives," National Bureau of Economic Research (2020), accessed April 20, 2020, https://scholar.princeton .edu/sites/default/files/zidar/files/slattery-zidar-taxincentives-2020.pdf.

27   Cailin R. Slattery and Owen M. Zidar, "Evaluating State and Local Tax Incentives," National Bureau of Economic Research (2020), accessed April 20, 2020, 15–16, https://scholar. princeton.edu/sites/default/files/zidar/files/slattery-zidar-taxincentives-2020.pdf.

28   Timothy J. Bartik, "'But For' Percentages for Economic Development Incentives: What Percentage Estimates Are Plausible Based on the Research Literature," W.E. Upjohn Institute for Employment Research (2018), accessed April 20, 2020, abstract, https:// research.upjohn.org/cgi/viewcontent.cgi?article=1307&context=up_workingpapers.

29   Cailin R. Slattery and Owen M. Zidar, "Evaluating State and Local Tax Incentives," National Bureau of Economic Research (2020), accessed April 20, 2020, 12, https://scholar .princeton.edu/sites/default/files/zidar/files/slattery-zidar-taxincentives-2020.pdf.

30   Jason Silverstein, "How Will Amazon Use the Data It Got from Cities Bidding on Its HQ2?," *CBS News*, November 15, 2018, https://www.cbsnews.com/news/amazon-new-hq2 -bidding-process-gave-the-company-priceless-data-on-cities-how-will-it-be-used/.

31   Associated Press, "Amazon's New Virginia Headquarters Get $23M in County Incentives, Despite Protests," *USA Today*, March 17, 2019, https://www.usatoday.com /story/money/2019/03/17/amazons-new-virginia-headquarters-get-23-m-county -incentives/3194172002/.

32   Jacob Passy, "This Is What Amazon's 'HQ2' Was Going to Cost New York Taxpayers," *Market Watch*, February 16, 2019, https://www.marketwatch.com/story /what-amazons-hq2-means-for-taxpayers-in-new-york-and-virginia-2018-11-14.

33   National Conference of State Legislators, "CON-Certificate of Need State Laws," December 1, 2019, https://www.ncsl.org/research/health/con-certificate-of-need-state-laws.aspx.

34   United States Department of Justice, "Competition in Health Care and Certificates of Need: Joint Statement of the Antitrust Division of the U.S. Department of Justice and the Federal Trade Commission before the Illinois Task Force on Health Planning Reform,"

September 15, 2008, https://www.justice.gov/atr/competition-health-care-and
-certificates-need-joint-statement-antitrust-division-us-department#N_25.

35   Thomas Stratmann and Christopher Koopman, "Entry Regulation and Rural Health Care:
     Certificate-of-Need Laws, Ambulatory Surgical Centers, and Community Hospitals,"
     Mercatus Center at George Mason University (2016), accessed April 20, 2020, 18, https://
     www.mercatus.org/publications/regulation/entry-regulation-and
     -rural-health-care-certificate-need-laws-ambulatory.

36   Angela C. Erickson, "States Are Suspending Certificate of Need Laws in the Wake of
     COVID-19 but the Damage Might Already Be Done," Pacific Legal Foundation (blog),
     March 31, 2020, accessed April 29, 2020, https://pacificlegal.org/certificate-of-need
     -laws-covid-19/.

37   Bentley Coffey, Patrick A. McLaughlin, and Pietro Peretto. "The Cumulative Cost of
     Regulations," Mercatus Center at George Mason University (2016), accessed April 20,
     2020, 8, https://www.mercatus.org/publications/regulation/cumulative-cost-regulations.

38   Matthew D. Mitchell, Scott Eastman, and Tamara Winter, "A Culture of Favoritism:
     Corporate Privilege and Beliefs about Markets and Government," Mercatus Center at
     George Mason University (2019), accessed April 20, 2020, 23–24, 47-48, https://www
     .mercatus.org/system/files/mitchell-culture-favoritism-mercatus-special-study-v1.pdf.

39   According to Gallup, the percentage of Americans with very little confidence in big busi-
     ness has increased since they began tracking business confidence in 1973. "Confidence in
     Institutions," Gallup, accessed April 22, 2020, https://news.gallup.com/poll/1597
     /confidence-institutions.aspx.

40   Mohamed Younis, "Four in 10 Americans Embrace Some Form of Socialism," Gallup (2019),
     accessed April 20, 2020, https://news.gallup.com/poll/257639/four-americans
     -embrace-form-socialism.aspx; VictimsofCommunism.org, "Annual Report on U.S.
     Attitudes Toward Socialism, Communism, and Collectivism," October 2019, https://
     www.victimsofcommunism.org/2019-annual-poll.

41   "Most Think Government, Big Business Work Together against America," Rasmussen
     Reports (2016), accessed April 20, 2020, https://www.rasmussenreports.com/public
     _content/politics/general_politics/july_2016/most_think_government_big_business
     _work_together_against_america; Matthew D. Mitchell, "Public Perceptions of Markets,
     Government, and Favoritism," Mercatus Center at George Mason University (2019),
     accessed April 15, 2020, 8, https://www.mercatus.org/publications/corporate-welfare
     /public-perceptions-markets-government-and-favoritism.

42   Russell Roberts, "Gambling with Other People's Money: How Perverted Incentives Caused

the Financial Crisis," Mercatus Center (2010), accessed April 20, 2020, https://www.mercatus.org/system/files/RUSS-final.pdf; John A. Allison, *The Financial Crisis and the Free Market Cure: Why Pure Capitalism Is the World Economy's Only Hope* (New York: McGraw-Hill, 2013), 14–15.

43   Joe Weisenthal, "The 4 Things That Worry Jamie Dimon," *Business Insider*, February 4, 2013, https://www.businessinsider.com/the-four-things-that-worry-jamie-dimon-2013-2.

44   FRED Economic Data, "Commercial Banks in the U.S.," accessed April 18, 2020, https://fred.stlouisfed.org/graph/?id=USNUM,US100NUM; Michael D. Bordo and John V. Duca, "The Impact of the Dodd-Frank on Small Businesses," Hoover Institution Economics Working Papers (2018), accessed April 20, 2020, 8, https://www.hoover.org/sites/default/files/research/docs/18106-bordo-duca.pdf.

45   Bianca Peter, "Bank Market Share by Deposits and Assets," *Wallet Hub*, September 16, 2019, https://wallethub.com/edu/sa/bank-market-share-by-deposits/25587/.

46   Rob Nichols, "Yes, Community Banks Are Struggling under Dodd-Frank," *Politico*, September 6, 2016, https://www.politico.com/agenda/story/2016/09/community-banks-dodd-frank-000197/.

47   Olivia Oran, "Big Banks' Relationship with Dodd-Frank: It's Complicated," Reuters, November 23, 2016, https://www.reuters.com/article/us-usa-trump-banks/big-banks-relationship-with-dodd-frank-its-complicated-idUSKBN13I1YA.

48   "Regulation Is Good for Goldman," *Wall Street Journal*, February 11, 2015, https://www.wsj.com/articles/regulation-is-good-for-goldman-1423700859.

49   Inti Pacheco and Josh Zumbrun, "The Steel Industry Gets What It Wants on Tariffs," *Wall Street Journal*, October 22, 2018, https://www.wsj.com/articles/u-s-steelmakers-early-champions-of-tariffs-shift-focus-to-making-them-go-away-1540200601; Peter Navarro, "Trump Steel Tariffs Bring Hope, Prosperity Back to Granite City," WhiteHouse.gov, July 26, 2018, https://www.whitehouse.gov/articles/trump-steel-tariffs-bring-hope-prosperity-back-granite-city/.

50   Gary Clyde Hufbauer and Euijin Jung, "Steel Profits Gain, but Steel Users Pay, under Trump's Protectionism," Peterson Institute for International Economics (2018), accessed April 20, 2020, https://www.piie.com/blogs/trade-investment-policy-watch/steel-profits-gain-steel-users-pay-under-trumps-protectionism.

51   Aaron Flaaen and Justin Pierce, "Disentangling the Effects of the 2018-2019 Tariffs on a Globally Connected U.S. Manufacturing Sector," Federal Reserve Board (2019), accessed April 20, 2020, 1, https://www.federalreserve.gov/econres/feds/files/2019086pap.pdf.

52   Joseph Francois and Laura M. Baughman, "The Unintended Consequences of U.S. Steel Import Tariffs: A Quantification of the Impact During 2002," Trade Partnership

Worldwide LLC (2003), accessed April 20, 2020, 12, http://tradepartnership.com/wp
-content/uploads/2014/06/2002jobstudy.pdf.

53   The Editorial Board, "Trump's Political Tariff Bureaucracy," *Wall Street Journal*, August 6,
2018, https://www.wsj.com/articles/trumps-political-tariff-bureaucracy-1533597856.

54   Christine McDaniel, "Investigating Product Exclusion Requests for Section 301 Tariffs: An
Update," Mercatus Center at George Mason University (2019), accessed April 20, 2020,
https://www.mercatus.org/bridge/commentary/investigating-product-exclusion
-requests-section-301-tariffs-update.

55   David Nicklaus, "Missouri Nail Maker Wins Tariff Exemption and Begins Planning a
Comeback," *St. Louis Post-Dispatch*, April 5, 2019, https://www.stltoday.com/business
/columns/david-nicklaus/missouri-nail-maker-wins-tariff-exemption-and-begins
-planning-a/article_6ef61b35-014f-5c57-bb52-50f7f3e4542a.html.

56   David Nicklaus, "Missouri Nail Maker Wins Tariff Exemption and Begins Planning a
Comeback," *St. Louis Post-Dispatch*, April 5, 2019, https://www.stltoday.com/business
/columns/david-nicklaus/missouri-nail-maker-wins-tariff-exemption-and-begins
-planning-a/article_6ef61b35-014f-5c57-bb52-50f7f3e4542a.html.

57   Chad P. Brown, "Trump's Steel and Aluminum Tariffs Are Cascading Out of Control,"
Peterson Institute for International Economics (2020), accessed April 20, 2020, https://
www.piie.com/blogs/trade-and-investment-policy-watch
/trumps-steel-and-aluminum-tariffs-are-cascading-out-control.

58   Jacob Bunge and Jesse Newman, "USDA Sets Plans for $16 Billion in New Aid to Farmers,"
Wall Street Journal, July 25, 2019, https://www.wsj.com/articles
/usda-sets-plans-for-16-billion-in-new-aid-to-farmers-11564065120.

59   Matthew D. Mitchell, "Public Perceptions of Markets, Government, and Favoritism,"
Mercatus Center at George Mason University (2019), accessed April 20, 2020, 9, https://
www.mercatus.org/publications/corporate-welfare
/public-perceptions-markets-government-and-favoritism.

60   NFU Government Relations Staff, "RFS, Corn, and the Farm Economy," Iowa Farmers
Union, accessed April 18, 2020, https://iowafarmersunion.org/rfs-corn
-and-the-farm-economy/.

61   Mene Ukueberuwa, "Boomer Socialism Led to Bernie Sanders," *Wall Street Journal*,
January 17, 2020, https://www.wsj.com/articles
/boomer-socialism-led-to-bernie-sanders-11579304307.

62   Institute for Justice, Melony Armstrong, Braiding Freedom, accessed April 18, 2020, http://
braidingfreedom.com/braiding-initiative/supporters/melony-armstrong/.

63   StandTogether.org, "How One Hair-Braider Unlocked Opportunity for Entrepreneurs,"

accessed April 18, 2020, https://standtogether.org/2020/01/09
/when-one-entrepreneurs-tenacity-creates-opportunity-for-others/.

64   Nick Sibilla, "New Mississippi Law Will Rein in Licensing Boards, Regulate State
Regulators," *Forbes*, April 13, 2017, https://www.forbes.com/sites/instituteforjustice
/2017/04/13/new-mississippi-law-will-rein-in-licensing-boards-regulate-state
-regulators/#1d094bc21715.

65   Morris M. Kleiner and Evgeny S. Vorotnikov, "At What Cost? State and National Estimates of
the Economic Costs of Occupational Licensing," Institute for Justice (2019), accessed April
20, 2020, 18, https://ij.org/wp-content/uploads/2018/11/Licensure_Report_WEB.pdf.

66   Trevor Smith, Timothy Lee, and Bryon Allen, "The Support for Freedom Index," The Fund
for American Studies (2017), accessed April 20, 2020, 40, https://tfas.org/wp-content
/uploads/2017/04/Freedom-Support-Study_2017.pdf?; Department of the Treasury Office
of Economic Policy, the Council of Economic Advisers, and the Department of Labor,
"Occupational Licensing: A Framework for Policymakers," White House Archives (2015),
accessed April 20, 2020, https://obamawhitehouse.archives.gov/sites/default/files/docs
/licensing_report_final_nonembargo.pdf; "Economic Report of the President," White
House Archives (2020), accessed April 20, 2020, 95, https://www.whitehouse.gov/wp
-content/uploads/2020/02/2020-Economic-Report-of-the-President-WHCEA.pdf.

Chapter Nine

1   Frederick Douglass, *The Anti-Slavery Movement* (Rochester: Press of Lee, Mann & Co. Daily
American Office, 1835), 33.

2   "Weldon Angelos," FAMM, Families against Mandatory Minimums, accessed April 14,
2020, https://famm.org/stories/weldon-angelos/.

3   "Public Trust in Government: 1958–2019," Pew Research Center (2019), accessed April 15,
2020, https://www.people-press.org/2019/04/11/public-trust-in-government-1958-2019/.

4   George Washington, "Farewell Address to the People of the United States," September 19,
1796, 14, https://www.govinfo.gov/content/pkg/GPO-CDOC-106sdoc21/pdf/GPO-CDOC
-106sdoc21.pdf.

5   Carl Hulse, "Bipartisan Criminal Justice Overhaul Is Haunted by Willie Horton," *New York
Times*, January 4, 2016, https://www.nytimes.com/2016/01/05/us/politics
/bipartisan-criminal-justice-overhaul-is-haunted-by-willie-horton.html.

6   "Key Statistic: Total Correctional Population," Bureau of Justice Statistics, accessed April
18, 2020, https://www.bjs.gov/index.cfm?ty=kfdetail&iid=487.

7   Roy Walmsley, "World Prison Population List, Twelfth Edition," Institute for Criminal

Policy Research, accessed April 18, 2020, 2, https://www.prisonstudies.org/sites/default
/files/resources/downloads/wppl_12.pdf.

8   Jeremy Travis, Bruce Western, and Steve Redburn, eds., *The Growth of Incarceration in the
United States: Exploring Causes and Consequences* (Washington, DC: National Academies
Press, 2014), 92–101.

9   Gary Fields and John R. Emshwiller, "As Criminal Laws Proliferate, More Are Ensnared,"
Wall Street Journal, July 23, 2011, https://www.wsj.com/articles/SB1000142405274870374
9504576172714184601654.

10   Brian W. Walsh and Tiffany M. Joslyn, "Without Intent: How Congress Is Eroding the
Criminal Intent Requirement in Federal Law," National Association of Criminal Defense
Lawyers and Heritage Foundation (2010), accessed April 20, 2020, 6, https://www.nacdl
.org/Document/WithoutIntentHowCongressIsErodingCriminalIntentReq.

11   John S. Baker Jr., "Revisiting the Explosive Growth of Federal Crimes," Heritage
Foundation (2008), accessed April 20, 2020, 1, https://www.heritage.org/report
/revisiting-the-explosive-growth-federal-crimes.

12   John C. Coffee Jr., "Does 'Unlawful' Mean 'Criminal'?: Reflections on the Disappearing Tort/
Crime Distinction in American Law," *Boston University Law Review* 71, no. 1 (1991): 216.

13   Harvey Silverglate, *Three Felonies A Day: How the Feds Target the Innocent* (New York:
Encounter Books, 2011).

14   Ram Subramanian and Ruth Delaney, "Playbook for Change?: States Reconsider
Mandatory Sentences," Vera Institute for Justice (2014), accessed April 20, 2020, 5–7,
https://www.prisonpolicy.org/scans/vera/mandatory-sentences-policy-report-v2b.pdf.

15   Kevin R. Reitz, "The Disassembly and Reassembly of U.S. Sentencing Practices," in
Sentencing and Sanctions in Western Countries, ed. Michael Tonry and Richard S. Frase
(Oxford: Oxford University Press, 2001), 224–25.

16   "Mandatory Minimum Sentences Decline, Sentencing Commission Says," United States
Courts (2017), accessed April 20, 2020, https://www.uscourts.gov/news/2017/07/25
/mandatory-minimum-sentences-decline-sentencing-commission-says.

17   "Criminal Justice Facts," Sentencing Project, accessed April 15, 2020, https://www
.sentencingproject.org/criminal-justice-facts/.

18   Erica Goode, "Stronger Hand for Judges in the 'Bazaar' of Plea Deals," *New York Times*,
March 22, 2012, https://www.nytimes.com/2012/03/23/us/stronger-hand-for-judges-after
-rulings-on-plea-deals.html.

19   Timothy Hughes and Doris James Wilson, "Reentry Trends in the U.S.," Bureau of Justice
Statistics, accessed April 15, 2020, https://www.bjs.gov/content/reentry/reentry.cfm.

20   "Collateral Consequences: The Crossroads of Punishment, Redemption, and the Effects on Communities," U.S. Commission on Civil Rights (2019), accessed April 20, 2020, 35, https://www.usccr.gov/pubs/2019/06-13-Collateral-Consequences.pdf.

21   Adam Looney and Nicholas Turner, "Work and Opportunity before and after Incarceration," Brookings Institution (2018), accessed April 20, 2020, 7, 10, https://www.brookings.edu/wp-content/uploads/2018/03/es_20180314_looneyincarceration_final.pdf.

22   Adam Looney and Nicholas Turner, "Work and Opportunity before and after Incarceration," Brookings Institution (2018), accessed April 20, 2020, 7, 10, https://www.brookings.edu/wp-content/uploads/2018/03/es_20180314_looneyincarceration_final.pdf.

23   Mariel Alper, Matthew R. Durose, and Joshua Markman, "2018 Update on Prisoner Recidivism: A 9-Year Follow-Up Period (2005-2014)," Bureau of Justice Statistics (2018), accessed April 20, 2020, 1, https://www.bjs.gov/content/pub/pdf/18upr9yfup0514.pdf; "Recidivism among Federal Offenders: A Comprehensive Overview," United States Sentencing Commission (2016), accessed April 20, 2020, 5, https://www.ussc.gov/sites/default/files/pdf/research-and-publications/research-publications/2016/recidivism_overview.pdf.

24   Bruce Western and Becky Petit, "Collateral Costs: Incarceration's Effect on Economic Mobility," Pew Charitable Trusts (2010), accessed April 20, 2020, 4, https://www.pewtrusts.org/en/research-and-analysis/reports/0001/01/01/collateral-costs.

25   Bruce Western and Becky Petit, "Collateral Costs: Incarceration's Effect on Economic Mobility," Pew Charitable Trusts (2010), accessed April 20, 2020, 18, https://www.pewtrusts.org/en/research-and-analysis/reports/0001/01/01/collateral-costs.

26   John Gramlich, "5 Facts about Crime in the U.S.," *FactTank*, October 17, 2019, https://www.pewresearch.org/fact-tank/2019/10/17/facts-about-crime-in-the-u-s/.

27   Christopher T. Lowenkamp, Marie VanNostrand, and Alexander Holsinger, "The Hidden Costs of Pretrial Detention," Laura and John Arnold Foundation (2013), accessed April 20, 2020, 3, https://craftmediabucket.s3.amazonaws.com/uploads/PDFs/LJAF_Report_hidden-costs_FNL.pdf.

28   Don Stemen, "The Prison Paradox: More Incarceration Will Not Make Us Safer," Vera Institute of Justice (2017), accessed April 20, 2020, 1, https://www.vera.org/downloads/publications/for-the-record-prison-paradox_02.pdf.

29   Jennifer Bronson and E. Ann Carson, "Prisoners in 2017," Bureau of Justice Statistics (2019), accessed April 20, 2020, 17, https://www.bjs.gov/content/pub/pdf/p17.pdf; "Race and Ethnicity," United States Census Bureau, accessed April 15, 2020, https://data.census.gov/cedsci/profilechartwidget?geoID=0100000US&metricFormat=percent&topic=Race&type=bar.

30   Sunha Choi, "Experiencing Financial Hardship with Medical Bills and Its Effects on Health
      Care Behavior: A 2-Year Panel Study," *Health Education & Behavior* 45, no. 4 (2017): 616-
      24; Malerie Lazar and Lisa Davenport, "Barriers to Health Care Access for Low Income
      Families: A Review of Literature," *Journal of Community Health Nursing* 35, no. 1 (2018):
      28-37; "Reforming America's Healthcare System through Choice and Competition,"
      U.S. Department of Health and Human Services, U.S. Department of the Treasury, U.S.
      Department of Labor (2018), accessed April 20, 2020, 30–94, https://www.hhs.gov
      /sites/default/files/Reforming-Americas-Healthcare-System-Through-Choice-and
      -Competition.pdf.

31   "The Budget and Economic Outlook: 2020–2030," Congressional Budget Office (2020),
      accessed April 20, 2020, 5–9, https://www.cbo.gov/publication/56073.

32   Cailin R. Slattery and Owen M. Zidar, "Evaluating State and Local Tax Incentives," National
      Bureau of Economic Research (2020), accessed April 20, 2020, 1, https://scholar.princeton
      .edu/sites/default/files/zidar/files/slattery-zidar-taxincentives-2020.pdf.

33   Jennifer Agiesta, "CNN Poll: 8 in 10 Back DACA, Supporters Hold Trump, GOP Responsible
      for Not Extending Program," *CNN*, February 28, 2018, https://www.cnn.com/2018/02/28
      /politics/cnn-poll-immigration-daca-trump/index.html.

34   Kim Hart, "Exclusive Poll: Most Democrats See Republicans as Racist, Sexist," *Axios*,
      November 12, 2018, https://www.axios.com/poll-democrats-and-republicans-hate-each
      -other-racist-ignorant-evil-99ae7afc-5a51-42be-8ee2-3959e43ce320.html.

35   Susan Page, "Divided We Fall? Americans See Our Angry Political Debate as 'A Big
      Problem,'" *USA Today*, December 5, 2019, https://www.usatoday.com/story/news/politics
      /elections/hiddencommonground/2019/12/05
      /hidden-common-ground-americans-divided-politics-seek-civility/4282301002/.

36   "Department of Justice Announces the Release of 3,100 Inmates under First Step Act,
      Publishes Risk and Needs Assessment System," Department of Justice (2019), accessed
      April 20, 2020, https://www.justice.gov/opa/pr/department-justice-announces
      -release-3100-inmates-under-first-step-act-publishes-risk-and.

37   Rachel D. Cohen and Ailsa Chang, "Federal Legislation Seeks Ban on Shackling of
      Pregnant Inmates," *NPR*, December 5, 2018, https://www.npr.org/sections/health
      -shots/2018/12/05/673757680/federal-legislation-seeks-ban-on-shackling-of
      -pregnant-inmates; "First Step Act," Office of Education & Sentencing Practice (2019),
      accessed April 20, 2020, 4, https://www.ussc.gov/sites/default/files/pdf/training
      /newsletters/2019-special_FIRST-STEP-Act.pdf.

38   "35 States Reform Criminal Justice Policies through Justice Reinvestment," Pew

Charitable Trusts (2018), accessed April 20, 2020, https://www.pewtrusts.org/en /research-and-analysis/fact-sheets/2018/07/35-states-reform-criminal-justice -policies-through-justice-reinvestment.

39 Lois M. Davis, et al., "Evaluating the Effectiveness of Correctional Education: A Meta-Analysis of Programs That Provide Education to Incarcerated Adults," RAND Corporation (2013), accessed April 20, 2020, 57, https://www.rand.org/pubs/research_reports/RR266.html.

40 HudsonLink.org, "What We Do," accessed April 22, 2020, http://www.hudsonlink.org /what-we-do/.

41 Jennifer Bronson and E. Ann Carson, "Prisoners in 2017," Bureau of Justice Statistics (2019), accessed April 20, 2020, 3, https://www.bjs.gov/content/pub/pdf/p17.pdf.

42 "2016 Crime in the United States: Crime in the United States, by Volume and Rate per 100,000 Inhabitants," Federal Bureau of Investigation, accessed April 18, 2020, https:// ucr.fbi.gov/crime-in-the-u.s/2016/crime-in-the-u.s.-2016/topic-pages/tables/table-1.

43 Deborah Barfield Barry, "Senate Passes First Step Act with Push from Criminal Justice Groups; Bill Goes to House," *USA Today*, December 18, 2018, https://www.usatoday.com /story/news/politics/2018/12/18/first-step-act-passes-senate-criminal-justice-bill -moves-house/2356547002/; Joel Achenbach and Scott Clement, "America Is Really More Divided Than Ever," *Washington Post*, July 16, 2016, https://www.washingtonpost.com /national/america-really-is-more-divided-than-ever/2016/07/17/fbfebee6-49d8-11e6 -90a8-fb84201e0645_story.html.

44 Curt Devine, Drew Griffin, and Nelli Black, "Report: Deadly Delays in Care Continue at Phoenix VA," *CNN*, October 4, 2016, https://www.cnn.com/2016/10/04/politics /phoenix-va-deadly-delays-veterans/index.html.

45 "Department of Veterans Affairs Access Audit System-Wide Review of Access," Department of Veterans Affairs (2014), accessed April 16, 2020, 22, https://www.va.gov/health/docs /VAAccessAuditFindingsReport.pdf.

46 "Review of Alleged Mismanagement at the Health Eligibility Center," VA Office of the Inspector General (2015), 11, https://www.va.gov/oig/pubs/VAOIG-14-01792-510.pdf.

47 Geoff Bennett, "Congress Passes Bill to Increase Accountability among VA Employees," *NPR*, June 13, 2017, https://www.npr.org/2017/06/13/531810565 /congress-passes-bill-to-increase-accountability-among-va-employees.

48 Donovan Slack, "Senate Passes Major VA Overhaul; Trump Expected to Sign Law within Days," *USA Today*, May 23, 2018, https://www.usatoday.com/story/news /politics/2018/05/23/veterans-choice-overhaul-passes-senate/629315002/.

49 "Americans' Views of President Trump's Agenda on Health Care,

Immigration, and Infrastructure," Politico and Harvard T.H. Chan School of Public Health (2018), accessed April 20, 2020, 6, https://www.politico.com/f/?id=00000162-20dc-d21f-abe7-feddbc1f0000.

50   Jo Ciavaglia, "34-Year-Old Northampton Dad of Three Facing Death from ALS Is Local Face of 'Right to Try' Bill," *Bucks County Courier Times*, August 11, 2017, https://www.buckscountycouriertimes.com/2454eee2-792b-11e7-9ea2-078fd5befef8.html.

51   Michael Maherrey, "The 'Right to Try' War Was Actually Won on the State Level," Foundation for Economic Education, June 4, 2018, https://fee.org/articles/the-right-to-try-war-was-actually-won-on-the-state-level/.

52   Matt Bellina, "ALS, Risk Factors, Strategies and How We Live with Them," *Tweed Thoughts* (blog), February 6, 2020, https://tweedthoughts.com/2020/02/06/als-risk-factors-strategies-and-how-we-live-with-them/.

53   Don Thompson and Adam Beam, "National Leaders Start Group for Bipartisan Criminal Justice Reform," *Christian Science Monitor*, July 23, 2019, https://www.csmonitor.com/USA/Justice/2019/0723/National-leaders-start-group-for-bipartisan-criminal-justice-reform; "Adversaries Unite to Achieve Historic Criminal Justice Reform," Stand Together (2019), accessed April 20, 2020, https://www.youtube.com/watch?v=BWjLCu4L_ps.

Chapter Ten

1   Martin Luther King Jr., *Strength to Love*, with foreword by Coretta Scott King (Boston: Beacon Press, 1981), 26.

2   R. Richard Geddes and Sharon Tennyson, "Passage of the Married Women's Property Acts and Earnings Acts in the United States: 1850 to 1920," in *Research in Economic History*, Vol. 29, ed. Christopher Hanes and Susan Wolcott (Bingly, UK: Emerald Group Publishing Ltd., 2013), 153.

3   R. Richard Geddes and Sharon Tennyson, "Passage of the Married Women's Property Acts and Earnings Acts in the United States: 1850 to 1920," in *Research in Economic History*, Vol. 29, ed. Christopher Hanes and Susan Wolcott (Bingly, UK: Emerald Group Publishing Ltd., 2013), 153.

4   S. J. Kleinberg, *Women in the United States, 1830–1945* (London: Macmillan Press Ltd., 1999), 143.

5   Leslie W. Gladstone, "Equal Rights Amendments: State Provisions," Congressional Research Service (2004), accessed April 17, 2020, 1, https://digital.library.unt.edu/ark:/67531/metacrs7397/m1/1/high_res_d/RS20217_2004Aug23.pdf.

6   Marcy Lynn Karin, "Esther Morris and Her Equality State: From Council Bill 70 to Life on the Bench," *American Journal of Legal History* 46, no. 3 (2004): 341.

7   Jone Johnson Lewis, "A Brief History of Women in Higher Education," *ThoughtCo*, March 25, 2019, https://www.thoughtco.com/history-women-higher-ed-4129738.

8   Nancy Weiss Malkiel, *"Keep the Damned Women Out": The Struggle for Coeducation* (Princeton, NJ: Princeton University Press, 2016), 3–6.

9   Jeffrey M. Jones, "New High in U.S. Say Immigration Most Important Problem," Gallup (2019), accessed April 20, 2020, https://news.gallup.com/poll/259103/new-high-say -immigration-important-problem.aspx.

10   "National Immigration Survey," New American Economy (2018), accessed April 20, 2020, 3, https://www.newamericaneconomy.org/wp-content/uploads/2018/09/NAE-National -Immigration-Survey-Deck.pdf.

11   "Frustration in the Schools," *Kappan Magazine*, August 26, 2019, K21, https:// kappanonline.org/wp-content/uploads/2019/08/pdk_101_1_PollSupplement.pdf.

12   Lydia Saad, "Americans' Take on the U.S. Is Improved, but Still Mixed," Gallup (2020), accessed April 20, 2020, https://news.gallup.com/poll/284033/americans -improved-mixed.aspx.

13   Ruth Igielnik, "70% of Americans Say U.S. Economic System Unfairly Favors the Powerful," Pew Research Center (2020), accessed April 20, 2020, https:// www.pewresearch.org/fact-tank/2020/01/09/70-of-americans-say-u-s-economic -system-unfairly-favors-the-powerful/.

14   "Most Americans Would Support Withdrawal from Afghanistan," YouGov (2018), accessed April 20, 2020, https://today.yougov.com/topics/politics/articles-reports/2018/10/08 /most-americans-would-support-withdrawal-afghanista; "Poll: Veterans and Military Families Favor More Health Care Choices for Veterans, Increasingly Support Ending 'Endless Wars,'" Concerned Veterans for America (2020), accessed April 20, 2020, 3, https://mk0wehezuhu1jcn3uqvn.kinstacdn.com/wp-content/uploads/2020/04 /2020-CVA-Survey_Interview-Schedule.pdf.

15   Mark Hannah and Caroline Gray, "Indispensable No More?: How the American Public Sees U.S. Foreign Policy," Eurasia Group Foundation (2019), accessed April 20, 2020, 11, http:// egfound.org/wp-content/uploads/2019/12/Indispensable-no-more-2019.pdf.

16   "Party Affiliation," Gallup, accessed April 16, 2020, https://news.gallup.com/poll/15370 /party-affiliation.aspx.

17   "Party Images," Gallup, accessed April 16, 2020, https://news.gallup.com/poll/24655 /party-images.aspx.

18   Timur Kuran, *Private Truths, Public Lies: The Social Consequences of Preference Falsification* (Cambridge, MA: Harvard University Press, 1997).

19   "The Success Index," Populace and Gallup (2019), accessed April 20, 2020, 6, http://populace.org/successindex.

20   "Attitudes on Same-Sex Marriage," Pew Research Center (2019), accessed April 20, 2020, https://www.pewforum.org/fact-sheet/changing-attitudes-on-gay-marriage/.

21   Andrew Jacobs, "For Gay Democrats, a Primary Where Rights Are Not an Issue, This Time," *New York Times*, January 28, 2008, https://www.nytimes.com/2008/01/28/us/politics/28gay.html; Simone Pathé, "How Democrats Came Around on Gay Rights," *Roll Call*, July 28, 2016, https://www.rollcall.com/2016/07/28/how-democrats-came-around-on-gay-rights/.

22   Abraham Maslow, *Maslow on Management* (New York: John Wiley & Sons, Inc., 1998), 286.

23   William S. McFeely, *Frederick Douglass* (New York: W.W. Norton and Co., 1991), 235–36.

24   Katy June-Friesen, "Old Friends Elizabeth Cady Stanton and Susan B. Anthony Made History Together," *Humanities* 35, no. 4 (2014), https://www.neh.gov/humanities/2014/julyaugust/feature/old-friends-elizabeth-cady-stanton-and-susan-b-anthony-made-histo.

25   William H. Chafe, *Civilities and Civil Rights: Greensboro, North Carolina, and the Black Struggle for Freedom* (Oxford: Oxford University Press, 1981), 80–81.

26   William H. Chafe, *Civilities and Civil Rights: Greensboro, North Carolina, and the Black Struggle for Freedom* (Oxford: Oxford University Press, 1981), 71.

Conclusion

1   Abraham Maslow, *Motivation and Personality*, 2nd ed. (New York: Harper & Row, 1970), 46.

2   Abraham Maslow, *Motivation and Personality*, 2nd ed. (New York: Harper & Row, 1970), 46.

3   Viktor Frankl, *The Unheard Cry for Meaning* (New York: Simon & Schuster, 1978), 21.

INDEX

abstract principles, 3, 8, 30–32

addiction, 117–18, 137–43

African Americans, 53, 212, 250–51

Amazon, 185–86

Angelos, Weldon, 205–6, 224

Anthony, Susan B., 250

Aristotle, 30, 46

Arizona State University, 170–71

Armstrong, Melony, 177–79, 201–2, 248

Arthur D. Little, 34

Auschwitz, 37–38

authoritarianism, 44

Baddour, Ray, 34–35

bailouts, 189

Bellina, Matt and Caitlin, 226–30

Bergamo, Italy, 75–76

Bible, 45–46

Bill of Rights, 206

Bingham, Caleb, *The Columbian Orator*, 105

Black Panthers, 130–31

Bloods, 109

border-adjustment tax (BAT), 194–95

bottom-up approach: in American society, 94–95; in business, 9, 12–13, 66–67, 72–81, 196–98, 200–202; in challenging injustice, 100; in community-based projects, 12, 133–47; in education, 12, 162–65, 171–74; effectiveness, xv–xvii, 4; explanation of, 3–4, 44; listening and learning as essential to, 136; local knowledge as key ingredients in, 4; ordinary people's contributions to, xvii, 52–53, 67–68, 72–73; in politics, 223–32; social movements built by, 236; three-step process in, 100, 136, 165–73, 230–31

Brown University, 166

Bush, George H. W., 209

Bush, George W., 159

business: anticompetitive regulations in, 177–79, 181–82, 184, 187, 189–90, 201–2; barriers to competition in, 177–78, 181–82; bottom-up approach in, 9, 12–13, 66–67, 72–81, 196–98, 200–202; control mentality in, 64–65, 74–76; culture of, 67, 75–78, 82, 180, 187, 192–93, 197–98; educational preparation for, 155; institutional role of, 93–94; profit motive in, 177, 179, 183, 195; public opinion on, 180, 188–89, 199, 202, 244; tax breaks for, 184–85; transformation of, 192–202; trial and error in, 64–65, 77–78, 81; value creation as purpose of, 72, 76, 78, 79, 163, 177, 179, 182, 188, 195, 199; virtuous cycles in, 9, 79–80. *See also* corporate welfare; Principled Entrepreneurship™; protectionism

Business Leaders Against Subsidies and Tariffs (BLAST), 200

Café Momentum, 132–36

Carney, Tim, *Alienated America*, 127–28

Case, Anne, 89

Catholic University of America, 196

certificate-of-need (CON) laws, 186

Challenge Process, 74–75

Chicago Statement, 168

Ciocca, Art, 196–98

Civil Rights Act, 251

civil rights movement, 250–51

Cleveland, Grover, 106

colleges and universities: alternatives to, 168–69, 173; career readiness provided by, 173; cost of, 156, 159, 161, 173; failures of, 155,

LEARN MORE ABOUT HOW YOU CAN
STAND TOGETHER TO HELP EVERY PERSON RISE

BELIEVEINPEOPLEBOOK.COM

Visit to:

• Read and watch more stories from effective social entrepreneurs

• Get tools and resources to transform your effectiveness

• Find out how to partner with Stand Together

to tackle the issues that matter most